K2
28,251'

GASHERBRUM 4
26,000'

MUZTAGH TOWER
23,862'

BROAD PEAK
26,401'

GASHERBRUM 1
26,470'

W9-BTD-258

Masherbrum Base Camp

Baltoro Glacier

Route Taken Out from Masherbrum

NORTH PILLAR

CHOGOLISA
25,148'

K7 Base Camp

Paiju

MASHERBRUM
25,659'

Trekking Route in to Masherbrum

K7
22,749'

Hushe Village

K A R A K O R A M   R A N G E

Khapalu

NORTHER

PAKISTA

MASHERBRUM RANGE

Trekking Route to K7 Base Camp

Shiaischo Camp

K7 Base Camp

K7
22,749'

Charakusa Valley

LINK SAR
23,100'

HAJJI BRAKK
19,636'

KAPURA PEAK
21,470'

K6
23,891'

Hushe Village

End of Road

Kms.

0   20

Miles

0

Beyond the Mountain

by Steve House

"What is there, beyond the mountain, if not the man?" – WALTER BONATTI

PATAGONIA BOOKS

BEYOND THE MOUNTAIN

copyright 2009 Patagonia Books
Text © Steve House
Foreword © Reinhold Messner

First edition
Printed in Canada

Preserving our environment
Patagonia chose Legacy Hi-Bulk White
100% post-consumer recycled paper for
the pages of this book printed by Webcom Inc.

© **Mixed Sources**
Product group from well-managed
forests, controlled sources and
recycled wood or fiber
FSC   www.fsc.org Cert no. SW-COC-002358
© 1996 Forest Stewardship Council

Cover photos: (front) Marko Prezelj, (back) Vince Anderson, (portrait) Steve House Collection
End maps: Anita Karl and James Kemp

ISBN 978-0-9790659-5-8 (regular edition)

ISBN 978-0-9790659-6-5 (boxed edition)

To the partners with whom I lived these stories: Vince Anderson, Scott Backes, Barry Blanchard, Rolando Garibotti, Dusan Golobič, Eli Helmuth, Joe Josephson, Alex Lowe, Bruce Miller, Marko Prezelj, Branko Starič, Mark Twight, and Mira and Zdenko Zorič. These stories are as much theirs as mine.

TABLE OF CONTENTS

Reinhold Messner and I share the view at the Nanga Parbat Base Camp in August, 2005.
VINCE ANDERSON

FOREWORD

The Message of Steve House

I ADMIRE STEVE HOUSE for his approach to the mountains. Step by step he has become the best alpinist he can become. In my view he is at the top of mountaineering. He climbs the right routes on the right mountains in a time when everyone is climbing Everest. Often we haven't even heard of the peak he is climbing on. But how, and with whom, he is climbing interests me.

In this book he gives up his experiences, his stories, his heritage. There are no words of the "climax" on the summit, no words of victory. Instead, Steve tells about suffering through freezing cold bivouacs, the discomfort of high-altitude, the deep emptiness after a high success.

Steve House is a great adventurer; he knows that "success must never be assured." He is also a great storyteller. He tells about doing, not about morals or lessons. His commitment to his goals lets him try and try again. The times he succeeds he learns that success is as temporary as the snow in spring.

I am keen to read these stories of one of today's best climbers – to know about Steve's mentors; his moments of learning, evolution and revelation; his heroes and dreams; the moments he excels and when he fails; his partners and his trust in them, and his sorrow when he loses them – to know about his life. These stories evoke strong emotions in me. I remember the loss of my own friends, my fears before great climbs, my care for my partners.

In this day, climbing has become a global phenomenon and most climbers around the world act like they are in a climbing movie with beautiful, colorful Gore-Tex suits and shiny aluminium. In contrast, Steve says, "My most rewarding days were days when I cut away everything." And with these few words he holds the same line as Mummery, Bonatti, and Robbins. It's the style that makes the difference.

"The simpler we make things, the richer the experiences become." But only if we remain active, only if we try, only if we risk – and especially when we fail. Failure is a part of learning. Through our failures we learn the most. "Action is the message."

– Reinhold Messner

PROLOGUE

I'VE NEVER BEEN A STORYTELLER. Most climbers are like me: quiet, introverted, physical people. But I wrote this book because I wanted to explain something about why I climb: to you, but also to myself.

Now that I've finished it, I am afraid I may have failed. Failed to answer questions such as why I take deadly risks, why I leave home for months at a time, and why I routinely spend my savings on air tickets to remote lands. But I see success in degrees, and failure provides valuable lessons.

The depth of any story is proportionate to the protagonist's commitment to their goal, the complexity of the problem, and the grace of the solution. Success must never be assured.

When I stood on the greatest summit I've ever achieved, success vaporized. As many before, I learned that the moment we think we have attained the goal, we lose it. Success is empty. The sum of all our luck, judgments, lessons learned and heeded, elevation gained and lost, our fitness and skill is zero.

When I climb, I know I will descend. When I grow to love my partners I know that they may die. When I run uphill my legs first get weaker, then stronger, and eventually weaker again. The sum is zero, and so the goals become the plotlines to our lives.

The stories in this book take place between 1988 and 2008. Each time I returned to the infinite canvas of the mountains with a new goal: to plot a new route, traverse a peak, climb a route faster than anyone before, or to climb alone what had only been accomplished by a team of men. My most rewarding days were days when I cut away everything; when I redefined my understanding of necessity.

Writing these stories has been unexpectedly cathartic. I have come to a clearer understanding that climbing has the power to distill the full spectrum of life into a few days, or even a few hours. At the same time I sharpened my realization that doing – climbing – is the only way to understand this. My hope for *Beyond the Mountain* is that it inspires a few to go simply, and to climb well: to see for themselves.

Remember: the simpler you make things, the richer the experience becomes.

Steve House
Terrebonne, Oregon
U.S.A.
April, 2009

Bruce Miller (left) and I show the signs of altitude illness at a 23,620-foot bivouac on the Rupal Face. The swelling in our faces is due to peripheral edema, or swelling of the extremities. BRUCE MILLER COLLECTION

CHAPTER ONE

At Any Price

22,000 Feet on the Rupal Face, Nanga Parbat, Pakistan: August 15, 2004

I TAKE A DEEP BREATH and push the honed edge of the knife against the rope. It doesn't cut. I whetted the edge for just this reason. Frustrated, I look at the small knife in the palm of my mitten. I have carried this knife upwards for four days, on a climb where every ounce counts both towards and against my own survival. The rope is sacred, both a symbol and the truest expression of partnership, but if I can cut it Bruce and I can rid ourselves of four pounds and climb to the summit.

Climbing ropes must be cared for, stored neatly, kept clean. When I was young, I skipped Sunday school, but knew that to step on a climbing rope was a cardinal sin. Panting, I straighten my cutting arm and lean in, sawing into the rope, pushing still harder.

Nothing. I sit back on my heels to rest; I have only a small nick in the sheath to show for my effort. I lean in one more time, holding my arm straight and letting the blade tip slightly. I feel it start to slice through. It is over quickly: the rope severed. I trumpet and thrust the two fresh-cut ends above my head, mocking the seriousness of our situation.

Bruce, on his knees in the snow, chuckles as he slowly coils the half we're taking with us. Tufts of unwashed hair protrude from his thick hat and hood. His eyes are alive, his weathered face radiant. In his mirth the swollen red skin of his lips crack; the fissures are caked with five days worth of lip balm and phlegm.

I am sure that we won't – that we can't – come back here, so I toss the discarded rope at the base of a black horn of rock. I push my helmet and our rock-climbing gear into a small hill of snow-covered gear.

Standing up, Bruce finishes organizing our shortened rope. He turns and regards my rough treatment of the gear we're leaving behind. I stand and start to climb off with the deliberate, comically rigid movements of high altitude. Five breaths are required to recover from moving one leg up one step. A few short feet take a few long minutes.

Bruce steps backwards, folds his lanky frame, and picks up the discarded rope in his thick, gloved hands. Kneeling, he wraps it forcefully to the rock again and again. He clips in my helmet and secures the rock rack. I shrug my indifference and stab my ice axe further up the slope, knowing that I'll never see this place again.

◇◇◇◇◇◇◇◇◇◇◇◇◇◇◇◇◇◇◇◇

Fourteen years earlier, in 1990, I celebrated my twentieth birthday at Nanga Parbat base camp. I was the youngest member of a Slovenian expedition that put two climbers, Jože Rozman and Marija Frantar, on the summit via the Schell route. It was my first Himalayan climbing experience, and the sour memory of it drove me from the greater ranges for years. The mountains were too high for my adolescent lungs, the walls too steep for my young legs, the experiences cut too deep for my thin skin. As I aged, those same memories fermented into something more complex: unresolved and alluring.

During that time Bruce Miller was unknown to me, a young carpenter living in Boulder, Colorado, working only when it was too hot or too snowy to climb. There he read Reinhold Messner's provocative book *The Seventh Grade* in a house crowded with seven other climbers. In Messner's book is a photograph of his brother Günther, a few days before his death, high on the snow-plastered Rupal Face with a small whiskbroom hanging inconspicuously on his harness. Armed with what he calls "this secret Rupal knowledge," Bruce swept his way up a number of snow-covered rock climbs above Boulder.

◇◇◇◇◇◇◇◇◇◇◇◇◇◇◇◇◇◇◇◇

A few hours higher, we dig a small platform on which to pitch our tiny tent. Diving inside, Bruce brews a pot of peppermint tea. He twists around to look at me, his face alight with excitement. "You know, I think we're going to do this thing."

"Yeah, I know." I answer, lying back on a thin foam mattress. "I didn't want to say anything yet." I close my tearing eyes to rest my pounding head on the relative comfort of our tiny coil of rope. "We still have tomorrow, which will be the big day. I don't know if we should take our bivy gear to the summit, or not." I breathe deeply at the thin air.

At dawn we pack our one sleeping bag, strike the tent and leave our bivouac.

I kick a trail of steps toward the top. We each carry 25 pounds of equipment, food and fuel to survive three more days. My footsteps don't sink more than ankle deep in the snow. The air is calm and clear. Turning, I can see the curve of the planet stretching into India and across China.

My head hangs. For me it has been another bad night of little rest. Glancing at Bruce I see his face is puffy from the altitude. I am in worse shape. Our internal organs are subject to the same swelling. We've climbed into the "death zone," the altitude at which nothing can live for long without supplemental aids, like bottled oxygen, something Bruce and I would never consider. For us sucking O is doping, cheating. Besides, carrying the heavy bottles of oxygen is physically impossible in our chosen style – alpine style – of climbing. The style is so named because it utilizes the same methods used to climb smaller peaks in the Alps. You climb with a backpack containing your food, fuel, shelter, clothing and climbing gear. And, if all goes well, you bring it all back down.

I wrap my fingers over a rocky edge and pull myself to the top of a short, 40-foot cliff. I pause to catch my breath and Bruce steps ahead and leads off. I follow at a slow, all-day pace. I'm happy to be in his track, drafting. Yesterday I felt strong, but last night I puked up half my meager ration of food. I am dehydrated and sluggish, and my headache is worse now than when we bedded down.

Suddenly I come upon Bruce, leaning against his pack on a nondescript snow slope. I am a little disappointed that his stint in front has been so short.

"How's it going Steve?"

I lean into the slope, put my head against my axe, and breathe hard. I am not going to lie; I'm not fine. But this pain is familiar.

"Uh. Okay." I say as I stand.

"I've been waiting forty minutes. What's wrong?"

"Forty minutes?" I don't understand. I pant rapidly. "I just stopped." Breathe. "To shit."

"You don't look so good." Bruce starts to chuckle, but the laugh is lost in a hacking cough that doubles him over.

He lifts his head and takes two awkward steps back up his track. His track? It suddenly registers that Bruce has down climbed to me. His pace has buried mine. He watched me struggle for 40 minutes; watched me take five steps, then rest my head on my ice axe taking 10 breaths. Sometimes more.

Bruce raises himself up; his eyes try to meet mine. The cracks in his lips are packed with drying blood. He looks away and says, "I want to go down."

I lean my forehead back on my axe trying to concentrate. I push back my mitten to look at the altimeter on my wrist. It reads 24,800 feet, just 1,900 feet below Nanga Parbat's summit.

"Down? Why?" I lift my head and stare at him. He has pushed his hood back, but dark sunglasses hide his eyes. His face is too thin, waxy like a mask. He doesn't look at me.

"We're almost at twenty-five thousand feet." I breathe. "It's still early."

"Then where are we going to bivy tonight? On the summit?"

Yes, I think, and then I say aloud, "Where we end up. Wasn't that the plan?" Breathe. "I think we'll be okay." I gather my breath and force the words out quickly. "We have three more nights."

I squat down on one knee and think. I try to imagine a logical argument against his decision to turn around. To keep climbing is flagrantly dangerous and selfish. Just like it always is. Not understanding Bruce's change of heart precludes me from arguing against it. Faintly, I see that I don't know this man. I nearly chuckle at the folly of us being here together, of not having tempered our partnership in the furnace of experience.

Three weeks ago, while climbing alone on K7, I had been so confident I rejected partnership. I knew that my trust in others had turned to dust, desiccated by ever-changing climbing partners, a failed marriage, and bearing witness to climbers trashing the mountain environments that I cherish. My desire to climb Nanga Parbat had usurped this knowledge.

There is no partnership, no marriage but convenience. There is just he and I. Separate in our desires. Mine to ascend at any price. Bruce's to cash out now, before we have committed everything. I wonder, "Who is this man?"

The Indus Hotel, Skardu, Pakistan: August 5, 2004

I sit with bare feet sticking off the two inches of foam that pass as my bed; the shoulder bones of my back grind uncomfortably against a gritty whitewashed wall. At the center of the room a low, scarred wooden table is strewn with the contents of my repair kit: two folding knives, a pair of black-handled trauma shears, white cloth tape, a sewing awl, a book of needles, scraps of thread and a near-empty tube of waterproofing paste for leather. My newly rejuvenated insulated climbing gloves are wedged against the coarse screen of a window that overlooks a gravel hillside streaked with trash. A fly buzzes past my face as it circles towards the closed bathroom door where the shower drains into the same hole in the floor that serves as a squat-toilet. A second door leads into a thinly carpeted concrete hallway that leads out past the five large tables of the hotel's lobby and restaurant and into Skardu's main street.

When I step onto the road my feet sink softly into fine, black sand drifted across the road. My imagination turns east toward the sunrise, running along the shiny, rippling pewter surface of the Indus River. Dark with silt when the sun is high, the Indus runs between the hulking behemoths of the Himalayan Range and the angular, sharp tips of the Karakoram Mountains. South of me the

Himalayas stretch 1,500 miles to the east reaching across India, Nepal, Tibet, Bhutan, and China. Forty miles away the range finds its western terminus in one final act of mountain building: Nanga Parbat.

Nanga Parbat is the ninth highest peak in the world. In Urdu the name means the Naked Mountain. Its Rupal Face, the largest mountain wall in the world, is so steep that winter snows do not cling to the smooth, black gneiss that glaciers slowly mill into the powdery sand piled in front of the hotel.

Our group of six is coming from the north side, the Karakoram side, of the big river. At the end of a four-wheel drive track sits the village of Hushe. A three-day walk past Hushe, through dusty goat-worn hillsides and across the rock-covered ice of the Charakusa Glacier, lies a cul-de-sac of mountains mostly untouched by man. In 1856, the British Great Survey of India named a dark-streaked granite mountain overlooking that glacier Karakoram-7. Its summit needle is a remote aerie of snow 8,000 feet above the valley floor.

Ten days ago I stood on K7's summit at sunset. I frantically scanned the serrated horizon as it was being swallowed by darkness. Through the fog of 36 sleepless hours the shadows of a million mountains stretched off into the dusk. A few hours before I summitted, when a cornice dropped right in front of my chest, I had watched holding my breath as it fell silently. I gasped for air when it finally exploded below me. To get to this final pinnacle required seven attempts over two expeditions. There had been moments where my survival seemed secondary to my need for acute experience.

There is a gentle knock on the door of my Indus Hotel room: lunch is ready. As I enter the dining room Bruce is helping himself to a fragrant saffron dish of steaming mutton. Oblong stainless-steel bowls hold piles of rice. I drop into the chair next to him.

"Man, I'm hungry," he says, big eyes fixed on the food.

Doug Chabot and Steve Swenson walk in together. "Alright! Lunch!" says Steve, pumping the air with his fist as he pulls out a chair.

Doug looks sideways at the 50-year old Swenson and laughs as he flops his thin frame into the heavy hand-hewn chair. "You'd think we hadn't eaten in like four hours!" he exclaims.

"I'm absolutely starving," says Swenson, looking deadpan at Doug, "and dead tired." His black thick hair is flattened and stiff from lying on his pillow.

The four of us have shared every meal for two months. Six weeks of that at the 14,500-foot K7 Base Camp. The neat and tidy Doug runs the Gallatin National Forest Avalanche Center from the Federal Building in downtown Bozeman. Steve has worked for over 25 years to make partner at one of Seattle's best engineering firms. Doug and the shaggy, sandy-haired Bruce summitted K7 just 24 hours behind me by following the first ascent route. After an avalanche swept his pack off the mountain, Swenson, Slovenian Marko Prezelj and Coloradoan Jeff Hollenbaugh turned back from high on K7-West, an unclimbed sister summit of K7.

Jeff was going to attempt the 13,500 foot-high Rupal Face with Bruce and I, but his motivation evaporated into thin air and his shaky post-divorce headspace. Jeff and Marko left for Islamabad this morning. Without Jeff, Bruce had cold feet about climbing the Rupal Face and has decided to join Doug and Steve Swenson to attempt the unclimbed west, or Mazeno, ridge of Nanga Parbat. We have allotted four days here in Skardu for resting, repairing, washing, and eating. Having been at altitude for so long our appetites are insatiable and the hotel cook is producing big meals full of the fresh vegetables and meats that we have been craving.

Between repairing, eating, and resting, I visualize climbing Nanga Parbat. I mentally dissect the wall into understandable pieces: I will carry a heavy pack across the cow pastures that run to the edge of the glacier. I will navigate the last crevasse and start up the narrow gully of snow transecting the rock buttress that leads to the first large snow slopes. Early the second day I will climb steep ice-covered rock to gain the ice slopes that lead to the glacier hanging onto the upper reaches of the wall. After another bivouac I will find a hidden passage to the broad gully that accesses the upper wall. Then I will traverse the final slopes to the summit pyramid.

Within my mental maps I weave the details of sharpening worn crampons, weighing rations of food, studying photographs to discover niches where I might safely rest.

As I mentally stand on Nanga Parbat's summit, the equanimity I discovered on my way to the 22,700-foot summit of K7 starts to dissolve in the acid of ambition. After so many hard days on K7, I am seduced by success: I lust after the thrill, yearn for the accomplishment, crave the closure.

I know I can climb Nanga Parbat, but others know us by what we've done, not what we can do. With K7 I have respect. But Nanga Parbat will bring more. Few mountains, not even Everest, are as coveted by climbers as the naked mountain, the killer mountain. Thirty-one men died attempting its first ascent. The Rupal Face has been successfully climbed twice. A route has been established on both the left-hand and right-hand edges of the wall. Reinhold and Günther Messner – supported by a large team organized by Karl Herrligkoffer – climbed the first route in 1970. A joint Polish/Mexican team climbed the second route in 1984. As my thoughts drift down from the summit I allow the question: Will Nanga Parbat be enough?

Base Camp, Nanga Parbat, Pakistan: August 10, 2004

Coming out of the mess tent I toss a stone at the herd of small, high-ribbed goats eating the grass behind camp. They scatter as I gather my sleeping bag

During the early morning hours of the second day, we climb close together to minimize the hazards of rockfall and the risk of dropping ice onto each other. STEVE HOUSE

dried by the morning sun. Slipping my bag into the half-zipped door of my tent, I bend down and reach for a daypack. Bruce approaches slowly.

"Hey Steve. Mind if I come along and have a look at the Rupal Face with you?" he asks as I pack the spotting scope and a collection of photographs. It is early morning, and the first full day in base camp. The weather is fine and clear. Clear weather on a big mountain may last only a few hours; I want to take full advantage of my first chance to study the wall in person.

"Sure." I stand. "But don't you want to go with Doug and Steve? They're going to check conditions on the Mazeno Ridge."

Bruce is wearing dark cotton pants, the cuffs worn to rags. His fleece jacket is rumpled, the collar twisted in. He kicks at the grass, and answers. "Well, when I saw the Rupal Face this morning. It's so amazing here." After a pause he looks up. "I figure I owe it to myself to have a closer look before ruling it out completely."

I stand from packing my backpack and turn to look at the wall as I cross my arms across my chest. "Well. I don't know."

I have been grappling with the idea of climbing this massive wall alone for the past two weeks. Now Bruce wants to come? I'm confused, but also relieved. It would be much safer to have two of us up there. Climbing K7 had taken seven attempts over two summers to learn the intricacies of route-finding on its 8,000-foot wall. The Rupal Face is even more complex, and the summit soars to the incredible height of 26,660 feet. The lightweight approach I used on K7 was an evolution of lessons learned on 20,320-foot Denali. Adapting those lessons to the 22,749-foot K7 took time. Climbing to Nanga Parbat's summit looms as another exhaustive, mind-rending evolution.

Seeing Nanga Parbat's summit being born into the red dawn of day, I just want to climb it. I want to stand on the summit and partnership offers the greatest probability of achieving that.

Dropping my arms to my side, I turn and say, "I guess that makes sense." I pause to take in Bruce's rugged, square-cut profile, his lean, fit body. He gazes up at the wall, fingers interlaced behind his head.

"Okay," I start slowly. "I'm up for it. I think we have to go back down across the lower meadow and out by the river to get the best view."

24,800 Feet on the Rupal Face, Nanga Parbat, Pakistan: August 15, 2004

Bruce is right. My vomiting has dehydrated me, nearly incapacitated me. If I go higher I am sure to get worse.

Ambition has fueled this drive towards the summit of Nanga Parbat. I have sacrificed everything to climbing: I am newly divorced, living out of a van, without savings and with no real job. I've paid too high a price to allow failure. I am willing to sacrifice my friendship with Bruce, but am I willing to die here?

In the sun on the windless upper slopes of the world's highest wall we stand and wordlessly decide our future with a single glassy-eyed look. I am in disbelief. I am soloing again. Soloing in my mind, but irrevocably tied to this partner for survival. I have no choice. Bruce is not going to allow me, or himself, to risk more than we already have.

At 10:30 in the morning on what should be our summit day, Bruce starts down. I lean against the snow, watching him descend. I think about striking upwards on my own. Then I remember that he's got the stove. I carry the fuel. We would both die.

I stare at the steep slope below. One set of closely spaced tracks leads up to my seat. Next to them, widely spaced prints mark Bruce's departure. Live or die, the two tracks ask. I make a few strides down before a confused wave of emotions engulfs me and I drop into a sitting position.

Looking out from Nanga Parbat, I am the highest thing around. In Indian Srinagar, cumulus cells build with the day's heat. To the east the backbone of the Himalaya marches across India.

My butt is cold and I have to stand. I'm already facing out, so slowly, I follow Bruce's track down. Rounding a rock tower, I hear Bruce calling.

"Hey!" I shout down. "I'm coming."

I remember that two years ago Bruce lost a partner who fell to his death on a similar slope. He must be worried. For a moment I wonder how long I sat there, but the thought is crushed by the painful drumbeat of my pulse in my head.

Together we down climb to where, hours before, we had cut our rope and abandoned the gear we no longer needed for the summit push. Mechanically, I uncoil the rope in my pack and tie it to the piece we left behind. Bruce rigs the anchor. We will rappel all the way back to where we spent last night. As he sets each anchor I pull the ropes and toss them off. He goes down first.

I wait for him to call up that he has the new anchor set before I go down. Each rappel is as long as the two halves of our rope: 120 feet. While the sun is still hot, we reach our bivy ledge hacked from the snow at 22,000 feet.

In the tent I close my eyes and pretend to sleep. Bruce melts snow for water and makes soup. I sit up when I hear the stove shut off and Bruce gently hands the pot to me. I slurp the thin soup. His eyes try to smile, but neither of us speaks.

The next morning we traverse into Messner's 1970 route. Bruce leads down, doing all the work. I think he may be going down the wrong way, rappelling over an ice cliff, but I don't care. I have given up, relinquished control of my fate.

◇◇◇◇◇◇◇◇◇◇◇◇◇◇◇◇◇◇◇◇◇◇◇◇◇◇◇◇◇

Two days later we are reunited in base camp. Doug and Steve have successfully traversed all of the previously unclimbed Mazeno Ridge to its junction with

Bruce back in base camp with what little gear remained after our descent from the Rupal Face. STEVE HOUSE

Nanga Parbat's flanks, which they then descended via the seldom-used Schell route. That night Doug, Steve and Bruce decide to leave for home. The next morning in the already harsh sun, a few thin leathery men load the trio's gear on abused donkeys, and suddenly everyone is gone.

I remain, alone with the base camp cook, Fida, and our government-assigned liaison officer. The departure of my mates leaves an unexpected vacuum that I cannot fill. I have nobody to talk to who understands my questions, no one to provide me with answers. I search my memory of those upper slopes for clues to what happened. There is no explanation. Everything had seemed to be going so well. We had felt sure that we were about to succeed. So why did we fail? How sick was I? Would I have allowed myself to die up there?

Yes, I entered into the partnership willingly. Yet I struggle with the power necessarily entrusted to my partner. Tying in with Bruce was the wrong decision because I wasn't prepared to share as a partner must. Yes, I would have died for Nanga Parbat. No, I can't expect others to feel the same. Why was I willing to go so far? Why was I so quick to trade familiar solitude for what I thought was a greater chance of success?

I felt invincible on K7; soaring on the euphoria of new experience. Perhaps Nanga Parbat was too big and I was simply too tired.

Before the morning's sun turns hot, I am out doing aerobic recovery tests. I step up on a knee-high rock repeatedly for five minutes, then measure how long it takes my heart rate to return to normal. It doesn't ever get below 90. Even in the mess tent an hour later, the monitor still reads 96. Before the attempt my resting heart rate at the 12,000-foot base camp was 48.

I sit in the meadow with the blank page of my journal and a thermos of tea. Looking up at the wall, I am tormented with another clear and sunny day. I can't know what would have happened had we kept going. Maybe the swelling would have caused fluid to leak into my lungs, disabling me near the summit. We might have gone to the top and then become lost trying to descend the opposite side of the mountain. Maybe we would have been crushed in an avalanche, like Günther. Maybe we would have walked out of Diamir Valley, flush with the experience. Proverbially speaking, we would have been rich, we would have been kings.

I know that had we succeeded it would have been the greatest American climb in the Himalaya since Willi Unsoeld and Tom Hornbein climbed the West Ridge of Everest in 1963. Theirs was the first traverse of a major Himalayan peak, a climb for which Willi sacrificed nine toes. President John F. Kennedy presented Unsoeld and Hornbein with the National Geographic Society's highest honor.

Climbing the Rupal Face would have been the greatest accomplishment of my life. I had to go down with Bruce because his no was necessarily stronger than my yes. That his no might have saved my life does not sit well with my ego.

Five days after my partner's departure, I start climbing the three-mile high Rupal Face alone. It is midnight under a new moon. At dawn I give up, not having climbed one-tenth of the wall.

My body is wrecked, my mind in chaos. I am not climbing with the lightness I had known on K7, but with a burden I have acquired on Nanga Parbat.

At the base of the wall I sit on my pack and spit green phlegm into the snow. I can barely lift my pack. I stumble beneath the crucifix of failure. Even if I had the physical strength to climb, it would be impossible to carry such a weight up the Rupal Face. Not the weight, I think, the imbalance. The imbalance created by my relentless drive for success.

I stand and face my twisting path downward, toward home. I hope to climb Nanga Parbat someday, but hope – this burning, blinding desire – now seems to be the problem. So I let go. I walk away. I begin the journey back. Back in time, back in place, back in mind. Back to the beginning.

Bruce heads down to base camp during one of the final rappels off Nanga Parbat. STEVE HOUSE

The 4,000-foot high north wall of Triglav. At 9,396 feet, Triglav is Slovenia's highest peak. We scrambled to the left at the thin horizontal snowband below the summit pyramid to reach the popular year-round hut on the mountain's shoulder. MARKO PREZELJ

CHAPTER TWO

The School of Slovenian Alpinism

Mount Štajerska Rinka, Kamnik Alps, Yugoslavia (now Slovenia): January, 1989

DUŠAN'S FACE IS PLASTER WHITE, his heavy beard and even his thick eyelashes are jeweled with snowflakes, which, amazingly, do not seem to melt. He looks up at me and blinks; the crystal mascara dissolves.

"*Ta suk je kar zajebon.*" He spits the hard tones of the Slovene words. "This next pitch is quite a bastard." He continues slowly in Slovene, as he would to a six-year-old. "Did I tell you? This route probably doesn't have a winter ascent. Hard it is..."

To see past Dušan's doubt I squint upwards. The steep limestone wall is split with a weathered crack running vertically into the mist. I hope to see Ljubo, who leads this pitch through the swirling fog. Occasional snowflakes drift upwards on the wind currents; clouds hide the half-dozen peaks that ring the Logar Valley.

I strain to see as the rope pays out slowly through the belay device on my harness and my ice encrusted, wool-clad hands. Inch by jerky inch. There is a pause and I hear the dull echo of a hammer driving steel. Above me in the cloud a piton is driven and clipped. Another unannounced avalanche of spindrift – snow accumulated and then released from the steep summit slopes hundreds of feet above – envelops us. I hear the faint tapping of the tiny flakes peppering our nylon coats.

The rope lies still in my hands for a long time. Suddenly, a few feet pay out in a rush. Then the rope stops again. I hear the heavy thud of more soft iron pitons being driven into limestone cracks. Again silence.

Then a distant sound: a muffled human voice, and a quick tug on the rope.

Our little stance becomes a flurry of activity. I take Ljubo off belay by freeing the rope from the figure-eight belay device. Dušan mutters something I don't understand as he digs the fresh snow away from the pitons and deconstructs the cobweb anchor of webbing slings and climbing rope. I ignore his comment and hasten to knock out a few of the pegs myself, leaving the aged, rusty ones for the next visitor who will arrive sometime after the spring thaw.

I move off the ledge and moments later I am standing on the steel points of my crampons, the front tips balanced on rock edges. My right hand grasps the rubber-coated shaft of an ice hammer to clean pitons out of cracks. My left hand holds an ice axe.

For a short time I feel weightless. I have felt this paradox of connection when climbing rock with bare hands. I feel the most connected the moment I minimize contact with the Earth. This time my support is crampons and the naked steel of my ice tools. The cold makes everything more vivid, more perfect.

The bright yellow and electric blue ice hammer in my hand, with its square-edged teeth purposefully cut into a cast steel pick, is a tool made for the modern alpinist. An alpinist, I already know, is a climber of mountains by difficult routes, by technical routes: real climbing to summits like this one. The ice hammer itself is a key to the world of legends that I've dreamed of in my fading boyhood: the world of climbers like Reinhold Messner, Hermann Buhl, Ricardo Cassin, Walter Bonatti, and Yvon Chouinard.

I reach above me and place the sharp steel tip of the axe in the limestone crack. I wiggle it in, teasing it deeper. As I start to pull on the tool it shifts and my heart races. I test it again by jerking my body down on my outstretched arm, tugging to feel whether it is set.

"Come on," I mutter to myself. "It's solid." I clench my jaw and my eyes squint involuntarily as I pull on the axe. As I step up onto a small ledge, the euphoria quickly dissipates into the chilled air. My crampon slips. My arms catch and keep me from falling onto the rope.

Regaining my balance, I stand, teetering on two small rock edges a dozen feet above the belay stance. The rush is forgotten. I have to concentrate. This pitch is graded as a V – a 5.9 for my American mind – that fact reminds me that it's hard, right at my limit.

I touch the rock with my gloved hand, the holds are small, but there is no crack here in which to place my ice tool. I drop my tools so they hang from their wrist-loops. My fingers wrap onto a rough-hewn edge in the limestone. It's only as wide as the first pad of my fingertips. I press the wool under my fingers, feeling the fabric compress into the edge as I start to climb.

I concentrate, remembering back to the tiny practice cliff near Maribor, toproping in the sun with Ljubo. "Climb up by looking down," he says in my mind. I look down at the pink front points of my new crampons. I find the places where the snow has settled, almost invisible horizontal spaces in this near-vertical landscape. Carefully, I put the tips of my crampon points on two. I stabilize my boots, hold my breath, and push into my toes. Slow and tenuous; I grunt and stand erect. Gasping I regain my breath in ragged gulps of frozen air.

I'm concentrating so intently that I nearly jump out of my jacket when the pink rope next to me, Dušan's rope, suddenly stretches and goes tight. Dušan, hanging in the fog below me, unleashes a string of epithets: Something about a mother that I'm happy not to understand. I look up and spy a new crack. I pull up my tool and find the crack is just within reach. The pick of my ice hammer fits perfectly. I smile to myself and climb upwards. Two hours later we reach the top of the wall.

"There is ridge," Ljubo shouts, pointing up into the streaming, windblown clouds, "to the summit, but it is too late today. Now we go down." Dušan hurriedly coils the rope, and Ljubo turns to face the wind and starts towards the valley.

Zagreb International Airport, Yugoslavia: August, 1988

I follow the crowd of passengers past signs written in the Cyrillic alphabet and in a second language I don't recognize. I gather my duffel and approach the wandering eye of a slouching, dark-skinned border guard. On the plane I had read about how, in 1945, Josip Broz Tito cobbled together Yugoslavia – land of the Slavs – from the bric-a-brac of post World War II Europe. The guard shuffles the pages of my passport, stopping to examine the holograph embedded in the photo page. Without a glance at the yearlong visa on page three, he stamps it, pushes it back to me and waves me through.

Tito has been dead eight years and the first cracks in his country are showing themselves in the international news. When I enter the arrivals hall a thin man with a light complexion and a dark, coarse swath of hair crosses the chipped tile floor towards me. His dark pressed slacks and ironed light blue oxford shirt contrast with the heavy, ill-fitting wool suits worn by almost everyone else. I stop, dropping my bag on the floor. A teenaged boy, wide glasses dominating his face and belted trousers pulled high, follows behind.

"Steve?" asks the man, swallowing the "v" to produce the word Stew.

"Yes?" I ask unsure if he's really saying my name.

"Špindler. I am Špindler, you call me Franci. This is my son."

"Jure," says the boy, pointing to himself. "Slovene for George." They both offer their hands, and I shake with my host father and brother for the year.

Three hours later the clattering Volkswagen diesel turns off the narrow highway and winds between potholes and the old town walls of Maribor, in the state of Slovenia. As we drive across the languid Drava River, I roll down my window to catch a fresh scent off the water. Instead I am met by a soon-to-be-familiar ammonia odor, the heavy smell of industry.

I am relieved as we pull up to one of the more spacious homes, driving through a wide gate and into the yard of a two-story stucco house. The front door opens as we get out.

"Stew?" My new host-mother steps out of slippers and into wooden clogs set outside the threshold. Stepping forward she puts out her hand limply, fingers angled towards the ground.

"My name Ani." Her skin looks Turkish, dark and smooth, and her black hair is pulled back tightly into a dense bun. She wears a large flowered apron over a dark gray pants suit.

"And this is Natasha." A young-looking 14-year-old girl peers around the doorway. Wearing a dark jumper, she has the same radiant face and beautiful skin as her mother, her large dark eyes shine with intelligence.

"Hello," she says shyly, clinging to the back of her mother's flower-print apron.

Franci changes into slippers. "Here," he commands, carrying my duffel, and I follow him inside.

"No. No." Ani yells. I freeze and look around. All four of them are staring at me. I turn towards Ani, "What?"

"Shoe." Ani points at my Nikes.

"No!" says Franci sternly. "No shoe in house. Take this, is for you." He indicates a huge oversize pair of slippers that I've stepped right over.

My feet slip on the wooden stairs as I follow Franci to a large bedroom facing the busy street. Unsure of what to do, I unzip my bag and begin to stack my belongings across a shelf at the end of a narrow bed: three pairs of Levis, seven T-shirts, a few undergarments, and four jumbo jars of peanut butter.

"I spoke with school today," announces Franci at dinner. He speaks better English than anyone in the family, having traveled to Australia twice where he earned more as a gray-market laborer than he makes as a chemical engineer in Slovenia. "They think it best if you go to school with Jure. This is science and English track. I think you are good in science."

I shrug, and smile. "Ok," I don't object. Not knowing any Slovene yet, it seems like I might have a chance with the language of numbers and symbols, especially since I'll be taking courses I've already had back home.

"And Slovensko?" I ask, using the word they call their own language. So far I've learned to count to 500, the verb "to tell," and the word for grass. I still can't get my tongue around "*piščanetc*," Slovene for chicken, though I've tried because there are six living in the yard.

"For this we have to see. Is not so easy," says Franci. He turns back to his plate of pocket-sized fried cabbage rolls.

∞∞∞∞∞∞∞∞∞∞∞∞∞∞∞∞∞∞∞∞

As Jure and I pedal towards the first day of school, I discover that only third gear works on Franci's bike: the shifter is frozen. Nervously, I shadow Jure through crowded streets bursting with diesel fumes and honking mini cars that swerve and turn with complete disregard for lanes. I wear Levis and Nikes, and a gray Patagonia fleece jacket, patched at the elbows.

"Do you like the Levis?" Jure asks. "I thought the American cowboys wore the Wrangler jeans?" He reveals for the first time that his English is pretty good.

I am surprised that he thinks I am a cowboy. I'm not. "Yeah, that's usually true, but especially for the movies. In the summer sometimes I worked on a ranch, and nobody really cared what jeans you had."

"Mmmm. Cool. So, do you have a gun?" He has an excited look now and I think that his bringing me to class might mean big points for him, especially if I have some good information.

"A gun?"

"Yeah, a pistol, like the, how do you say, sick-shooter?"

"Six-shooter?" I laugh. "Six. Six bullets inside it. No, no. I don't have a gun." I lie, kind of. Guns back home don't belong to anyone. They belong to a family. One old Parker shotgun we have was 100 years old before I was born. Guns are passed on and cherished. But guns, I have been taught, are tools, not props. I had always thought these Hollywood stereotypes of Americans were over stated.

"Do you have horse?"

"Horses? No." The movies reach further than I thought. "I live in a small town. In town. I have ridden a few times. But I don't know anything about horses. I have a motorcycle though. And we rode four-wheelers on the ranch."

"What is four-wheeler?"

At school, the kids Jure introduces me to are either too shy or too self-conscious about their English to talk to me. Class time is very serious and during the lessons the students are strictly attentive. The math and chemistry look familiar, but due to the language barrier, I haven't the faintest idea what they are talking about. Bored, I write a couple of letters and absentmindedly gaze out a large wall of dirty windows.

Next to the school a construction pit yawns. Bulldozers push dirt, cranes lower bundles of steel to a clutch of waiting men. Trucks idle on the perimeter. Tearing a page from my notebook, I sketch the scene and pass it to Jure who sits next to me. He's focused on the lesson, but I push the paper in front of his notebook anyway.

Startled, he looks up, looks at my picture, and passes it back. "Nice." He mutters.

"No, no," I shake my head. Taking back the drawing I scribe a line to the lawn beside the construction pit. "*Trava*," I write the Slovene word for grass. Then I draw lines to all the objects in my sketch and push the paper back across the desk.

Soon I have a list of words: man, truck, hat, crane, fence, rock, wheel, wall, driver, and pencil. Two verbs: to dig and to write. I make a list; 10 nouns and two conjugated verbs. On the bike ride home I practice reciting my new knowledge to Jure.

My first Saturday I take off on the bike to explore. I pedal down the back alleyways that lead into a huge war cemetery and exit near a series of hulking square, gray apartment buildings. Children play outside on a steel swing-set in the center of a broad, dead lawn. Across the busy bridge the new frontage street is lined with promising new buildings with empty plate-glass windows. I bike past a crowded bus depot and through a long park; the firm gravel path crunches and snaps as I pedal past three ponds.

The trees show the fatigue of late summer as I climb the narrow road leading up, out of town, and into the countryside. The concrete road becomes more and more broken, and the houses more spaced apart and less well kept. I start to sweat and as the oppression I feel builds, I pedal harder.

Past the last house the road narrows to one lane and passes fields of drying cornstalks and bare patches that just last week held cabbage. On the hills I strain to pedal the squeaking bicycle. I do not find the untouched wilderness I grew up with so near to my Oregon home. The deer, elk, beaver, bobcat, foxes, hares, trout, and fall-run salmon are not to be seen. No pine-scented breeze lifting the limbs of the forest. I see nothing like the cattle ranches I worked during my summers. Even here the acrid city odor hangs over me and the leaves sag under a strange coating of grime. I feel sad. I have left behind the freedom I'd earned by way of summer jobs. I had been admitted to a good college, had respectable savings, and a fast Yamaha motorbike. I exchanged that for a vague fantasy of adventure.

Back at the Špindler's home I sit in the kitchen, the warmest place in the house. Writing in my journal I examine my new situation. "Life seems oppressive," I theorize, "because there is so little outlet for aspiration." Franci has the television tuned to the evening news. The sharp edge of political rhetoric reverberates across the language barrier. I continue to write: "Or, more likely, the fatalistic feeling I have from these people is derived from the fact that the very future of this nation seems to be in doubt. In such an environment there can be no funnel for ambition. Only waiting for better times."

<><><><><><><><><><><><><><><><><><><>

A month later I roll out of bed and drop my feet to the floor. I pull on some dirty jeans and let out a great sigh. Barefoot, I enter the kitchen late; Jure and Natasha are finishing their fried egg breakfast.

"*Hočeš* (you want) American breakfast?" Ani asks in the brand of Slo-English we've developed. The family quickly adapt to using the Slovene words I've learned with my notebooks full of lists, and substitute English when they use a word I haven't yet learned.

"No thanks, I think I'm sick." I reply in Slovene.

That sets off a cascade of words I don't understand. Ani shoos me out of the kitchen with her apron, and I understand that I'm to stay in my room. Five minutes later Ani delivers a liter pot of strong chamomile tea.

"Homemade," she says proudly in the simplified Slovene she uses with me. I had noticed the chamomile flowers ringing the garden.

"Here is sugar. Now work," she says pointedly, and heads down the stairs and out the door to her job as a civil engineer inspector.

In the evening I am invited back into the kitchen. I'm happy for that, because my room is cold. When everyone else has cleared out after dinner, Ani looks up from her cleaning, sets the oversize wooden spoon down and gently turns to me.

"Štef," she says. Since no one can pronounce Steve, I have quickly been renamed Štef. "You aren't sick, you are homesick." She sits down and is quiet for a moment. I am unsure if I should be grateful for her sudden attention. Her big, round, dark eyes look into mine and she asks, "Why?"

I look at her with startled eyes. Yes, of course, I hadn't seen this myself. "I, I, ... " I stutter and drop my gaze to summon my courage. "I am bored. I don't understand the school lessons. The students only have time to study. There are no athletics." I stop and look at Ani.

"Which sports do you like the most?" Ani asks.

The next day I follow Franci and Ani into the basement and down a dark, low-ceilinged hallway toward the furthest corner of the Maribor Mechanical School. We turn a corner, step over a stone threshold, and duck into a brightly lit room. Inside I see quarried stone walls and an uneven terracotta floor. Twenty people, mostly young men, twist on the benches, halting their meeting to see who has barged in.

A blonde man with hair feathered back hunches at the desk with large hands crossed in front of him. He looks at the Špindlers, glances at me, and waves us forward. After a short conversation in fast Slovene his blue eyes - so uncommon here - look straight at me. He puts out his hand, and addresses me in English.

"Hi, I'm Ljubo. Welcome to Mountaineering Club Kozjak. You climbing before?" I nod and he continues. "You sit and see how we make things here. Afterwards we go on one beer and we make plan for climbing. No? You have bus pass to go home? No?"

Three days later Ljubo and I are climbing on a small slab of rock in the forest of Pohorje, Maribor's patron mountain. I had toproped many rock climbs and led easy multipitch climbs at Smith Rock in Oregon. But Ljubo's lessons are strict. More directed. Definitely more purposeful than the school-of-hard-knocks lessons a teenager with a climbing rope and a rack of hexes learns on his own.

After allowing me to scamper up, eager to show off my skill, he lowers me back down. "Štef, again. Now slowly and be sure."

I have found a new school: one whose language I readily understand. The school of Slovenian alpinism.

Karavla Bivouac Hut, North Face of Triglav, Yugoslavia (now Slovenia): February, 1989

I lie down on the bunk and snap off my headlamp. I squeeze my eyes shut. Thinking about tomorrow makes my head spin in the confines of the small bivy hut. Outside, in the darkness, looms the 6,000-foot north face of Triglav: Slovenia's biggest wall and Yugoslavia's highest peak. I mentally go through my gear, food, and water. I have little: a sandwich, a green apple, a liter of sweetened tea, and a sweater. Everything else I will wear for our predawn start, now a scant three hours away.

A moment later, a boot steps down onto my bunk and dismounts onto the worn wooden floor. I sit up sharply, suddenly aware that I had been in a deep, dreamless sleep. A spark ignites under a kettle. Groggily I sit up and stuff my feet into plastic boots and fold the hut blankets. A few gulps of warm and sweet tea and the four of us – Branko, Zdenko, Mira, and I – step into the darkness. For a brief moment before Mira illuminates the icy trail with her headlamp, I see that half the hemisphere before us is black: the dark, looming mass of an alpine north face. Looking above it and behind us, a canopy of stars pierce the cold sky.

After a short walk we stop and the broad, mustachioed Branko flakes out the climbing rope that he has carried coiled over his shoulder. I join him on a broad ledge coated with frozen gravel. As he starts climbing his crampons scrape and then spark. Already the lanky and quiet Zdenko and the short, round-faced Mira, a piston of energy and determination, have moved well past us. My rope comes tight from Branko, a tug and a distant grunt and I'm off, scrambling as hard as I can. I am slowed only by the occasional blank slab or broken crust of ice.

At the top of a steep crack I find Mira smiling as she belays. Branko chatters something about the route and pulls off his sweater. Above us I hear the thud of a heavy soft iron piton finding its way home. Zdenko suddenly shouts; I look up to see an ice axe flying towards me, bouncing off the wall and sailing past out into the abyss thousands of feet below. He unleashes the now-familiar curses as he turns back to the wall and starts off again.

The pitches of climbing end with hasty monosyllabic shouts from Branko. Each pitch leads to another. The day is short, and in the darkening evening I switch on my headlamp. I'm cold, but I'm already wearing my spare sweater. I'm hungry, but my sandwich is long devoured. I'm thirsty, but my thermos is dry.

I lead off – finally I am allowed to lead! I tail Mira as closely as I can, clipping my rope into the many fixed pitons that mark the route. Gradually, the

Ljubo Hansel, Dušan Golobič, and I (from left) take a break on a ski approach into the Logar Valley during the winter of 1989. DUŠAN GOLOBIČ COLLECTION

wall becomes less steep, and suddenly we're on nearly flat ground. I brace myself behind a boulder and belay Branko up.

"Summit?" I ask, my Slovene still limited to short sentences.

"*Ne, ne,*" says Mira with wide eyes. "*Jutri.*"

"Tomorrow?" I don't get it. How can we climb all night? Aren't we near the top? But I don't ask more. Branko crests the wall, finally silent, and I stand, hurriedly coiling the rope as he unties and skips off toward Mira and Zdenko's receding lights. I finish with the rope and start off after them, trying to tie the finishing knot on the coil as I run and stumble across the scree-covered shoulder of the mountain. I catch up with Branko just as another light appears and we start downhill to a large, well-lit hut.

Outside the door we take off our crampons and I follow the three of them through the front door. Here in a small entry room, Branko searches through a huge bin of mismatched and threadbare slippers and hands me a pair. I slip my tired feet into them, placing my boots on a shelf among dozens of other boots, and step into a crowded room that has the look and feel of a tavern back in the valley. The place is heavy with split-log benches, sturdy, worn tables. A few people look up at us from plates of hot food with half-empty pitchers of beer in front of them.

As we sit I begin to understand. We're staying here tonight. This was probably explained to me, but I did not understand. Branko, Mira, and Zdenko approach the counter where bills are exchanged for bowls of soup, plates of mashed potatoes dashed with meat and gravy. They each return to the table balancing a tray and a glass of beer.

I sit sheepishly until finally Mira asks, "What's up Štef? Aren't you hungry?"

After a few minutes of unintelligible shouting and backslapping between Branko and the hut master, I am in the kitchen. The hut master unbuttons the front of his blue smock and leans against the counter. He extends one arm towards me in laughter and says something I don't quite catch about America, pronouncing it Ameri-ka. He seems quite amused at having an American doing his dirty dishes.

I stand at the sink and pick up a large pot. The hut master laughs again, folding his large hands in on himself and twisting with his own hysterical joke. He steps away and I start to fill the pot with water, searching for detergent.

The hut keeper walks over to me, holding a full mug of beer. I wipe my wet hands on my pants, thanking him for the beer, and take a long drink. I set the glass on a high shelf and survey the pile of plates before me. One holds a half-finished meal of sausage and sauerkraut. This time, I laugh myself as I pick up the plate and start to eat the abandoned food to the cheers of the hut master.

"Good, Štef. Good!"

At Camp One on the Schell route on Nanga Parbat in July 1990. The T-shirt was a gift from my boy scout troop, and I'm sporting five weeks of facial hair. STEVE HOUSE COLLECTION

CHAPTER THREE

Nanga Parbat 1990

13,000 feet, Advanced Base Camp, Nanga Parbat, Pakistan: July 5, 1990

AN HOUR AFTER WE DEPART from the rubbish pit of the Korean advanced base camp, I start to fall behind my five teammates: Tomi, Silvo, Robi, Jože, and Marija. Once behind them, I lose the benefit of group momentum and my footfalls drag ever slower. I see the endless loose brown dirt and rocks ahead of me. I draw deeply of the thinning air and often pause under the labor of doing so.

I am tired; not tired like I have no strength remaining, but tired like I have no will left. I can't understand this after all the preclimb training. My mind drifts to all those pounding circuits on my bike out Steamboat Island Road, leaving campus just as the rain had started to pour down.

I plod on, resigned to my weakness. The afternoon sun drops behind the mountain, and my doubts start to boil over when suddenly I see the others. They've pitched the silver tent against a small cliff and are sitting among the rocks, sharing a pot of food.

"Oh, Štef! Welcome." I plop down heavily near Robi who slaps me on the thigh as I lean back against the support of my pack, gasping for breath, and glance at my altimeter: 17, 200 feet. Jože, who was squatting near the tent door, stands and moves around behind me and starts to open my pack. I'm carrying the second tent.

"Wait, wait." I lean forward and take the pack off.

"You okay Štef?" Marija asks, leaning forward from her seat on a nearby rock.

"Tired. I think just tired," I say, exhaling sharply.

"Here, take some noodles. You can have the rest," Marija offers.

I slurp down a few cold ramen noodles and drink the salty broth, but refuse the tinned mystery-meat Robi passes me. Jože has his down jacket off now and is moving rocks to build a small tent platform on this loose slope. Robi and Tomi stand to help him. Marija starts unrolling the tent. I lean forward, press my palms against my knees to get up. Slowly, I assemble the tent poles. At 6:30 I crawl in and fall asleep.

I wake panicked. I have to get outside to vomit. Badly. But I can't get up. I can't move. Summoning all my will, I sit up. As I do, my head screams like a locomotive blasting its whistle. I flop back down, panting. My desperation builds, and I sit up again, but it's hard to do anything. I'm robbed of all my strength. I push my toes into my boot shells and stand up. Outside I teeter on the end of the small platform before taking a step down into the loose gravelly slope. Two steps down, I slip but catch myself, and then I throw up in the pallid pool of light cast by my headlamp.

With relief, my willpower waxes stronger; I crawl back through the blackness and back into the safety of my sleeping bag. Lying down I feel heavy and very tired. My head hurts terribly. I am very nauseous. I start to drift away as the night melts into a field of tall green grass coming up knee-high all around me. Then Anne, my girlfriend, is walking towards me. She's wearing cut-off jeans and has her hair in two long braids. She says something I can't quite understand, as if I'm too far away. She has a picnic basket. She kneels down next to me and opens it. Talking to me, she begins to unwrap a large sandwich.

I bolt upright and pull down the tent door with a single sweep of my arm. I get a half gasp of air, when suddenly, with a violence I've not known before, I am thrust forward, out of the tent door, and vomit onto the loose rocks. The liquid splashes off of the rocks and onto my hand. I collapse onto my elbow and am wracked by more powerful convulsions. I mutter an apology to Robi and Tomi who now have their lights on me and are sitting up. They talk hurriedly as I lie motionless in the doorway. Robi says something to me about tablets. I drag my body out of the tent, wearing only long underwear. A few feet away I lie with my head uphill in the rocks in a loose fetal position. The painful contractions return again and again. I shiver alone on the rocks, sticky with my own fluids.

Robi coaxes a foam pad under me, and blankets me with my sleeping bag. He offers me water; I sit up on my elbow and take a shallow sip. The convulsions immediately rumble low in my bowel before they mercilessly ram into my body, rolling over me again and again. I lie in the rocks, drifting in and out of consciousness, in and out of hallucinations. Anne is a part of many of them, as is base camp, and fields of green grass.

Robi returns to squat next to me, wearing unlaced boots and a down coat. "Štef, come back to the tent."

I sit up; Robi puts his hand under my arm and gently pulls me back to the tent. After a very, very long time, the sun strikes the tent. Good, I think, as I squint into the rays streaming around the mountain. I can go down now.

Tomi and Robi rise and exit the tent. I lie there, berating myself to get up, get my pack, and stuff my sleeping bag. The heat in the tent becomes unbearable. Still, I can't will myself to move. I'm paralyzed. Marija, fully dressed for climbing, brings a pot with water. I am so thirsty. I sit up, take a sip, and seconds later throw up again. Like before, I can't stop. Wasted, I collapse back into the tent, even more exhausted.

Tomi approaches with my rucksack, hands it to me, and starts to dismantle the tent with me still in it. I don't manage to get out of the tent before it comes down. Jože has scouted a better location for Camp 1 a few hundred feet higher.

I lay out my sleeping bag where the tent had been and doze in the sun. A few short hours later they return. I push my unstuffed sleeping bag into my empty pack and start down, my mind avoiding the discomfort as I slowly make my way back to base camp, where I sleep for two days. During waking moments I think that I am done with this mountain, that I've been defeated. The self-pity helps me sleep.

Latoba Meadows Base Camp, Nanga Parbat, Pakistan: July 4, 1990, (three days before)

The day before I foolishly rushed to 17,000 feet and got sick, I wrote in my journal, "I am glad to be here, it has been such a long journey. The summit looks so far, far away. The whole day we walked to base camp I tried not to think about it." I look up, knowing that I do not know a fraction of what there is to know about myself. In the long silences between avalanches I wonder whether my unknown interior contains bravery or cowardice, strength or weakness.

With a rock for a pillow I stretch out and gaze at Nanga Parbat: the ice suspended thousands of feet above base camp blushes gray as the afternoon storms begin to clear. The clouds are lifting on the first thermals of the day, unveiling buttresses of dark stone. Skyscraper seracs show iridescent blue ice where they have calved off, cleansing the wall at random moments. When they go big they deposit iron-hard boulders of turquoise ice on the flat goat-shorn meadow.

◇◇◇◇◇◇◇◇◇◇◇◇◇◇◇◇◇◇◇◇◇◇◇◇◇◇◇◇

Our expedition was organized from the Mountaineering Club Kozjak in Maribor by the fresh-faced engineering professor, Tone Golnar. It is Tone's dream to open a new route on the Rupal Face. During the spring of 1989 he traveled across Slovenia canvassing the alpine clubs for willing expedition members.

Tone spread the large, crisp photographs of Nanga Parbat, all resplendent mountain and piercing blue sky, across the desk in the Mountaineering Club

Kozjak's basement meeting room. When I saw them I knew I must go. This moment would begin a 17-year obsession with the Rupal Face. This was the opportunity I craved: my chance to step into the pages of history, to climb in the big mountains. I saw those photographs one week before I returned home to Oregon from my year abroad. Immediately I started working to save money towards the $1,800 cost. I wrote Tone a letter expressing my interest in the expedition; to increase my chances of being accepted I lied, claiming to be 20 instead of 18 years of age.

◇◇◇◇◇◇◇◇◇◇◇◇◇◇◇◇◇◇◇◇◇◇◇◇◇◇◇◇◇◇

A year later we are assembled in Nanga Parbat Base Camp in Pakistan: 18 Slovenes, a Bosnian, a Serbian, and me.

Since then, a new influence has emerged. Marija Frantar vibrates with the confidence of a driven woman. As a vegetarian among omnivores she lives on fried potatoes and dandelion salad. She is quick to smile, and often blushes at a joke. She is one of the most experienced among us, having climbed three 7,000-meter peaks. She has convinced Tone to abandon his pie-in-the-sky scheme of climbing the Rupal Face in favor of the less technical Schell route, the easiest route to the summit of Nanga Parbat from this side of the mountain.

"The first task of the expedition," announces Tone as we finish a dinner of ramen soup, fried potatoes, and a few curried green beans, "is to establish Camp 1. To do this we will divide into teams of five or six. Who wants to be on the first team?" Everyone but me raises a hand.

"Štef," whispers Robi, a fellow youngster on this expedition. "Those on the first team will be the first to try the summit!" Understanding this, I too raise my hand.

"The most experienced should go first. Jože and Marija, of course. Tomi, Robi and Silvo." Tone pauses as he looks around. "And Štef." I am surprised to hear my name. I am the youngest, the least experienced. But Tone is a close friend of Ljubo's, and my suspicion that Ljubo has asked Tone to look out for me has just been confirmed.

A few people protest, but this time it is lanky Marija who speaks up, her square-shorn hair accentuates her gaunt, hollow-cheeked, über-fit look. "If we make the camps good and have some luck with the weather," she pauses to look at each of the members, "and we work well together, everyone will climb to the summit. It is early in the season. We all will have an opportunity to work."

In the morning the six of us rise to warm and calm conditions. The top third of the mountain is shrouded in a singular cloudbank and a thin pane of cirrus cloud fans out across the southwestern sky. Wordlessly, Jože distributes the group gear: tents, stoves, fuel, and a bit of rope. I slip my assigned tent into my backpack and head across the green pasture that cradles base camp.

After three hours we arrive at what the last expedition, a group of Koreans, had used as their advanced base camp. Tone and Jože have started to prepare some soup in an aluminum pot perched on a tiny stove. A bit of water dribbles through the nearby boulders. The small flat area against the wall is stacked full of rubbish: plastic and foil wrappers, empty fuel canisters, most of it with an Asian script.

As we ascend higher and higher I feel weaker and slower. We set up Camp 1 on a barren rock field, and a few hours later I have my first experience with altitude sickness.

Latoba Meadows Base Camp, Nanga Parbat, Pakistan: July 8, 1990

Weakly, I pick up my journal. "On the morning of the 5th we went up to establish and occupy Camp 1. It's no coincidence that I haven't written about it until two days after my return. It was a very harsh 48 hours. The kind of experience that you see in a person's eyes years after the fact."

As the days wear on, the rest of the team moves in and out of base camp, establishing a rhythm of work and rest. Watching them on the fourth morning after my bout with altitude sickness, I feel the desire to climb creeping back. I talk to Tone and we decide to work me back into the rotation. I will take up the end of the line by joining with the oldest expedition member, Željko from Bosnia.

The next morning I am awakened by the sound of rain on the tent. I immediately realize that we won't be going up today. I am relieved. Seconds later I reproach myself for this feeling. I am anxious about what will happen my next trip up, frightened that I will get altitude illness again. Heavy clouds sag across the mountains like a wet dishrag. Somehow the fresh and cool morning brings honesty and rawness.

The following morning the weather is clear and Željko and I set off at dawn. I gladly fall in behind him, matching his pace, step for step, foot for foot. The familiar brown scree rolls by. My rucksack feels light. Hundreds of tiny wildflowers pierce the brown dirt. By 3 o'clock we reach Camp 1 and I climb inside the narrow tent. The warmth of the sun on the tent relaxes me. The tent door frames clouds drifting gently past my view. I am hungry and nip into a can of tuna fish and then polish off a few granola bars. It has warmed enough that the dripping sound of melting snow has changed to the hollow gurgle of water percolating down through the boulders where a few days ago I knelt, sick and weakened.

At midnight we wake. Željko is already outside the tent, dressed in dark blue climbing pants and a button-down cotton flannel shirt befitting his occupation as a farmer. Standing, he shuts off the stove and hands me a thermos of tea. Pulling on my boots, I step into the lacquered darkness of a moonless night.

While still fastening his helmet on over his hand-knit wool cap, Željko starts off toward the ropes that have been fixed above Camp 1.

I fall in behind, steadying my breathing as we work upwards, each slow step feels awkward until finally, we slip into a pattern. One crampon at a time bites the frozen snow. Step up, swing the other leg around and up, drop it just a bit higher. It is good to feel the crunch of the snow under the machine-like efficiency of my crampons. I lift the axe in my uphill hand, then plunge it back down, the tip striking the snow with a hollow twang.

On reaching the crest above camp we follow a faintly scuffed path toward the base of a rock tower, inked even blacker in silhouette against the sky. There, at the base, a piton is fixed with a carabiner which in turn holds a knotted white rope; the fixed line that will safeguard our passage across the most difficult sections of the climb.

Željko stops to attach his ascender to the rope. With a quick tug to assure himself it's working, he resumes climbing. Taking advantage of the wisdom that we should never climb on the same section of rope at the same time, I remove my pack and sip some hot tea from my thermos. Once Željko is across the icy couloir and has moved his ascender past the next piton, I lightly shoulder my load of ramen, pasta, tea, sugar, powdered milk and stove fuel bound for Camp 2. The couloir passes under my crampons without event, and the route crosses onto another rib of icy rock.

The monotony of climbing starts to weigh on me as section after section passes. I move along the rope, every step secured by the fixed line. I soon realize that when confronted with a difficult section the quickest thing is to forego any climbing technique and simply pull on the fixed rope. In fact, this is the only way I can keep up with the plaid blur of Željko, whose robotic pace remains steady.

Camp 2 is perched on a house-size ice shelf formed by the confluence of the mountain's south face and the smaller, but still several-thousand-foot wall, to the west. We unload our supplies into the empty tents. As I finish unpacking my load I catch a short, hoarse yodel on the wind. I look up; it's Tone and Robi on their way back down from supplying Camp 3 several thousand feet above.

I hoot in reply and put on my parka to wait for my friends. Željko sits on his pack, dons a patched down parka, and pulls a stove from the tent to start preparing a drink for the descending pair.

"How is it?" I ask as Robi steps a cramponed foot onto the tent platform chopped into the ice. His faded yellow parka hangs loose and oversized on his gaunt steelworker's frame.

"Good. It's good. Glad to see you on the mountain again Štef. Hello Željko."

"Hello, hello," Željko says, muffled by the hiss of the stove working away at the ice.

I had not expected conditions to be so warm. At 19,000 feet I'm wearing only Midweight Capilene, and no gloves. This was my first time using fixed lines; the experience was not a positive one. STEVE HOUSE COLLECTION

"Maybe we will go down to base camp with you after a short rest. No?" Robi looks at Tone.

"Yes," replies Tone, pulling out a sleeping pad to sit on. "It is better to sleep in base camp tonight, but we should start down soon, the sun will loosen the rocks. It will be too dangerous to cross the couloir in a few hours." Tone ponders Željko with a professorial look. "Željko, leave the stove and start back with Štef. We will finish here and follow behind you. Go before it gets too warm."

"Okay. I understand." Željko stands and takes off his coat. "Lucky trails." With that familiar mountaineers' farewell, he shoulders his pack. I strip off my own parka. It's too warm now for the down jacket, even at rest. When I look up from stuffing my jacket into my pack, Željko has already set off down the lines. I clip in with my locking carabiner and start down after him.

I chase Željko's crampon marks down the ice ridge, where we switch to rappelling down the lines, and then down the mixed face of rock and ice. The ropes are starting to show a few nicks, signs of rock fall, that I didn't notice as I came up by headlamp. I blast down the lines; Željko always just a bit ahead. I work harder to keep up, transitioning from one rappel to the next as fast as I can. When I almost catch up, he is across the final couloir and working down the slope above Camp 1.

At the start of the traverse I pause and look up the couloir to see if any stones are falling towards me. Nothing. I hold my breath to listen. A rush of wind lifts a cloud over the ridge crest revealing a sudden view of the peaks on the horizon. No other sound but the wind. I look down at my feet and start across.

Once on the other side, I pause to catch my breath. I'm losing strength now; I am hot and fatigued, and long since out of tea. It has taken us three hours to descend from Camp 2. From Camp 1 it is a simple hike down 5,000 feet of loose scree to base camp: a bitch to go up, but quick to descend. I turn and spy two dots of color a few hundred feet above. Robi, in yellow, is followed closely by Tone's purple parka. They're just 20 minutes behind me.

Five minutes later I step down and drop my pack near the biggest tent at Camp 1. "Good. No?" says Željko, as he glances at his watch. He already has his few things out of the tent and is packing to go to base camp.

"Yeah, three hours. I think that's good for the first time down. I'm tired though."

Just then, a large clatter of stones is followed by a sharp, distinct human shout. I spin around in time to see a barrage of loose stones fall past Robi and strafe the couloir below him. The sound is deafening as the rock fall passes 40 feet to the right of camp. Above us Tone is yelling. Robi is not moving.

"Shit." I turn back to the pack I just took off. Željko is already on his feet, bounding up the hill. I shoulder my pack and trip over the guy-lines to the tent in my haste. I can't tell what is going on above us. Raggedly I breathe and scramble upwards toward Robi and Tone. Faster and faster, until I have to stop, gasping for breath, lungs burning.

Željko flies ahead of me. I look up. Both Tone and Robi are in the middle of the snow couloir now. And both are moving off to the side toward us. Relief. Robi is okay, I think. "He's okay. He's okay." I slow my pace but continue to climb toward the descending pair.

Leaning heavily against Tone, Robi walks towards me. He's holding his left elbow and his left hand is curled into an unnatural snarl. Željko shadows them, eyeing Robi cautiously.

"It's my arm," he says, his face red. "It's broken I think. Shit! I don't believe it." A rock rolls under his foot and he stumbles. Tone catches Robi before he topples over.

"Slowly," Tone coaches softly. "Slowly now."

"Give me your pack, Robi," I say.

"No, no. At camp," he replies. I turn around to retrace the hundred feet back to Camp 1.

Two days later a pair of small black dots noisily beat the sky as they make their cautious descent across the rock-strewn glacier and circle above our barren little meadow. A few moments later the first Pakistani Army helicopter dips towards our camp and lands a few hundred feet away. The second one lands a few hundred feet further down valley. The pilot waves us forward. Robi grasps his injured arm in its sling, and in a slouch, he jogs towards the waiting chopper. Taking a seat on the pilot's left-hand side, he clumsily fixes his seat belt before returning the pilot's curt nod. With a deafening rattle he is gone. No good-bye. No chance for hopeful words. Robi is lifted into the bosom of civilization and is on his way to a hospital in Islamabad where his arm will be X-rayed, the cracked bones set and cast.

Robi was one of our strongest climbers, and the mood of the expedition shifts down from one of youthful exuberance to measured stoicism. Željko and I continue to cycle loads up to camps 1 and 2. On the third trip we try to carry two sleeping bags to Camp 3 but are turned back by our slow progress in the recent heavy snows.

Latoba Meadows Base Camp, Nanga Parbat, Pakistan: July 29, 1990

In base camp the radio handset buzzes to life. "Base camp, base camp. Speak up." It's Jože.

"Base camp." repeats Tone.

"Yeah, Tone. The weather seems fine, so Marija and I will start for the summit tomorrow." They're attempting the summit? How can that happen so fast, I think.

"Good. You have everything?" Tone replies stiffly.

"Ya, Ya. The light tent and the one sleeping bag and the new rope that Štef brought." My rope? I think. How did my rope get up there? But I know, it was the best one, the only new one, and part of the expedition gear. I just wish I was up there, using it.

"Lucky trails. Call us each night at 8 o'clock if possible." Tone signs off.

"Thank you. Lucky trails. Tomorrow we will call." The radio crackles and goes dead.

The next day the expedition is quiet. No one goes up on the mountain. In camp we all rest: reading in the tents, playing nervous games of cards, scanning the skies for approaching storms. Waiting. That night the radio is silent and the next day the card game doesn't formulate.

"Tone, weren't they supposed to call every night?" I ask.

"Ya, Štef. They are supposed to call. I am worried. It is again after the time they should call. This is not good."

On the third day, our liaison officer, Assad, offers his assistance. He has access to army communications and there is an army camp just down valley. Perhaps Marija and Jože descended the opposite side of the mountain. In our imaginings this is certainly possible. So Assad contacts an army officer who is stationed in Chilas, on the mountain's far side; this officer agrees to send two men up to the Diamir Base Camp to see if they descended the easier far side of the mountain.

Five days later and still no word from Marija and Jože. I am shaken from my sleep by visions of the bivouacked pair, thousands of feet above me, cold and freezing, while I lie here comfortably warm. Unable to get back to sleep, I write a long letter to Anne: "They haven't called in for five days now... we're all thinking that the worst has happened."

At first light I head across the meadow to send it out with the Sierra Club trekking group that camped nearby last night. Just as I am returning to my tent, I hear something I haven't heard in a long time.

"Base camp, base camp, speak up. Over." It's Jože!

Within seconds Tone is outside the tent and is quickly surrounded by the rest of the expedition, standing tiptoe on the dewy ground, half-dressed, and clamoring to hear the radio.

"Base camp here. How are you? Tell us everything!" Tone demands.

"Yeah. All is okay. On 31 July at five in afternoon we reached the summit. We are both tired. Both okay. Marija has little frostbite on her fingers, but it is fine. We are at Camp Three now. We come down to base camp today if possible."

A great shout of group relief goes out. Tone looks like he might cry. Everyone is talking in fast breathless sentences. I run over to the trekkers, reclaim my letter, and quickly scrawl the good news on the outside of the envelope.

At dusk Marija and Jože walk into base camp. A few members have climbed up to them to help them with their packs. I watch the small, tight pack of climbers move down the valley toward base camp. At dinner we all excitedly fire questions at them: How were the conditions? Where did you bivouac? What took so much time? Why could they not call for five days? What did the summit look like?

At breakfast the next morning the conversation has shifted. "Tone," Željko asks. "What now. Who is going up next?"

"No Željko, no one is going up. Only to clean the camps."

"But we want a chance at the summit now!" Željko cries.

Tone's reply is drowned in the din of reaction. Finally, Tone stands up to assert his voice, jabbing the air to make his points. "Twelve hours ago half of you thought Marija and Jože were dead!" His face flushes red with emotion. "Now you want to go up? No. It is too difficult. Too dangerous. This expedition is finished." He sits down.

Two days later at Camp 1 Željko and I lift our massive packs. Of the 20, we were the only ones willing to come and clean out the camp and bring the tents down. I glance up, our fixed lines stretch off, we do not have the time or the willing manpower to clean those ropes off the mountain. I turn and plunge down the loose dirt and scree below me. Leaving the ropes fixed is inexcusable littering. My disappointment in my teammates propels me all the way to base camp.

Three weeks later I perch on a large white granite boulder peering up the Batura Glacier valley. I've traveled hundreds of miles by jeep, bus, tractor, and finally by foot. When the expedition dissolved I wanted to see more of this country, while the others elected to return to Islamabad for an early flight home. I pick up my journal, shifting uncomfortably on the rock. As far I as I can see there are unclimbed mountains of striking danger and uncommon beauty.

"What I have learned about myself on this expedition I will be assimilating for a long time," I write. "There were many valuable lessons. I have been shown how much I did not know. Marija and Jože have also shown me how much can be done. Becoming an alpinist, an alpinist who can reach these summits, including Nanga Parbat. That is what I want to become."

I pause, focusing on the tiny points of the summits piercing the horizon. I put the pen back to the paper. "Rereading what I just wrote, I realize that I'm not even sure exactly what that entails. I suppose I need to get more experience. I know that I need to improve my own climbing. And organize my own climbs. I need to get good enough not to need fixed ropes. What a disaster fixed ropes and camps are! I have to find a way to surround myself with good climbers. Good partners will make me a better climber. And that's what I want to be, the best climber I can become. If I could climb the Rupal Face some day, that would be the ultimate. I can't imagine ever becoming good enough for that."

Marija Frantar summited Nanga Parbat with Jože Rozman on July 31, 1990. In 1991, Marija and Jože attempted Kanchenjunga. Near the summit they called base camp to say they were lost. Their bodies were found at 24,000 feet. Disoriented and exhausted, they had fallen to their deaths. SILVIJ MOROJNA

CHAPTER FOUR

No Place to Hide

Bellingham, Washington: August, 1991

"MARIJA AND JOŽE ARE DEAD?" I think the words and then repeat them out loud to myself. Spoken, they sound painfully true. I sit down and reread the letter, then refold it and replace it in its envelope. Holding the envelope gently, I stare at the floor. In my mind I see Kanchenjunga, the mountain that killed them. I recall from a photograph that it's broad and narrow, covered in chaotic broken glaciers, with three distinct summits. My eyes move to the window where summer's rays are already heating a fine day.

"It can't be."

It is 6:45 in the morning, and I am at the guide service office to meet my six-day mountaineering class. I stand and tuck the envelope into the top of my backpack.

"They're just someplace better now." I think to myself. "I bet that Marija convinced Jože to go down the other side of the mountain and join a Buddhist monastery. I can see her doing that. That would be fun to hear about. Eight, ten years ... they'll be back."

I step out onto the stairs and greet the first of my students.

Bellingham, Washington: June, 1992

"Mugs is gone."

At first I can't absorb the words. The door to the red van is drawn open, throwing sunlight across thin vinyl seats bolted school-bus style to a bruised metal floor. I sit quietly in the back, an exhausted youth struggling between testosterone-surges of arrogance and powerful doses of mountain-induced humility. Julie Cheney-Culberson, Matt's wife, looks tiny in the doorway.

"Matt." She pauses to look him in the face. Matt has drawn a tense breath. Tears well up in her eyes. "Mugs is gone, Matt. Mugs is gone."

Mugs was one of the best alpinists in America. His Cassin Ridge solo eventually would inspire my own Alaskan climbs. He fell into a crevasse while guiding Denali. He walked up to the crevasse edge to make a routine route-finding decision. He didn't have a belay. His clients were unable to extract him.

Matt goes to her, both needing and providing comfort. Uncomfortable, I slip out unnoticed. "Mugs Stump? Dead?" I think. "That shouldn't happen. Not like that."

Soon I'm walking downhill, toward Tony's Coffee House, wondering if that cute brunette I met last week might be working today. "Yeah, this is the same day, same time, as last week." I take off down the sidewalk, a renewed purpose to my step.

Skagit, Washington: August 11, 1993

"This will just take a minute," I announce to the van full of mountaineering students as I pull into a familiar gas station parking lot. "Why don't you guys get some ice cream. I need to call the office to let them know we're down and safe."

I drop 35 cents into the phone, it rings twice. "Hello?" I ask when I don't hear the normally cheerful "American Alpine Institute" greeting on the line.

"Hello. Who's this?" comes the reply.

"Hi Sheilagh, it's Steve. I'm just calling to let you know we're off Mount Baker and heading your way."

The voice on the other end of the line is quaking as she starts. "Steve, it's Julie. We just found out. Julie's dead."

"How?" I demand. I had just seen Julie earlier this week.

"She and Matt went up to Canada. We don't have any details yet. I only know that they fell down the Aemmer Couloir on Mount Temple. Matt is badly hurt, but he's going to be okay."

I hang up the phone and walk back to the van. The climbing stories I read as a youth had been full of avalanches, rock fall, crevasses, storms, exhaustion, and extreme altitude. Men – for they were mostly men – succeeding, but also failing and dying. It's not just a story anymore.

Dexter Falls, Ouray, Colorado: February 25, 1995

I hear the growl of the falling stone before I see it. "Rock!" I scream. "Lean in. Lean in!"

Dan and Caroll both lean into the ice. Dan is turned towards me and I see the fear reflected in his eyes. Behind Dan, Caroll faces straight in, his nose to the ice, his hands gripping the ice screws at our belay stance. I smash my body into the ice, and I lift my head in time to see the rock spinning assuredly, fatefully towards Caroll. Caroll senses it, I think, because just then he looks up.

I see the rock, but there is no time to feel anything. It is roughly the size and shape of a small microwave oven. It is dark, dark brown, nearly black. One end of it is crusted with shiny dark mud that had been holding it to the mountain. The mud is laced with crystals from the morning's frost. The rock is more trapezoid than square. Bits of snow spin off of it as it flies. It smashes into Caroll's helmet. The corner of the trapezoid goes into the turquoise blue helmet. Caroll is gone.

"Caroll!" Dan and I both scream. Caroll isn't at the rappel station anymore. One of the ice screws we had placed for our anchor is bent or broken; I can't tell. There is a flap of webbing that should be part of our anchor, swinging impotently between us. A broken carabiner lies on the foot-wide ledge where Caroll had been standing.

I look down. Caroll is sprawled in steep snow 30 feet below, unanchored, and 10 feet away from a sheer 120-foot drop to the base of Dexter Falls, a moderate ice climb an easy hour's walk from the highway. He isn't moving. There is no sound.

In earning my alpine guide's certification I had trained for emergencies like this. I had hoped that they would never happen to me. But I always suspected that if I stayed in it long enough they would. My training takes over: take care of the survivors, allow no more victims. I rebuild the anchor. One ice screw is still good. I replace the damaged one with a new screw. Tears are streaming down Dan's face as I clip him to the new anchor. I rig the rappel rope and descend to Caroll.

"Don't hurry, Steve." I recite to myself the mantra of the rescuer, "You don't have any time to waste." When I get to Caroll he is motionless but breathing deep, irregular, labored breaths.

"Caroll! Caroll!" I yell.

Dan hangs in his harness, his forehead against the ice. He is sobbing quietly. Besides Caroll's heavy breathing, it is the only sound I hear. I shake Caroll's shoulder. No response. I attach his harness to mine to ensure he doesn't roll off the ice cliff.

His helmet is split open, sliced like a pie. The sharp tip of the broken plastic is smeared with an opaque, gooey red. There is a sharp odor I've never smelled before. Pungent, like dilute ammonia. Gently, I reach down and remove the helmet. He groans, but the helmet is loose and slips off easily.

Holding his head out of the snow I see that the backside of his skull is strangely flattened and covered in thick blood blended with an opaque gel and clumped strands of hair. I start to touch and press around the wound. It is soft.

My stomach turns. I see all of this as if I'm a distant observer.

"Do something! Help him!" my mind screams. I place a big roll of gauze onto the wound and use another roll to secure it to his head. I put his helmet back on to hold the compress. I pull out a long piece of cord, double it, and tie a knot near the center, improvising a system for us to rappel simultaneously.

"Let's go Caroll." I kneel and place his right arm over my shoulder and grab his harness with my free hand. Standing, I tip him up. He is heavy, but once he's up, his legs seem to hold him. I gently move his body back down the slope to a position where he is half hanging on the rope, half standing. He is rigid but unstable, and I hold his harness firmly to keep him upright and keep pushing him against the rappel device. I step to his right. I see eyes under lids that are heavy, almost completely shut. I get behind him and grab hold of his climbing harness with my left hand. My right controls the rappel and I let slip a few inches of rope to get us moving downhill.

He grunts, and I lower a few more feet, gaining speed now. With sudden strength Caroll twists towards me swinging at me with closed fists. I am in close, almost to his chest and his blows swing wide and round to hit the back of my head. I feel like bawling, crying at this betrayal. I look up at Dan as Caroll hits me again and again. Dan looks away. Just then, Caroll hits me in the side of the face with his elbow. He is pushing in all directions. He levers himself out of my grasp and knocks himself down into the snow.

"Caroll! Dammit! Stand up!" Dan suddenly yells. I look up at Dan, his face a red mass of tears and terror.

A thought flashes in my head: Caroll's combativeness is a result of the head wound. I reach for his harness. He is bigger than I am. I pull and he doesn't budge. I am mad now. I work under him again, forcing my arm into the snow beneath him, and then with a heave, I thrust him into a standing position and for a moment he stands on his own.

I step back, moving us a few feet down. My crampon scrapes at something. It is dark brown. Partially covered in the snow it looks almost black. I push at it with my foot. The rock is very heavy. It is more of a trapezoid than a square.

For a moment Caroll is motionless. His lids are raised now and he is looking at me with eyes that no longer see: unfocused, dark eyes. Before he can strike at me, his unknown attacker, I shove him down the hill. The harness catches his weight as I lower us down the rappel line.

I have myself rigged just below him, so I swing down, adding my own weight to the anchor. Capitalizing on our momentum, I move down into position and wrap my arm around his middle to get a strong grip on the front of his harness. I lean against the rope and pull Caroll down the slope with me.

The top of the ice wall drops off and Caroll's weight is fully on his harness now. This makes it easier to control our descent. Still he rages, thrashing and punching. His harness keeps him facing up and I am held just below and behind him, coincidentally sheltered from his blows. Time recovers its normal scale and within a few seconds we are safely on the ground.

"Dan!" I yell. "You must rappel down to us now."

I hear nothing. I test the ropes with a light grip to see if he is rigging his rappel device a 120 feet above us. The rope is still.

"Dan! Come. Down." I pause and there is no response. "Do. You. Hear. Me?"

Still no reply, but the rope shakes a little and I know he is starting down. Slowly, bravely, he makes his way down the rope to us.

"Over there. Help me," I command as we each lift Caroll by an arm and half carry, half drag him off to the far side of the waterfall, clear of the possibility of more falling rocks. Dan sits with his legs outstretched and holds Caroll's head in his lap; his hand over the gauze.

"You stay here. I'm running out to get help." It's only 1 pm. Search and Rescue will get here soon and we'll get Caroll out of here and to the hospital. Caroll's breathing is deep and regular now, his chest rising and falling peacefully. Dan is crying again.

"You're doing good, Steve." Dan stutters through his tears, and wipes his nose on a sleeve. "This is just a bad hair day. Caroll will be alright." I wince at the poor timing of his favorite saying.

As I run down the trail I can't shake the vision: The black hair gelled into thick strands. The opaque, viscous fluid mixed with blood. Some of it almost clear, some pink, some dark red. The softness I felt when I pressed on the white edge of his fractured skull. When I let go, startled, how more gel and blood came up. I tried to push it back in. But the hair was matted. Black, thick strands of unclean hair.

<hr/>

It is my turn to stand in front of the church congregation in Charlotte, North Carolina, 10 days later. Caroll had died in the ICU, four days after the accident. I had watched as his wife's hand shook so hard she couldn't legibly sign the order to terminate life support.

I walk toward the pulpit and look out across hundreds of faces and realize just how out of my element I am. A young, white, atheist mountain guide from Washington state standing in front of a congregation of Southern Baptists. I am 24 years old and have never bought alcohol without being carded. Today I'm wearing my sport coat and my one necktie for only the second time. The first had been my senior prom six years earlier.

I wish I could tell them about the black, secret pride worn by those climbers still living. How we share knowing glances among us when one of our brothers dies. I want to deride the outsiders – or those wishing to justify their decision not to climb – who are quick to point out how suddenly death can come to an alpinist.

"You never know who will be next! You might be next!" they cry.

This is true. I justify continuing to climb, my comrades' deaths notwithstanding, by attempting to learn the lessons of their fatal errors. But this time the errors are mine, and Caroll is dead. I cry for Caroll, but mostly for myself. Before I was better, smarter, stronger. Luckier.

But I wasn't. I'm not. I shouldn't be alive. Tears stream down my cheeks for this injustice. There is no place to hide.

"I am Steve House." My too loud voice booms and cracks over the speakers. I step back a little. "I'm the certified alpine climbing guide who was there with Caroll in Colorado."

Though nothing I might have done would have held that nearly black stone in place, I want to tell them how I feel that I fell short as a mountain guide: not giving sufficient weight to the warming temperature, not cracking the whip a little harder when Caroll and Dan got a late start. I wish I could explain these transgressions. I can't ask for their forgiveness when I can't make them understand my sins.

"I climbed with Caroll many times over the last few years." I blink away a few tears and gather enough courage to continue. "I know he loved climbing, that he was at peace when he was in the mountains. If it's any consolation to you all, I think that his last days were joyous ones." I step away from the microphone, hating this justification. Death is death. Irrevocable. Forever.

Eli Helmuth (right) and I pose at the top of Motorcycle Hill, July 2, 1995. The Father and Sons Wall is bathed in afternoon sun behind us. We staged our first ascent of the wall from the West Buttress route's 11,000-foot camp. ELI HELMUTH

CHAPTER FIVE

A Punk in Crampons

Father and Sons Wall, Denali, Alaska: July 1, 1995

WITH MY BOOT I PUSH the downy snow off the top of the small rock outcropping. The black steel of the crampon scratches as it drags against the ice. Eli hacks away rhythmically. With a slow 4/4 count, he swings from his shoulder, slowly flattening and smoothing our little perch. With the snow cleared, I take up my axe and join in. *Whack-whack. Whack-whack. Whack-whack.*

"Looks good, huh?" Eli says 30 minutes later. His worn bibs come high on his chest. With the thick white sun block on his cheeks and the dark mountain glasses he looks like an extra in a zombie movie.

"Good enough for government work," I say, my arm aches from chopping. Using the axe, I brush snow from above the ledge and place a couple of ice screws. We both tie in.

Clipping off my two mismatched ice tools – the hammer blue and short, and the axe black and longer – to the anchor, I work off my crampons and then carefully clip them in as well. Balancing on the slick blue ice, I pull out my bivy sack, sit down on our small ledge, and pull the nylon sack over my feet and up to my chin. In turn Eli kicks his toe into the ice, reaches down, and snaps off his crampons. In the bivy sacks we wear our parkas and mittens, but we have no sleeping bags to insulate us. I grunt and twist to adapt to the lumps, half-lying on my backpack, half-leaning against the slope above me.

Eli laughs. "Comfy?"

"Yeah, great."

Warmth and comfort have been sacrificed to our credo of light and fast. It is

2 o'clock in the afternoon. We've been on the move nonstop for 22 hours. We're hungry and thirsty. I lie back, Eli flicks a lighter and the stove sparks to life as he lifts his glasses, pushing back his thick, unwashed hair. He turns up the gas and the stove starts to growl. It feels good to lie down after so much effort. My muscles are still warm from the climbing; the tension seeps from my legs out into the refreshing coolness of the ice underneath me.

Due to Eli's attentiveness to the small aluminum pot, we soon have water. Water means we can eat: ramen soup, a bag of molasses cookies, energy bars. I look down and across the wall to where I can pick out climbers on the normal, West Buttress route. I imagine them gazing back, taking in the view of the massive wall. We are hidden by the wall's vastness. The summer sun bakes down, warming us as an afterthought.

Light and fast means cold and hungry. As the hard hand of shadow replaces the caress of sunshine, I am pulled from slumber. We have dozed just two hours. With a shrug, Eli shifts and turns away from me. Neither of us offer any words against the silence. This is our second straight month together, having just guided Denali's West Rib route. After that trip, we tossed around a few ideas for a climb. It was too warm for lower-elevation objectives, like the Ruth Gorge. So between pints of Häagen-Dazs, we settled on the Father and Sons Wall. It's a well-known objective; Mugs Stump had been attempting it the year before his death.

To shake off my drowsiness, I push back the green hood of the bivy sack. Below us a cloudbank, gray and thick, laps at the base of the wall, a great lake on a steep, inaccessible shore. I look out across the clear sky. It has darkened to a lovely midnight blue.

It is my turn to work the stove, and once I have the blue flame melting ice, I stare into a glacier wilderness. The Peters Glacier flows down and gives in to the darkening greens and browns of tundra that march north into the Alaskan interior. I can't identify anything human anywhere. The climbers visible earlier have moved on. We are supremely isolated. I find this strangely comforting. Not long ago, I would have been profoundly discomfited by this solitude. Fears are overcome incrementally. Increasing skill, ambition and experience has eroded my fear of exposure and isolation. Experience has dispelled my existential fear of this universe of rock and ice and snow.

But then I look down, and it hits me that we are 4,000 feet up a previously unexplored, unclimbed wall on North America's highest peak. I close my eyes and take a deep breath against my building anxiety and look up. Break it down, I think. We have 2,000 feet of technical ice climbing above us, and maybe four hours of easier climbing beyond that to regain the West Buttress route. Rejoining the normal route will allow us to circle back down and around to the tents we left at the 11,000-foot camp.

There is no way now that we can retreat down our ascent route with the little equipment we have: two 165-foot climbing ropes, a half-dozen ice screws, and a small handful of rock-climbing hardware. Up is the only way home.

Neither of us has ever been out this far before. We're living the science fiction of legendary climber Mugs Stump soloing the Cassin Ridge in a day; the ideal that Mark Twight and Scott Backes lived the year before while climbing and descending a new route on Mount Hunter in 44 hours. The stories we've read of men climbing the biggest mountains, even Everest, in marathon 30-plus hour days.

Thinking about the climbers who preceded us renews my confidence. I can see that without heavy packs we can go much farther than I ever imagined. By embracing one kind of risk – not being equipped to stop for more than a few hours, no matter what the situation – we are stretching the safety net of speed to another level. The less time we're on the wall the less chance we have of being caught in a storm. With our crampons and ice tools we're climbing this idea into action.

A pewter twilight filters our world; all is shades of gray and black. Darkness itself is held at bay by the recent summer solstice and our northern latitude. Our strategy relies on the never dark Alaskan night. Assuredly, we clip dulled crampons back onto boots, pack our few belongings into our small packs, and resume climbing.

The climbing now is easy, but dangerous. We take more risks to climb faster. We place one ice screw and clip the rope to it, simulclimbing together – both climbing at the same time with the rope stretched out between us and the screw serving to keep us from going to the bottom of the wall if one of us slips. Nevertheless, such a fall would likely result in a painful, slow demise. Broken legs and arms a more likely outcome than the quick finality of a ground-fall death. I wonder if it wouldn't be safer simply to unrope. In my frazzled state the prospect seems too harrowing to suggest. With our partnership as a crutch we hobble up the last few hundred feet.

I'm in front, and having placed the last of our six ice screws, I drive my ice hammer solidly into the ice and clip our rope into it. I climb to the end of the rope and I place my one remaining ice tool and belay Eli by knotting a sling over the head of the axe, using the tool as the belay anchor.

Eli leads through wordlessly, glancing sideways at my ice-axe belay. He already has all the gear from cleaning the last pitch and there is no need to discuss, critique or dwell on risks already taken.

Trance-like, we move together up the wall; the features that we memorized from photographs morph into place and actual scale. A couloir that we thought would be two feet wide is 30 feet wide. Aspects we thought flush, angle sharply off to the side.

As soon as the angle relents, about 200 feet below the top of the Northwest Buttress, Eli stops. We've climbed the last several hundred feet without a running belay; just soloing while roped together. No shared anchor to arrest us as in simulclimbing, thinking we are only moments away from topping out. I shiver in the thick chill of the Arctic night. Eli kneels in the snow, bent over with stomach cramps from dehydration.

It is too cold to stop in the middle of the night and wait for the stove to cheer us. "Straighten up, man," I admonish. "We can't stay here."

"I know. I know. Just give me a minute."

I lie down on the hard snow, arms flopped to my sides, digesting my own pain. The cold seeps quickly in. I roll onto my stomach, press onto my hands and knees, and slowly stand up. "Come on," I say, and we strike for the top.

The apex of the Father and Sons Wall is at 15,400 feet. From there the ridge crest curls a lazy design to Denali's north summit, 4,000 feet above. The top looks close in the still, blue light of Alaskan midnight, but we know better. We are briefly tempted by the romance of climbing all the way to the summit. Our goal, however, has been to climb the wall, not necessarily to reach the summit. Planning otherwise would have compromised our 20-pound packs. Eli and I stand at the top of the Father and Sons Wall at half-past midnight.

We stumble down through snowdrifts and crevasses, unaccustomed to the flatness. The glacier here is windblown and we walk across bare ice, jumping thinly veiled crevasses. Soon we start up the snow-laden northern slope of the West Buttress. We have 1,200 feet to ascend and it goes slowly. I pause every few steps to catch my breath, leaning against snow so deep it comes to my belly. I shovel and collapse the snow by hand and move up two steps. I switch leads with Eli. He does five steps.

The temperature drops further and an icy breeze trickles down from the upper mountain, numbing our faces. I work my jaw to keep my face from freezing; the skin feels wax-like and stiff. When we finally arrive at 16,200 feet we are on familiar ground, the normal route, and our descent. We walk past gently flapping tents while people snore peacefully inside. Our survival is assured. In a couple easy hours we are back in our own tents.

American Alpine Institute, Bellingham, Washington: September, 1995

Neither Eli nor I have seen our pictures in a magazine before. But now our photographs accompany the news of our new route, which we named First Born, in the pages of *Climbing, Rock and Ice,* and eventually the estimable *American Alpine Journal*. I am torn between excitement and dismay at the publicity.

"Those people don't care. They don't understand what we went through to do that climb." I toss the magazine back into a pile at the climbing shop.

I need a new goal. I recall a potential route that Eli and I saw on our way to First Born: an unclimbed direct line on Denali's Washburn Wall, which is accessed from the same approach we used for First Born. Having just completed my undergraduate ecology degree, I decide not to apply to a masters program and choose instead to spend the winter guiding in Ecuador, where I log time at altitude and bank most of my pay. Though I earn only $75 per day, it leaves me plenty of free time and allows me to build fitness and gain valuable experience at high altitude.

My college classmates write from their graduate school jobs with tales of endless titrations completed in science labs, of 80-hour weeks researching their professor's theses. I slowly kick steps up 20,000-foot volcanoes and resent my lack of intellectual challenge. Knowing my goals are solely mine, I scoff at those who went to grad school, or took so-called real jobs. That is the ultimate sell-out: to work for the man. To cast your only soul into a hell of cubicles and workstations and dollar bills. And if they don't see this, they don't deserve the chance to find out who they might become.

I am a punk in crampons. Living to climb. Climbing to live. A lucky rabbit, saved not by my own brilliance, but by the odd-chance that in Slovenia I had been shown the Wonderland trap door of climbing. I am sure that alpinism can reveal everything I need to know as a human being.

My boyhood friends turn detractors. They try to take me down with logic borrowed from their church of success. "What are you going to do when you're old and your knees are shot? Are you saving for retirement?" I laugh at them, the laugh of the cornered villain who knows his escape. I will succeed because I must. Their slings and arrows are excuses for their failure to be brave enough, their failure to believe in themselves, their failure to commit to an unmapped future.

Their born-again indoctrination makes them blind to the benefits of process. I trade stock in the future for cash in hand. I equal their fervor in my admonitions that their notions of success are meaningless. I charge that they are motivated by expectations that are not their own; busy with empty dramas that belong only to them.

I have exorcised my own expectations and embraced life in the moment. The socialistic Slovenes showed me the way with their actions, their spirits, and their thoughts. They lived in a country with no future. Redemption, they taught, can be achieved only by showing great spirit, style, and fortitude.

That is how I see it. Time may soften my piety. Maybe I will gain a greater appreciation for teachers and scientists and taxi drivers. And perhaps alpinism will not be able to teach me everything that I need to know.

I have read all the books and know that none of the legendary climbers had done their first great climbs later than the age of 26. At 24, Reinhold Messner soloed the north face of Les Droites in eight hours, thereby revolutionizing ice climbing. Deep down I know that I have something great in me, something that will suit my strengths. Something alpine, icy, and committing.

To achieve it, I will need to commit everything to my art.

By chance, my wife of seven months, Anne, and I are reunited at the 14,000-foot camp on Denali. It is her birthday but she's too embarrassed to let anyone know, limiting our celebration to a hug and a kiss. I am descending from guiding a successful trip up the West Rib route. Anne is apprenticing as a guide on the West Buttress. Eli, my co-leader on the Rib trip, gracefully offers to continue down to base camp with the clients. Secretly I am overjoyed to be left here alone. I've kept my plans for a new route to myself. I have not told Anne.

Flexibility is one key to success in the Alaska Range. I plot a couple objectives: The new route I saw last year on the Washburn Wall or a fast solo of the Cassin Ridge. I scrounge a good stockpile of food and borrow a second ice tool. Anne's group heads up to high camp. I say goodbye and begin recording cloud cover, barometric pressure, and wind direction in my journal.

After several days the weather seems to have acquired a pattern: clear and cold in the morning, breezy in the afternoon, squally and showery in the evening. I decide to go look at the new route: the northwest face of the West Buttress. Commonly known as the Washburn Wall, a gesture of respect to Bradford Washburn who explored, photographed, suggested, and climbed many of the mountain's major routes.

Putting my climbing harness on over patched nylon pants, I leave the camp at 14,000 feet and jog down around Windy Corner in plastic boots and crampons. I carry only a water bottle, one extra pair of gloves, and a couple of energy bars. I meet with more than one admonishing glance from the heavily laden mountaineers plodding their way up. My own thoughts are equally reproachful. "There ain't nothing light or fast about those guys."

Forty minutes later, I veer off this well-worn path, take a deep breath, and follow the descent route Eli and I pioneered last year. Facing in toward the slope I down climb steep snow to an ice gully that after two hours deposits me at 10,000 feet on the Peters Glacier.

From there I can see 1,800 feet of 50-degree ice stretching to meet the steep granite rockband in the middle of the face. I take large bites off an energy bar and a few measured sips of water as I trace white streaks of what may be climbable ice cascading through the rock. Above that a web of gullies and ice slopes connect the remaining 4,000 feet in a simple, direct pattern.

I cruise up on soft, polished ice. No rope, no partner. Just two, three, sometimes four metal points holding me to the mountain. Occasional spindrift hisses harmlessly to my left as I weave along the edge of the icefield. I focus on the rhythm of the climbing. As I get higher the vastness of Denali looms large, blocking the sun. Into the shadow I climb.

Near the rockband I pause to look up with increasing frequency and concern.

I lead one of the first steep pitches of First Born on the Father and Sons Wall. I established three new routes on Denali: First Born in 1995, Beauty Is a Rare Thing in 1996, and Mascioli's Pillar in 1997. ELI HELMUTH

I stop, chop a small platform in the ice, and clip into my tools. My path has ended as quickly as it began. There is no ice where I had imagined the route would go. The bare rock is too steep, too blank, to climb alone.

The traverse to the right, over to the only existing route on the face, doesn't look bad. That route was climbed a few years before by the veteran team of Phil Powers, Greg Collins, and Tom Walters and looks to be easily within my capabilities.

Allowing my disappointment to digest, I scan the wall above me, suddenly noticing a vertical flow of tan water ice camouflaged by the copper colored stone. It is not more than a 100 feet from where I stand. My heart beats faster as I nervously trace the undulations for several hundred feet to where it disappears over a bulge. I force myself to sit and study my options. For an hour I watch, but nothing falls down my newfound line.

As I move towards the icy corner I remind myself of the stakes: my life. Part of the beauty of soloing is that the risks are so high and so obvious. I whisper my promises. "Don't climb up anything you can't climb down. Listen to your intuition."

With the first easy stick of the ice axe's swing I scream, "*Aaarghh.*" I shout to banish doubt and to make sure I'm awake. A buzz of adrenaline lights me; I've never been more alive.

Each foot of altitude gained deepens my commitment. I have no rope with which to rappel or make a belay. No radio to call for help. One Denali guide, an old friend from years before, knows where I went today. I'm on a smooth smear of gray ice 200 feet into the rockband. The ice is barely a foot wide here and near vertical. I think of my sister's wedding next week. I mustn't ruin that with my funeral. Above me the ice widens and rolls back to 60 degrees before kicking up to vertical again and disappearing out of sight.

While climbing I talk to myself. "This kind of steep climbing can't last on an alpine face." And "the ice is incredible." Farther up, "I could belay off of that ice tool." As the runnel steepens I am forced to call upon my strength. I step a foot out left and place my crampons on a good square edge for balance. My self-talk continues. "Climb smart Steve. Technique. Relax and breathe. Climb smart Steve. Relax. Breathe."

I look down at my feet to step up; the face is laid out below me. Fields of snow-streaked ice and bands of wet rock fall unbroken to the virgin-white glacier. Fear grips me and I see myself skidding down this ice, slamming into the rocks, and spinning out away from the mountain. Dead before I hit bottom.

The ice slips back from vertical. I scramble carefully into a small alcove where I can stand without fear that a small slip will kill me. Above to my left rises a large gully that steepens to where it is stacked with plates of loose, rotten rock. Three other ice smears run up the right side of the chimney, each white and nearly vertical. The first smear is less steep, the middle is the broadest, tallest, and steepest, and the highest is less steep still, but rocks pierce the thin ice.

I climb up the first ice flow, each step is a decision, the summation of time-tempered judgment. I feel vastly experienced, invincible. The smear rolls back and I pause. To the right a small icefield tapers off and ends in steep, blank, and impassable rock. Above, lower angled mixed rock and ice climbing offer a possible exit. A few body-lengths higher I pause again. Here I will have to either commit to steep drytooling or descend. Pick by careful pick I reverse the last 100 feet of climbing.

The highest flow is less steep and the mixed climbing required there looks easier than what I just retreated from. I scurry up to its base and make a few moves. Two body-lengths into it I test the rock by striking it with my hammer. The veneer of ice holding it in place gives way and a shower of stones sail past my feet. I step back down.

My remaining options are to climb the middle flow or to down climb the entire face. I've down climbed vertical and near-vertical ice many times on toprope to train for this possibility. By necessity I down climbed vertical water ice on lead once. If I climb this vertical pitch, and am later forced to down climb, it won't be for practice, it will be for keeps. I focus my eyes, take three deep breaths, and swing an axe into the middle flow. The ice at the start is thin and close to vertical. I try my tools in several areas, testing the ice's strength and thickness. Satisfied that it will support me without breaking, I step my right foot out, push against it in a stemming position, and strike high with my tools.

Each moment requires precise judgment. The consequence of a single erroneous decision is beyond contemplation. I employ every instinct, every sense. To that end I have ears to hear the staccato crunch of a well-placed crampon strike. Eyes to see the warm-blue of solid ice. Skin to feel whether the temperature may be creeping above the all-important mark of 32 degrees, or plunging below zero and into an inhuman zone in which only the mountain itself can exist.

The ice thickens at the top as it blends into easier, 55-degree ice that I follow to the left. I can see the easy gully now. From there I will still have 4,000 feet of climbing, but it will be simple compared to this, and I will be able to move quickly and make good time. But I'm not out of the woods yet.

Between me and salvation is a short section of mixed climbing. The rock is nearly vertical and blocky. But it's not that far, 10 feet of horizontal climbing. I place one ice hammer solidly in the ice, as close to the rock as I can get it. The tool is bomber and will catch me if I fall in the first few feet. I reach to a large foothold, and kick it. Satisfied that it is solid I step onto it. Reaching out with my other tool I tap a few possible handholds. They all stay put. I drop the hammer so it hangs from my wrist and wrap my fingers around the best hold.

I reach the gully and let out a hoot. Looking back over what I just climbed, I feel satisfaction and immense joy. I glance at my watch and altimeter: 6:45 pm and right at 12,000 feet. Later I name the route Beauty Is a Rare Thing.

I wonder what is it, exactly, that I expect alpinism will teach me? Today,

Denali from the west, showing the Father and Sons Wall on the left and the Washburn Wall on the right.
BRADFORD WASHBURN

climbing has shown me a courageous, strong side of myself, a beautiful bravery. Other days I've seen pitiful weakness. I've watched myself crawl, belly-flat, across a mountainous landscape of fear. Climbing has shown me that I am all of these things: strong and weak, brave and cowardly, both immune to and at the mercy of the fear of death, all at the same time.

Risk is the fee to learn these lessons. The cost is not negotiable. It is a price that, for now, I pay gladly.

Alex Lowe on the second ascent of Legal at Last; he made the first ascent two years earlier. The route, Barely Legal, that I led, is to the left. In December 1995, both were among the hardest mixed leads in the world at that time. BRAD JOHNSON/PEAKS AND PLACES PHOTOGRAPHY

CHAPTER SIX

Alex Lowe

Cody, Wyoming: December 16, 1995

THE SIGNBOARD ACROSS THE STREET alternates big red digital numbers: 6:20 am, – 7°. Another wind gust rocks my tiny red car. As the heater blasts I am worried that I have the wrong place. I twist in my seat to see the hotel's sign. Big Bear Inn. I am worried that I have the wrong day.

I met Alex Lowe and Steve Swenson on an Alaskan glacier six months ago. Last week, Alex and I arranged to climb ice together above the south fork of the Shoshone River outside of Cody, Wyoming. Alex is one of the best-known climbers in the world right now. He is notorious for climbing thin ice and mixed routes nobody else can touch. Add into that his rock-climbing prowess – he's able to regularly on sight 5.12 – his long record of expedition climbs, an engineering degree, a growing family, and his lead role on the North Face's "Dream Team." His mystique is palpable. Hardly an issue of *Climbing* magazine is without news of some groundbreaking ascent done by the great Alex Lowe.

I'm nervous about climbing with him. I'm just a young guide who he happened to meet on the glacier. I sew my own clothing to save money. I drive a tiny fuel-sipping car. I just finished my B.S. in Ecology, which had taken me six years and garnered no special honors. As I check my heater to make sure it's on high, I wonder how I ended up here. I look up as a tall SUV wheels into the parking lot and drives toward me, the only car in the lot. I get out to say hello, wearing a stained yellow down jacket I bought at a second hand store. Alex jumps out, the passenger door opens, and I'm surprised to see another man.

"Hey," Alex says. "How are you? Good drive?" He grabs my hand and slaps me on the shoulder enthusiastically. I open the back of my car for my gear, and the new guy, Brad Johnson, takes my hand and introduces himself. Alex tosses my pack into his truck before I can shut off my car and grab my boots. I climb into the back seat and the wind slams the door for me.

By sunup we're hiking uphill through windblown sagebrush and across the odd snowdrift. Nervous about whether or not I can keep up, I fall immediately behind Alex, not wanting to slow him down. Brad, his pack filled with cameras, film and many lenses, falls off the pace after just a few hundred yards. At this I relax. Alex notices Brad's pace and slows down himself. We pass under cones of our own frosted breath, the heavy winter silence broken only by the dull crunch of boots crossing bare, frozen ground. As we turn a corner in the trail, a frozen waterfall comes into view and Alex accelerates up the hill at a fantastic pace. I let him go, happy to stay ahead of Brad who has now found his second wind.

We unload our packs below the ice climb and I step into my climbing harness. Alex already has his harness cinched up and pulls out a clanging bag of ice screws. I adjust my helmet as Brad kneels to snap a few photographs of Alex in his element.

Alex glances at my gear and grabs my lime-green ice hammer. "Cool. Piranhas. These things are great!"

Piranhas are made by Simond, an uncommon French ice tool and crampon company whose reputation seems to rest on the fact that their factory is based in the capital of alpinism: Chamonix. The gray axe I'd inherited from Caroll, whose death earlier this year still weighs heavily on me. The green hammer I'd purchased from another guide for 40 bucks so I'd have a matched set.

"Only good tools around, besides these." Indicating a pair of the latest Charlet Moser offering. "I climbed on Piranhas too, before I started working for these guys." Working for sponsors must surely be a misnomer, I think. Doesn't he just climb every day? I have often thought to myself, "Imagine what I could do if I climbed full-time and went on free expeditions."

This is Alex's first reference to sponsorship, but the fact is obvious comparing our gear. His all-new North Face yellow and black one-piece suit retails for over $1,000, more than my August earnings. The fleece tights I wear were sewn out of $12 worth of fleece remnants, as can plainly be seen from the mismatched colors. My square-cut, 11-year old bibs are faded and patched. Alex's gear matches, even down to his yellow and black crampons.

I pull the rope from my pack and flake it out so we can start climbing. Brad is shooting again. I try to act natural, though I'm unsure of exactly how to do that.

Alex offers me the lead. Realizing that this is going to be the easiest pitch of the day, I am about to accept when Brad jumps in.

"I'll go," he shouts. I'm not disappointed. In fact, I'm relieved.

"I'll give you a belay," I say.

Brad climbs somewhat slowly and Alex grouses. Not meanly, but clearly it frustrates him that the rope doesn't pay out more quickly. He is antsy to climb. I'm glad I didn't lead, but I guess that I could have moved a bit faster since I would not be carrying camera gear.

At the next belay Alex doesn't offer me the lead; he just takes it. I don't mind and I don't object.

"I'll belay you, Alex." I look at Brad. "That way you can take pictures."

Alex climbs quickly. I almost expect something supernatural to happen: sparks shooting off of his crampons, or each tool placement being perfect, one swing, one stick. But while his movements evince a high degree of certainty and strength, I am somehow relieved to see that he also swings two or three times to get the pick to stick into the cold, brittle ice. He climbs 30 feet, not dangerously far, places a solid ice screw, and keeps climbing smoothly, but carefully, towards the top. He is proficient, for sure, but human after all.

Brad and I join Alex on a large ledge where we can safely unrope and walk around. We're now high above the broad, wind-swept Wyoming valley. Frozen braids of the Shoshone River empty Yellowstone Park to our west. Alex has belayed us from underneath a huge white icicle that hangs 20 feet above his head. I know this ice hanging above him is a route called Barely Legal that Alex was the first to climb.

As he recounts the story he laughs loudly at how pumped his partner was following it. How he hung there "like a haul-bag. Wish I'd had a pulley! Ha!" Quickly he adds that he too was pumped. "It's supersteep!" Obviously.

A hundred feet to the right another frozen squid of ice hangs, dozens of long, white tentacles reaching towards the ground, none touching. This route also has had only one ascent, also by Alex. I have done a few dozen big ice routes but all of them had ice touching the ground.

Alex hikes over to this second route, Legal at Last, and begins to rack up with rock and ice gear. I am unsure of how he will climb something this steep. Brad, brandishing his camera, scurries around looking for positions from which to shoot.

I flake the ropes below the squid and put Alex on belay as he ties into the ends. With a silent, direct glance to acknowledge that he is going, Alex steps off the ground. He climbs a body-width pillar of vertical ice for 10 feet, pausing just long enough to drill an ice screw at its top. Leaving the ice, he fits the picks of his ice tools into a crack in the rock and pulls out on the shafts of the tools to make the picks flex and bite. Just like we did in Slovenia years ago. But it wasn't steep like this, I think to myself.

Fifty feet up, Alex slings a large rock thumb with a nylon cord. Helmet-sized chunks of ice randomly glued to vertical rock continue above him. The bits of ice grow slightly larger as he ascends closer to the big frozen ice tentacles that hover just above him.

He pauses before the hanging icicle to place a rock piton for protection. As he hammers I realize I am witnessing a redefinition of ice climbing. In Slovenia I had climbed many lower angled rock routes in winter. But here the terrain is vertical, even overhanging, and splashed with water ice, which is rarely found in the mountains.

In the 45 minutes it takes Alex to lead the pitch and anchor to a tree 200 feet above me, my understanding of what is possible in climbing has forever been altered.

"Climbing!" I yell. Taking a few quick, hyperventilating breaths, I step off the ground. I am vibrating with tension, hardly able to control my excitement. With difficulty I focus on my movements. After 60 feet of climbing my arms are so engorged with blood, so pumped, that I nearly fall. The thought of someday being described as a haul bag keeps me moving despite the burning muscles. I move through the steepest part quickly and join Alex at the belay just before my strength fails completely.

∞∞∞∞∞∞∞∞∞∞∞∞∞∞∞∞∞∞∞∞∞∞∞∞

"What do you think, Steve?" Alex asks the next morning. "You want to try it?" He looks up at the climb we didn't do yesterday, Barely Legal. "Come on, give it a shot?"

Dumbfounded my head cranes back to take in the enormity of the ice pillar hanging in space above me. "Barely Legal, indeed." I reply.

"Come on, Steve! I could see those wheels turning yesterday. Smoke was virtually pouring out of your ears!" Alex laughs, and I can hardly refuse such encouragement.

In fact as I drifted off to sleep last night I had been wondering if I could lead something like this. I had hauled myself up Legal at Last without falling yesterday. That got me to thinking. Now I want to do it myself.

"Climb up there onto that stance." Alex points to a one-inch by eight-inch edge 10 feet off the ground. "Then you get a blade in there." He points at an incipient fissure 15 feet above. "And an angle in there, in the pod. Then hook your ice tool in the sling, reach out and snag that bad-boy!" Alex is practically jumping out of his suit at this point. So excited that I half-wonder if he will renege on his offer to let me lead.

I pick up the gear as Alex continues to coach enthusiastically. "Rack that knifeblade in the front. You'll have to stab it into the crack with one hand, while drytooling on that edge with your left tool."

My palms burn hot and sweaty despite the sub-freezing chill as I rack the knifeblade piton handily on the right side of my harness. An angle piton goes just behind it. I select my newest, sharpest ice screw and hang it behind the angle

74

piton. That will be my first piece of protection once I climb up to where the ice dagger attaches to the wall. Below the point of attachment, it is dangerous to have a screw because if you kick too hard and break the icicle as you climb past, the force of the falling ice attached to the lead rope will pull you to the ground.

"One thing, Steve," says Brad. "Would you mind wearing this?" He is unzipping his own brightly colored one-piece suit.

"Um. Sure. I guess." I realize that Brad is here to make a paycheck and since Alex isn't climbing he might as well get me to wave the flag.

"Hope you don't mind. But your dark pants aren't going to show up at all up there."

"Yeah, no problem. No conflicts of interest there!" I joke about my lack of sponsorship.

"Sorry, Steve," says Alex, once Brad has moved off and I'm pulling the suit on over my shoulders. "I didn't know we'd be whoring you out. Usually that's my job."

"It's okay... It's kind of a nice suit!"

I pull my harness on over the fresh nylon suit and add a few more screws and a handful of slings to round out Alex's recommended gear selection. Nervously I check and recheck everything. Finding everything in place, I have no choice but to pick up the ends of the climbing ropes and tie in. Alex already has me on belay.

Alex gives me one more pat on the back. "Go get 'em Steve!"

The first six feet are easy; a few good rock edges to stand on before the wall starts to rear steeply back. Stepping onto smaller edges now, I must stretch my left tool to set the pick on the flat edge.

"Yeah!" Alex yells up. "That's the one. Now step up and get the knifeblade in there by your tool."

Glancing down to find the footholds, I am buttressed by Alex's intense gaze, his posture reassuringly alert and ready at the belay. I focus on the wall and see a couple small edges in the rock. Stepping up I get eye level with the edge that supports my tools and spy the thin crack. Dropping my right arm and letting the ice hammer dangle by its leash from my wrist I grab the piton off my harness. Eyeing the crack, I fumble with the piton, trying to get the grip that will let me stab it into the crack.

Reaching up, I aim the thin metal tip at the crack and stick it perfectly into the narrow fissure. Though it is only in a couple millimeters, it stays put as I gingerly take my hand away. The muscles of my left arm are screaming from holding my body weight. I catch the rubber grip of my right tool and quickly place its pick over the rock edge and release my left tool. This lets me drop my entire left arm so it hangs behind me. It's pulsing from exertion. I shake my hand vigorously, and breathe hard.

"Good, Steve. Get it back. Breathe." Alex's calm voice comes from below.

Alex and I toast the day with a second large pot of espresso in the Big Bear Hotel in Cody, Wyoming.
I brought along an electric griddle to cook our breakfast on. Alex woke Doug Chabot and I with café lattes
in bed. DOUG CHABOT

The fire in my left arm subsides, but now my right feels the strain. I replace my left tool and pull back up to where I'm eye-to-eye with the ledge. I release my right tool and flick my wrist to turn the hammer side of the tool to the front. Unconsciously, I hold my breath as I start to lightly tap the piton in. One mis-strike could send the piton flying out, and with the fire in my arms, I'd be hard-pressed to reverse the moves to the ground without falling.

With each gentle blow the piton sinks a little further and I gradually increase the force of the blows. As I pound harder the steel begins to sing as it goes all the way into the crack.

"Right on," Alex celebrates below. "Right on, man!"

A second later I have my ropes clipped into my first piece of gear, protecting myself from a possible fall to the ground.

I start climbing toward the pod, the slight flaring in the crack, where I'll place the angle piton. With a few relaxed movements I am there and quickly sink the second piton while standing on a big rock edge. After clipping a sling to the angle I clip it to the rope. Here I must use a point of aid. I hook the sling with one ice tool and reach out to snag the icicle with my other tool.

Aid climbing is when you pull directly on gear normally used for fall-protection. Though less pure than free climbing – climbing the rock and ice with your hands and ice tools – it is sometimes necessary. This is just such an instance.

With my right tool looped in the sling I reach out and find I can just barely touch the tip of the dangling ice with my other tool. My stomach turns a knot as I pull back, my breath coming more rapidly now.

The plan is to get my pick into that ice. Then I have to let go of the sling and swing my entire body weight out onto that frozen wisp of drool and hang by one arm.

"Now what?" I ask myself. It looks really hard and the icicle is anything but close. I've already committed to climb this – or fall off trying. I've never fallen ice climbing. Ice climbers live by the unwritten rule that the leader must never fall. There are two reasons for the rule. One, the strength of ice screws, hand-drilled into the ice, is notoriously difficult to judge. Two, with so many steel points connected to you, even short falls can result in injury.

As if reading my mind, Alex shouts up, "Go for it, Steve. You've got two good pitons protecting you. You're safe."

I take a few forced deep breaths, plumbing for my focus. Then I lean out, straining against the sling to reach as far as I can, and swing for the center of the dangling icicle.

It sticks. Though I'm just in the tip of it, I have threaded my pick through the melt hole I'd been aiming for. This is one of the best placements as it fractures a minimum of ice. I take one big breath, unhook my tool from the sling and pendulum monkey-like out into space. My legs swing wildly and my body twists on my one arm.

Hanging at full extension I don't have the power to pull myself up with one arm. Feet flailing, I hook the pick of my right tool over the head of the left tool and am able to pull up on both arms. I pull my chin to hand level and lock off. I lift my right tool to swing higher into the icicle and my left arm starts to fail. In desperation I swing for a higher purchase on the icicle but miss and strike lower than I had intended. At that instant the icicle lets out an ear-popping crack, the ice snaps and I am swinging gently on the end of the rope.

"Yeah, way to go. You got rid of that fragile stuff." Alex hollers wildly from below. "Ride 'em cowboy!"

I am totally gassed and dangle for a long time, nursing the rest and wondering if I have the strength for another try.

"You want to come down?" Alex asks gently.

"No," I respond, steeling my resolve. "One more try. If I fall again you can go up there."

I reach over, hook the sling again with my tool, and call for slack. Repeating the reach, I find I can get just a bit higher where the icicle is thicker. Like a good cowboy, I get back on and ride. This time I have the strength. I climb up the dagger to the thick ice flow above and place my ice screw, twisting it in with exhausted arms. Soon I'm on top, tying the rope around a big tree. Alex hoots and hollers with joy as he follows the pitch.

∞∞∞∞∞∞∞∞∞∞∞∞∞∞∞∞∞∞∞

Later that night back in Cody, the Silver Dollar Bar is filled with equal parts cowboys and climbers. So far, the only point of contention between us is the jukebox. Our set just started off with the strong beat of a Led Zeppelin song. A weathered cowboy with a crisp-brimmed gray hat looks over at our group with obvious displeasure at the music selection. I follow him over to watch as he drops a meaty fistful of quarters into the machine. He cues up a long set of Alabama, Dolly Parton, and Vince Gill. Just as he finishes his last selection, the power-chords of AC/DC's "Highway to Hell" boom through the bar.

Chuckling, I walk back toward the crowded round table where Alex sits drinking a beer. There are no empty chairs here and I walk past as someone finishes a story, "...and then when we finally hit it. It was awesome. A big ball of fire went up and it lit up the whole desert."

I sit down at an empty table on the far side of the crowd as everyone laughs at the story. There are many climbers here I know by name and reputation. Barry Blanchard, the godfather of Canadian alpine climbing. Jack Tackle, one of the first to tackle big new routes alpine style in Alaska and a pioneer of ice climbing in Montana. John Sherman, all-around great rock climber and a father of modern bouldering. Joe Josephson, perhaps the hottest ice climber in North America after Alex. And Mark Wilford, one of the world's best alpinists, rock climbers, ice climbers, and boulderers: a true climber's climber.

Looking at the group, I'm not sure what bothers me more. The fact that half my climbing heroes are in this room, or the fact that they all seem like regular people.

Mark Wilford, holding a longneck bottle of Coors Light, turns in his chair and asks, "So. You guys were up on the Barely Legal wall?"

"Yeah. It was pretty wild," I reply. "Watching Alex climb was something else."

"Well. If there was ice on those routes, then a lot of stuff must be in shape," Mark continues.

Just then a balding guy wearing small wire rim glasses and a dark sweater stands up behind Wilford and lifts a heavy beer mug. "Be here or be talked about!" He toasts. Laughter erupts as the 20-odd climbers clank glasses.

Wilford has turned back to the group now, and as if on cue, he starts into another tale. "So after Christmas we took my truck out to the desert. And somehow I had ended up with this big, hollow glass Santa Claus. You know, about this big. So, John had the idea to fill this thing up with gasoline…" He points at Sherman, and laughs.

The Nant Blanc Glacier drains the cirque below this magnificent group of peaks soaring above Chamonix: the Aiguille Verte, the Aiguille Sans Nom, and the magnificent Grand (hidden) and Petit Drus. I was nearly entombed in a crevasse there. I returned the next summer and soloed the North Face route of the Petit Dru in six hours. MARKO PREZELJ

CHAPTER SEVEN

The Crypt

Nant Blanc Glacier, French Alps: August 22, 1996

SUDDENLY MY FOOT SLIDES out from under me; I slam to the ice and start accelerating quickly. I try to arrest my fall by dragging the pick of my ice axe into the slope. I slow a little, and then my legs are weightless. And then my body. I'm spinning and falling backwards through the air. Walls of ice race past.

I crash into soft, wet snow. I have hit a snow bridge down inside the crevasse. I can't see. I kick and squirm to get my head out of its hole. Immediately, automatically, I try to bridge the gap, my left leg touching one side and my shoulders the other. My right leg screams in pain.

What's wrong with my leg? I think.

The pain is so intense, so unlike anything I've felt before. I can't focus my eyes. I lean back squinting, and reach down to touch the leg, but can't feel the pressure of my hand.

Shit. This is bad. Nobody knows where I am. This is really bad.

My vision starts to close from the periphery, going black. I open my eyes wide and shake my head. I stare at my right boot. I wiggle my toes, but can't feel them. My thigh sears with pain – a white-hot, slow beat of pain. With difficulty I use the pick of my ice axe to tear a rough, round hole in my pant leg to examine it more closely. I see only skin.

I press my head back against the ice wall. I'm in a crevasse. Holy shit. I'm in a crevasse, I'm alone, and no one knows I'm here.

I look to my right, the slowly tapering walls of hard ice slither into darkness. I know that it isn't bottomless. The pressure of the deep glacial ice will press the walls together at around 60 or 80 feet. That's how people die in crevasses. They become slotted into the narrow, gently tapering crevice. Their body heat melts the ice a little, and their body weight wedges them deeper into a self-made sarcophagus. They get compressed and it gets harder to breathe. Their body temperature drops steadily, fatally, until they are 32 degrees and dead. The snow bridge – for now – has saved me from this, my most frequent nightmare.

I press on my leg, grabbing and torquing the femur to see if it's broken. It doesn't seem to be. This is good. Earlier this year my friend and guiding mentor Julie Cheney-Culberson broke her femur after a cornice collapsed and sent her and her husband Matt tumbling down a Canadian couloir. She bled to death.

The front of my thigh feels okay. The muscles behind my knee to my butt hurt badly. My lower back aches and my knee burns with a sharp pain. I lie still and gradually the pain ebbs. Once the sensation has subsided, I try to sit up and pull my leg towards me. Instantly, without pity, the pain comes. It cuts to the center of my being and I jerk flat. The pain spreads and radiates like heat filling my entire body and my entire awareness. It's impossible to think of anything else.

I groan. Each moment is an eternity. Only my chest moves, I keep the rest of my body still to allow the pain to subside.

I lie there quietly, taking rapid, shallow breaths. I can hear my heart beat hollow and loud. I think about where I am, my mind drawing a map. I'm in a crevasse on the right bank of the Nant Blanc Glacier, just across from the north face of the Petit Dru, which had been my objective. Not the climb itself, the weather has been too poor today. So I'd slept in, eaten two croissants and a pain au chocolat, but after the second espresso I had to start out. I wanted to see the mighty wall, long a goal of mine. I should have left a note for Mike, my roommate at the Hotel le Touring in Chamonix, telling him where I'd gone.

My mind's eye pulls out further. The Nant Blanc Glacier flows towards the Mer de Glace Glacier, whose waters flow down to Chamonix, France. The Alps. Europe. My life spills into the flowing ice, spreading out across this foreign continent. Cold snowflakes drop heavily from the sky to bury me. I can't breathe. I can't escape.

<><><><><><><><><><><><><><><>

I will die alone here, forever unfound, buried in ice. To die is one thing, to disappear elicits a deeper terror.

I squirm my shoulders farther up off the snow bridge to take stock of my situation. I'm more than 20 feet down. The uphill side of the crevasse, from which I fell, is overhanging concrete-hard ice. The other side is slightly less than vertical. I might be able to climb that. I have a pack containing a pair of crampons, a water bottle, and a camera. I'm still holding my axe. I soloed Beauty Is a Rare

Thing earlier this summer. I should be able to climb out of here.

When stepping off the rocks onto the edge of the glacier above, I didn't put on my new lightweight aluminum crampons to cross the few feet of steep snow to the flatter glacier. I didn't want to risk wearing the soft-metal points on rocks hidden in the snow. Because of that I slipped on an unseen ice patch and fell into this crevasse.

"If I wasn't such a cheap bastard, I might not be in this hole!" I say the words out loud. For the first time since my fall I hear my own voice.

"Hello." The human sound is comforting. "Hello, hello, hello. Listen up crevasse, I'm getting outta' here."

The aluminum crampons are still in my daypack. I look at my watch: 12:45 pm. Being careful not to drop it, I take off the pack and retrieve the crampons.

Holding the crampons in my lap, I stare at my feet. My left leg is braced against the far wall. My right leg hangs limply, supported by the snow bridge. I can't flex it. The only way it feels better is to hold it as straight as possible. The pain from the back of my leg laps at my consciousness.

If I bend my left leg towards me to put on the crampon I will lose my safety net – my bridged position across the gap – and commit my full weight to the snow bridge. A chill passes over me. I have no option. To stay here is to die.

"Okay. Here goes," I say out loud, and slowly press my back onto the snow bridge, ready to attempt to catch myself should it collapse. It holds for now. I slowly retract my left leg and bring it up across my right. The crampon snaps on and I push my left foot back into the far wall; the metal points grind reassuringly into the ice and small chips bounce down into darkness.

I look at my useless right foot. "Now what am I going to do with you?"

I lean forward to reach the outstretched foot, and my leg screams in pain. I sit back quickly, close my eyes, and let out a low-decibel moan.

I slip my right hand into the hole I cut in my sodden pants and touch the cold skin. My hand cups the back of my leg; it feels like its full of fluid.

"Or blood." I announce to the crevasse. This is how Julie died, fighting for consciousness as she lost more and more blood. Alone and battered among the rocks while her injured husband went for help, which did not come in time.

I try to examine my leg but can't see much through the dark hole. I place my crampon down on my lap and wrap my fingers firmly around my leg above the knee with my thumbs on top and my fingers sunk into the painful hamstring muscle. Very gently I start to draw my foot to me by pulling on my leg, but my hamstring quickly raises another protesting scream. I am exhausted with pain. I press my left foot against the ice wall, fearing that the bridge will collapse.

I wish I had worked today, I think. Then I wouldn't be in this mess. I would be racing up ahead of my client, setting a belay anchor, carefully coaching and guiding them up the route. Watching that satisfied grin spread across their face on some windy summit.

I begin to relax my grip on the far wall. What would I do if this bridge collapses? This thought is too private to announce to the abyss. If I can't get the crampon on that foot I can't climb out. "And if I can't climb out I'm going to die here." I say aloud. From the crevasse only menacing silence.

I sink back into the snow bridge and grasp my near-inert leg just below the knee with both hands. I exhale sharply, grit my teeth, close my eyes and pull. I try not to let the moan out, but it comes through my teeth and tears pool in my eyes. Blinking them away, I work the straps on my crampon until it is securely fixed to my right boot.

I leave the leg flexed and lie back down on the snow bridge, turning to look across the length of my crypt. The two walls arc away from me in parallel for 50 feet and then pinch off to the end of the crevasse.

"The Petit Dru would make one hell of a tombstone." My voice is flat in the icy box. How many are already buried in this glacier? I do not want to stay here. I want to see my wife again. I want to eat Mom's peach pie again.

I twist onto my side to a lying position. I flex my quadriceps to straighten the damaged leg. Strangely it doesn't hurt as much as I expect. I sit up, this time letting my right leg swing off the side of the bridge. I sit up and swing my axe into the solid ice of the crevasse's downhill wall. I pull myself onto my left knee and eye the snow bridge warily.

"If she's gonna go, now's the time." I wait as a few bits of snow crumble and noiselessly slide into the blackness. Nothing happens. I take the axe out, and quickly replace it as high as I can. With this new anchor I pull to a standing position; my right leg bounces and protests every movement. I grip the axe tightly and wrap the fingers of my left hand over its head, bracing for the plunge. I exhale. The bridge still holds.

"I'm not gonna stay here." I take the axe out again to gain another few feet.

With dread I realize a new problem. Once I step off the bridge I will be climbing near-vertical ice with fatal fall potential. Even if I manage to land on the bridge again and avoid falling into the narrowing icy void, it is not likely to withstand another blow. I have only one foot and one useable hand. My right leg is useless. The crampon on my left foot is securely kicked into the ice. Today I brought just one ice axe designed for walking on a glacier, not climbing vertical ice.

I can't remove the axe to replace it higher. I need all four limbs to climb out. Experimenting, I snuggle my body against the ice and loosen my grip on the axe, balancing on my left foot. I start to fall as soon as I loosen my grip on the axe. I'm stuck.

"I. Do. Not. Want. To. Stay. Here." I push the words through my teeth, smacking my forehead against the ice with each.

I step back to the snow bridge and settle my weight firmly onto my left leg before loosening my grip and removing the axe. I have an idea. Using the pick of the axe I cut a small handhold for my left hand and another one above it. Chipping away, I cut footholds for my right foot. I make these large. I come down with strong blows and ice chips spray into my face. I finish with a two-inch deep step. I make five of these every foot or two in a line as far as I can reach. Finished, I wipe my face of melting ice and plant the pick of my axe with my arm extended straight above me.

I pull on the axe and hop my left crampon onto the steep ice. Holding the head of the axe in my left hand, I thread my right hand through the leash at the base of the shaft. I look down and grit my teeth as I flex my quadriceps again, straightening my crippled leg. I cock my hip to lift the leg and delicately place my crampon's front points on the chopped ledge. Experimentally, I grip an edge chopped as a handhold and loosen the grip on my right hand.

"*Aaaah!*" My right leg collapses under the weight and pain shoots into my head, making me dizzy; stars flicker before my eyes. I step back down onto the bridge and lean my face against the bracing cold of the ice.

"Breathe. Breathe." The filtered blue light of the crevasse comes back into focus and I look up at the top. Summer mountain snowflakes fall wetly and are quickly engulfed by the pit. The sky is gray and heavy, but oddly bright. I exhale again and look down at my lame leg. I face the ice wall I must climb, and step up with my left foot. Flexing my quadriceps I again place my right crampon on its premade step. Keeping the quads flexed I again loosen my grip on the axe and let my weight come onto my legs.

It works. If I keep my quadriceps activated I can weight my injured leg. I reach for the ice handhold with my left hand and carefully remove my axe. For a moment I hold myself balanced on my good left leg with crampon points stuck into the ice and my right crampon balancing on the small icy edge. I extend my right arm and swing the axe firmly into the ice. Chips fly into my open jacket. I grab the axe with both hands and pull up on my arms, step my left foot up and drag the right foot behind.

I reach the last step I chopped from my stance on the bridge. The angle has relaxed slightly. I balance on my two legs and my last left handhold while I chop the next set, making sure to make the last left handhold large enough so I can hang on it with one hand and chop the next set of holds with the axe in my right.

Soon, I near the lip of the crevasse. The sky is light, despite continually spitting wet flakes of snow that stick to my face and itch as they melt. I can't let go to wipe them off.

"Now what?" My voice sounds more alive up here. I need to get my axe over the abrupt change from vertical to horizontal. That will require me to get high enough to reach over the edge with my entire right arm.

I work the fingers gripping the axe. They're getting tired, aching slightly, the familiar harbinger of a pump: an exhausted state caused by the buildup of lactic acid. I relax my grip and bear down on the head of the tool with my left hand to relieve the right. I'm going to need a last solid burst of strength to get out of here. Leaning my forehead on top of my left hand, I look down. Below me, the bridge looks frighteningly small.

Lifting my head I take one deep breath and reverse my last step. Deliberately, I grip the last good handhold and take out my axe. I use sober, short swings. I hack out a good hold with a big edge two feet below the lip. I exhale and climb back to my high point. My heart races. I relax the fingers of my right hand as much as I dare. I reach for the high left handhold I just made and place my axe high, just below the lip before stepping my feet up. Left first, then, delicately, my right.

Standing as tall as possible I can just peer over the lip of the crevasse. I test my grasp of the ice-handhold by loosening the pick of my axe. I take the axe out and teeter; one slip means death. I straighten my arm to measure my reach; my elbow just reaches the lip. It's a dangerous position from which to swing. If I misjudge, my arm could strike the ice first and catapult me back into the icy void.

I drop the hand holding the end of the ice axe shaft back behind my ear, and wind up for a strong swing. I need a solid placement to pull myself out. I wail the axe with everything I have left. It sticks solidly above the lip, but the pick is sunk at an angle. It's not as good as it must be. I remove it. Drops of water ooze from my gloves and spray my face as I unleash another hard, fast swing. I grunt with the effort, but the axe thunks solidly. Now I can I pull down and kick my left crampon into the ice. I wrap the cold fingers of my left hand around the head of the axe and pull myself, finally, onto the flat, snowy glacier.

I lie in the snow as heavy snowflakes cover me. My hands are numb, my pants soaked.

It is just past 2 o'clock. I have less than three hours to get off this glacier and ascend 1,600 feet to the cable car station at the Grands Montets. I twist around, my leg screams again, but I ignore it the best I can. I will have to crawl. It might be awhile before I guide again. But I will see Anne soon. Maybe I can visit my sister in Portland. I'll be convalescing for a while. But first I have to get to that cable car. Before the pain ebbs, I start off.

I am surrounded by crevasses. I head downhill to get off the glacier, but the glacier below me is badly fractured. Knowing that these are lateral crevasses – formed by the friction between the bedrock and the relatively thin ice of the glacier's edge – I crawl toward the center of the glacier seeking solid ice.

Fog hangs low and visibility is only 20 feet. The snow comes faster now. Not knowing if I can extricate myself from this maze of deadly ice, I turn the corner only to be met by another crevasse. I weave past two smaller cracks and with a sigh of relief, pull myself onto the dripping snow-covered jumble of boulders at the glacier's edge.

I look up into the fog, and consider the obstacles ahead. If I miss the last cable

Aiguille du Dru in winter. MARKO PREZELJ

car I could freeze to death in these wet clothes. Grasping the top of my axe like a cane I take a hop, then another, and another, and a fourth. I bend over, winded.

"This is going to be hard." I gulp a determined breath and start again, counting to myself. "One, two, three, four." Frazzled breathing and another count to four. A few iterations of this and I rotate around to sit on a boulder's edge. I'm exhausted.

At 4:30, fifteen minutes before the last car departs I mount the stairs leading to the station. The conductor squints at me as he takes a drag off his cigarette. Exhausted and steaming from exertion I sit on the galvanized metal landing in front of the station. I am finally out of the drizzling snowfall. The man considers me for a moment longer, rocks back slightly on his heels, exhales smoke through his nose as he looks away, and lifts the fag back to his lips.

On the ride down a well-fed tourist asks about my leg. I tell him it's broken. He is skeptical, but offers me a ride to the hospital in Chamonix.

I limp into the Emergency Room entrance of the Chamonix Hospital. I go to the desk and a nurse looks at me, saying something quickly that I don't understand.

"*Ma jambe.*" I point at the leg I've drug up towards the counter. She asks something, again I don't catch it, but then, "*Anglais?*"

"*Non, American.*" The nurse turns without a smile and walks away.

I'm not sure what to do, but I'm too tired to stand so I work my way to a row of hard plastic seats. I set my backpack on the floor and try to sit on the edge of the end seat. My leg hurts and I can't relax, so I grab the edge of the chair with my hands and lower myself onto the tile floor of the empty room. I push off the chair and lay my head on my pack, closing my eyes.

"*Hallo. Hallo.*" I am being shaken. I open my eyes to see a man in a white coat with jet-black hair pushing his toe into my rib cage. It's the doctor. I glance at the clock. I've been here over two hours.

"Can you stand?" He asks.

"*Oui.* Yes. If I flex the quadriceps." I start to get up to show him.

"You are okay. Go home." And the white coat turns and walks away. I pull myself erect. I want to follow him. Shouldn't I get an X-Ray. Shouldn't he at least examine me? Touch me?

"Fucking French," I say as I knock open the emergency-room doors.

It has started to rain again. I shoulder my pack, flip up the hood of my jacket and start to limp across town towards my rented room. I wish I had a pair of crutches.

I fly home a week later. I have neither health insurance, nor money to pay for medical treatment. I had been stupid. I was lucky. My right leg will never be the same. But I will pay more attention next time. It's the easy ground that kills you.

Joe Josephson on our first attempt of the Emperor. This attempt ended one-third of the way up the wall when we encountered steep, unprotectable climbing. STEVE HOUSE

CHAPTER EIGHT

Acceptance

Northeastern Oregon: March, 1997

CRUSTY PATCHES OF SNOW lie scattered across the hundred acres of private timberland we are supposed to plant with trees this week. Winter lingers in the Blue Mountains. Worse, the 14,000 seedlings – one year old and four-inch tall miniature ponderosa pine, Douglas fir, blue spruce, and western larch – are still in the ground at the nursery in central Oregon.

Over the weekend I pass the time with an odd job. Using a tractor I push up slash piles from old clear-cuts and burn what I can. Preparing the ground for the coming seedlings is hard, dirty work. The oversized industrial chain saw leaves my hands numb, my back aching, my ears ringing.

My morale takes another hit when we learn that the seedlings won't be here for at least another week. That night, I'm reading in my parents' small living room when the phone rings. It's Joe Josephson calling from Canmore, Alberta. Trying to hide my excitement, I ask how he's doing.

"Well, actually, not great." Jojo replies. "See, Barry and I are planning on heading up to Mount Robson, and Whipper, our third man, can't go. So we were wondering if you would be interested in going in there with us."

"Where?" I question him, though I think I heard him the first time.

"Robson. We're going to try a new route on the Emperor Face. Robson man, the King."

Forty hours later I steer my little car into the Mount Robson Visitor Centre. A loose engine-belt screams as I push in the clutch and coast to a rest next to Jojo and Barry. Their gear is strewn across the tarmac in the sunshine.

Emperor Face of Mount Robson, Canadian Rockies: March, 1997, (10 days later)

I shove my arm behind the base of the icicle, and the fabric of my jacket crackles from the cold. I can just reach around it; feeling the end of the cord with my fingertips I pull it through the back. I tie off the cord and clip my lead-rope to the icicle. I kick my crampon points into the icicle, being gentle as I pass, climbing into a shallow gully filled with snow, edged by vertical walls of black rock.

It is my block, my set of leads, and the short winter day is waning. There is no hint of a place to sit or lie down for the approaching night. The gully gently rises up to another steep section, which looks to be the day's crux.

I see Jojo's huge red parka lean back on the belay. "Nice work," he shouts. As I move past the slung icicle I hear Barry's more subdued baritone. "Good, Steve. Good."

During the last 10 days, we tried and failed to climb an audacious direct line up the center of this face. The steep snow-covered rock offered neither protection nor belay stances. The climbing became desperately hard after two pitches. After Barry nearly fell on lead, we retreated to our skis and quickly traveled two miles across frozen Berg Lake to a log cabin shelter. Over these 10 days we have become fast friends; quickly bonded by a love for what we're doing. Barry and Jojo accepting me into their world.

"It was the weirdest thing," Barry revealed one night as I stoked the wood stove with a dead log we had scavenged from the stunted spruce forest. "I was at my desk writing." I turned and saw him holding out his hands, palms down, wrists flexed, as if he were at the computer. "I was working on a story about the time David and I climbed Mount Fay with Carl Tobin." David Cheesmond had been one of Barry's closest friends, and was a driving force in Canadian alpine climbing, but died on Mount Logan in 1987. "I was getting into it, writing about the storm. And there was this point where David led this amazing pitch in the storm. He got us off of that wall, saved our lives. So, anyway, I was there writing that part of the story, I was really struggling with it, and this song came on, Jackson Browne's 'Running on Empty.' It was David's and my favorite song. I could feel David's presence there. I swear he was there with me, right in the room. I could feel him. I immediately grabbed a new sheet of paper and wrote David a letter. I can't explain that kind of shit man. Think whatever you want. But I can't explain that kind of shit."

〰〰〰〰〰〰〰〰〰〰〰〰〰

Now we are two-thirds of the way up a system of gullies on the right edge of this 6,000-foot wall. I smile as I reach up and clear snow out of the wide crack that rears up in front of me. I plug in our biggest piece and start torquing my picks into the narrowest part of the crack. Pulling on the tools, I step my feet

Barry Blanchard grimaces at the very cold, very foodless, and very waterless bivy near the top of the Emperor Face of Mount Robson. The rope strung above him is part of our anchor. JOE JOSEPHSON

With the day's first light, I lead the first pitch, of a new route called The Silver Lining that Barry, Jojo and I climbed in the spring of 1998 as a result of our commitment to "try again next year." JOE JOSEPHSON

up on small bits of ice and finally reach past the crux with the solid thunk of a well-placed ice tool.

I lead several more difficult pitches; ice gullies weaving through hard, clean rock. The best pitches of the route. Pitches Alex would love to climb, I think. By the last glimmer of day, Barry sees a ledge off to our right. We don headlamps and I lead across 200 horizontal feet to a three-tiered ledge: the perfect "room-with-a-view."

As I set up the anchor I ache with the day's effort. The cold and the 20-odd hours of climbing have been costly. Nevertheless I am elated beyond words. I am living my dream, climbing a new route on the King, with two of the Rockies' best. Barry and Jojo seem confident in my ability to climb securely and quickly through the difficult, complex terrain. That is the ultimate compliment.

As I belay them across to the ledge, I think about the seriousness of our situation. We are 4,000 feet up a north face; the temperature is quickly dropping towards –20 degrees. We finished the last of our water four hours ago and a north wind is picking up, threatening to freeze our exposed faces. Despite this, I'm really having fun. I am exceeding my own expectations. Worries about dying, or getting injured have dissolved in the momentum of the climbing.

I chuckle and look up at the full moon cresting the horizon. My worries about failure are also fading. The hardest, the worst, is surely behind us. The summit, and success, is ensured. Tomorrow will be cold and clear: a magnificent summit day. I let loose a long howl. In the darkness 100 feet away, Barry joins in.

Barry joins us on the ledges and we set up an anchor for the night. My crampons spark as I kick a few offending rocks off my soon-to-be bed. Opening my pack, I pull out the stove and hand it up to Jojo. I keep digging, looking for my mittens. The cold is creeping in.

"Hey Steve, the pump isn't on the fuel bottle."

"No? Seriously?" I reply and Jojo holds the bottle for me to see. "Shit! Well it must be in my pack somewhere!"

I hold my pack, the faded yellow cloth displays dozens of small, and some not-so-small, tears. Carefully, I go through everything. I take each item out and clip it securely to a carabiner so it doesn't fall. I put my numb, naked hand into the pack and shake it to convince myself that it's empty. No fuel pump.

Slowly, I put everything back in, checking each stuff sack. No fuel pump. I can't believe it. I can feel Barry and Jojo's eyes on me now. Again I remove each item carefully, inspect it, and clip it to the anchor. I check my pockets. I look up and Barry is staring at me from his sleeping bag. I check the top pocket of the pack. I put everything back inside. I am shivering. I examine the ledge I'm standing on, picking up my feet to see if I'm standing on it. I shine my headlamp down the face. A few feet of steep rock and snow give way to blackness.

"Well," I say letting my arms fall limply to my sides, "I definitely don't have it."

Jojo and Barry look at each other. I am nauseated. I feel like untying and chucking myself off this ledge. My mind quickly does the math. Without a fuel pump we have no stove. Without a stove we have no water. Without water we have no food. Without food and water we cannot continue. We will not stand on the summit tomorrow. Even tonight's open bivouac in these temperatures, in this worn out state, could end in disaster. Frostbite, hypothermia, even death, stalks climbers in our condition: exhausted, hungry, dehydrated.

I lean miserably against the wall. "Definitely. I definitely don't have it." Barry and Jojo say nothing.

"It fell out. It must have fallen out of my pack. I mean it came detached from the fuel bottle and maybe I dropped it when I unpacked. But I think maybe it just fell out. I'm sorry. I'm so sorry. Shit. I'm sorry."

Jojo gets into his bivouac sack. No words. I turn and unpack my elephant's foot, a short sleeping bag that zips to the bottom edge of my parka. Once inside that I sit on my small chunk of a foam pad and pull the bivy sack over my legs.

There has to be some way to get pressure into the fuel bottle, I think. With pressure we can have fire. Immediately I start to fiddle with a piece of wire from the climbing equipment and some athletic tape that makes up our first aid kit. I desperately want to pressurize the fuel bottle so I can light the stove and melt some snow.

After two hours I have created enough flame to produce one cup of water. I pass it up to Barry. Reaching for the cup he looks at me with his light glaring in my eyes. I hold up my hand to block the glare.

He directs his light away and says in his gravelly voice, "Steve, you're young. You know, when you sum up all the fuck-ups that you are going to make in your life, this is going to seem like pretty small change." Jojo laughs.

"Thanks Bubba," I say meekly, "but I'm not so sure about that."

Jojo laughs some more. Barry chuckles and passes the half-empty cup to Jojo. Tomorrow we will have to traverse to the Emperor Ridge and descend that route for 3,000 feet – without water. We'll walk a couple of miles around to the base of the Emperor Face, collect our skis and ski 18 miles to the road. Without a stove, and with all the water within a few hundred miles locked up in ice, we need to get back to civilization as soon as possible. We will do it, together. Barry and Jojo have already accepted my mistake, forgiven my faults. That's partnership.

◇◇◇◇◇◇◇◇◇◇◇◇◇◇◇◇◇◇◇◇◇◇◇

It is dark when we get to the road. We drive together in Barry's truck for 30 miles to the nearest brewpub; actually the only brewpub. We've been in the mountains for 12 days and not had a sip of water for over 30 hours.

We take refuge at a dark corner table. When the waitress approaches, Barry looks up calmly. "A pitcher of water please. Wait, make that two pitchers of water," he says, holding two fingers up for emphasis. "No ice. Oh, and a pitcher of ale please."

For once the water tastes sweeter than the beer. With both water pitchers drained, Barry hails the waitress for another round. Jojo fills our beer mugs and then hefts his own. "Here's to the King!"

We drink. Then Barry slaps me on the back and grins at me. "And here's to trying again next year!"

Steve Mascioli bathed in evening light at a bivouac five pitches up the Moonflower Buttress route on Mount Hunter's north buttress. He was killed 72 hours later by a dislodged snow mushroom as he belayed Alan Kearney on the route's 17th pitch. ALAN KEARNEY

CHAPTER NINE

Empty Chairs

Bellingham, Washington: July 1, 1997

THE TIRE OF THE OLD TRUCK bounces against the curb as I park hard against the steep side street. I double-check the address, and look out at a low, brown wooden building. I'm relieved not to be going to a church, knowing that Steve Mascioli wouldn't have wanted his memorial in a house of religion. I get out under the heavy rain-soaked boughs of an evergreen tree.

Inside the double doors, I pause and wait for my eyes to adjust to the dim light. I am early and, as my sight returns, I realize that the people here are family. I see a woman in a black, knee-length dress at the center of the room. That must be Lisa, I think.

We've spoken on the phone many times, but met just once when I approached her front door to help Steve with his rucksack one dark morning before we headed east to climb an ice couloir in the North Cascades. Steve played the band Morphine on the stereo while we were driving. I had never heard them before, but the heavy bass lines would underpin the rhythm of our climbing together.

I start towards her and as I near she turns, puts her hand on the shoulder of a child and kneels to speak to him. I swerve away, into a row of folding chairs, cross the small aisle, and sit down on the far end.

"Steve." I turn around, awkward in the fact that I share a name with the deceased. "You're here." Alan's eyes are edged red and sunken into sadness.

Alan Kearney had been leading a pitch on the north buttress of Mount Hunter when a huge chunk of snow unexpectedly broke off and killed his partner, Steve Mascioli. Leaving Steve, Alan rappelled the buttress alone and met two climbers skiing on the glacier who safely escorted Alan back to base camp. Coincidently, Steve Swenson and I had been there for a resupply.

"Looks like Lisa didn't want to talk to you." He speaks to the back of the chair, sitting down behind me.

"No. She never was too fond of us climbers to begin with."

"Please be seated!" I am cut off by a strong, loud voice and look across the room to see a tall, commanding man in a dark sports coat.

In front of me the chairs are empty. Alan sits in his spot. I turn and notice that a dozen men and women have filed in and are sitting behind me: climbers, wearing plaid button down shirts, tattered brown sweaters, and faded green and blue nylon parkas. With unruly beards and long double-braids, they sit perched on the front edges of their folding chairs in the last two rows of chairs. The family sits across the aisle. They all wear formal black. They have lost a son, their only husband, their only father.

A second tall man, maybe Steve's brother, approaches the podium. "Please. If any of you would like to say a few words about Steve." A few climbers fidget with a slide projector in the corner. The man waits, looking expectantly across the room.

Steve Swenson and I comforted Alan for two days, trying to prepare him for his return to the world of Steve's family, reporters, his own grief. We made him pancakes, poured whisky in his hot chocolate, and packed Steve Mascioli's climbing gear. I kept his plastic coffee cone. Mascioli loved a good cup of hand-brewed coffee.

Someone places a tottering projection screen behind the podium as the man waits. A climber stands up from behind me and walks to the front of the room. With relief Steve Mascioli's brother steps aside.

"I climbed with Steve many times over many years," he says upon turning. "And I wanted to stand here and say that Steve was a great man. I loved him dearly. And I mourn with all of you."

"Thanks, Scott." Lisa says.

Another climber walks up. "Steve was one of those guys who read all of the books you wished you'd read. And he understood them. And could discuss them." She turns towards the family. "I'm so sorry for your loss."

Lisa again, "Thank you, Lydia."

"Hey, can you dim the lights over there?" I turn and see the man at the projector straighten himself over the machine. An image of Steve flashes into the room. Half turned, I see some of the family wince and look away. A few start crying. I smile, recognizing Steve on a well-known climb he did.

"Steve was my great friend," starts the curly-haired man at the projector, "besides being a devoted son, husband, and father." A chair screeches against the floor and Lisa stands up and walks out carrying her young son. The speaker pauses for a moment, and then continues. "This is Steve on Mount Combatant a couple years ago. I didn't know him much before this expedition, but we had a fantastic time together."

Click. Another picture of Steve, this time sitting at a bivouac at sunset or dawn, tucked into a sleeping bag, clinging to a steaming mug. It has to be coffee, I think. Instantly I am reminded of Steve in similar places at different times. I look behind me. The climbers are leaning back in their chairs now. Each transported to their own moments in the mountains with Mascioli.

I turn at a great gasping sob from the family side of the room. Steve's mother is nearly hysterical. I notice that Lisa's sister has also left the room and that his brother Paul has also gone.

"How can you do this?" the mother blubbers, nearly unintelligibly. "Climbing took him away. How can you sit there and celebrate it with these, these horrible pictures?" Before she finishes, a new image appears on the screen.

Steve Swenson and I had gone back to our advanced camp after Alan flew out with Steve Mascioli's body. The next morning I brewed coffee with Mascioli's coffee-cone, and we ascended an unclimbed 4,000-foot rock pillar. We named it Mascioli's Pillar.

Click. The next image is of Steve climbing a steep granite wall, arms relaxed, expression focused, toes pushing into tiny footholds. He wears a slight grin. He is grinning at all of us. I lean back, comfortable, at home with this. I eagerly await the next slide as one of Steve's favorite Morphine songs plays in my head:

Listen young people I'm seventy-four
And I plan to live sixty or seventy more
Yeah, I've been all around,
I've done a few things,
And I spent a few nights on the floor.

Did everything wrong,
But I never got caught,
So of course I would do it all over again.
I surprised many people who'd written me off years ago,
Now they're way underground.

Nobody asked me,
But here's my advice,
To a young man or woman, who's living this life.
In a world gone to hell, where nobody's safe,
Do not go quietly unto your grave.
Do not go quietly unto your grave.

Scott Backes leads a sunny pitch on the east face of Howse Peak. That afternoon I lead what became known as "The Pitch," an extremely difficult line of thin ice, that as of this writing, over 10 years later, has not been repeated. STEVE HOUSE

CHAPTER TEN

Farmboy

Canmore, Alberta, Canada: March 27, 1999

KNOCKING THE SNOW OFF my boots, I push open the door to the Drake Pub. A large cheer hits me. I smile and step aside to let Scott in. Someone lets out a shrieking whistle and applause scatters across the room. I see Barry sitting on top of a large table near the center of the room surrounded by people. He has one foot on the ground. The other straightened leg, encased in a hip-length plastic brace, is extended on the table in front of him. Two full glasses of beer sit next to him; he holds another above his head to signal us.

"Hey," Barry chuckles, his still damp hair hangs around his shoulders. His roots are the color of pewter; the ends show the jet-black of his Native American heritage. "It's the great white hope of American alpinism, and the old guy."

"Yeah, Bubba," Scott says, slapping Barry on the shoulder and pulling him into a one-armed hug. "I may be old. But at least I'm a has-been."

"Beer? They keep bringing them," he says, gesturing with his glass to the surrounding crowd. "Catherine did all of this. I knew she was organizing a party, but I didn't know it was going to be like this. I'm glad we made it off the route when we did. She was pissed, and rightly so, that we only got off today. Plus this, eh?" He raps one knuckle against his braced leg. "Doc said I have a hairline fracture of the tibial plateau. Six weeks."

"Could have been a lot longer than six weeks," Scott says. He stretches for both glasses and passes one to me. "Here's to having Bubba alive." Raising the glasses we each look the other in the eye. Scott's eyes are shimmering and intense; Barry's dark and distant.

"Here's to Steve's pitch," says Barry, lifting his glass again as he smacks the beer foam off his unshaven upper lip.

Scott gives me a half-serious look. "The great white hope."

I drop my gaze to my glass. "You know I hate that name." And I draw in the bracing bitterness of the beer.

Scott laughs. "I know. I know you do. And that just proves my point."

East Face of Howse Peak, Canadian Rockies: March 22, 1999, (five days earlier)

The rope comes tight; I reach up and swing one ice tool into the white icicle that dangles over the black stone lip. *Thunk.* It makes a hollow sound followed by the rattle of ice chips cascading down onto the front of my new mango-orange Patagonia parka. The jacket is one piece of the free kit the company sent me six weeks ago, apparently on Barry's recommendation. I gently thread my pick into a hole in the ice that Scott left behind. I start upward, straining to move quickly. The weight of the pack increases as I kick up the vertical ice.

I reach the belay panting. The rock leans out above the ledge Scott stands on. Forty feet above him, like the tail of a mythical frozen serpent, hangs a great dagger of ice.

As I make the last steps to the anchor, I examine the nearby rock for cracks. One or two good cracks lead up from the ledge, but are squeezed shut by the dark monolithic limestone that caps the rock roof 20 feet higher.

"No gear," Scott says. "The cracks all pinch off. What this route is sayin' is fuck all y'all."

I'm disappointed; this icy snake had been our new goal, having decided, once again, not to go into Mount Robson due to an unstable weather forecast. Just then Barry pulls onto the belay ledge. With his head bent upward, he takes two blind steps, and sinks to his knees in the snow.

"Doesn't look good," Barry says. "Not good at all. No cracks. No cracks, no gear."

"No gear, no go." I finish the little mantra. It's the same mantra Alex taught me in Cody. As long as you can get gear in, there's no harm in going for it.

Barry looks down, plunges his tools into the snow and shifts his gaze to Scott and me. "Well, I thought that might happen. But we're here. Wanna head over that away and have a look-see?"

"Where?" I ask. I'm hesitant to give up so easily on our main objective, but it obviously isn't possible without going back down, bringing a bolt kit, and drilling holes in the rock, which none of us are willing to do. Reinhold Messner famously derided such tactics as the "murder of the impossible." Uncertainty is the essence of alpinism; ignoring that destroys the experience.

"This way," Barry says, pointing to the right. I was focused only on the route ahead. The topography of the rest of the wall is completely foreign to me. Barry, however, seems to have an inkling of another possible route.

"Okay. Lead on Bubba." Scott passes Barry the rest of the rack and Barry traverses right.

When we regroup, Barry has the anchor set far off to the right, near a bare, black rock wall. Up and to his left is an ice smear that looks like a giant under-cooked pancake. Most of it is batter-white; it's not really ice, but instead a thin frosting of vertical snow plastered on rock. Blue areas do reveal some solid ice in places. I check my ice screws and reach for my ice tools.

Scott leans back on the tangle of gear and looks up at the vertical veneer, then says, half to himself, half to Barry, "How come House ends up with the hardest pitches?"

"You've not climbed much with the Farmboy, have you Scotty?" Barry's wife Catherine, who thinks me wholesome, has nicknamed me Farmboy. Barry puts his hand on the taller Scott's shoulder. "He always gets the hard ones."

"How does that happen?" Scott asks, looking at me with feigned incredulity.

"God only knows man, God only knows," Barry slowly shakes his head.

"Well," Scott says, digging into his pack and pulling out a big down parka. "I'm just here for the show."

Canmore, Alberta, Canada: March 12, 1999, (10 days earlier)

"I came out of retirement for you. I had to see for myself," Scott says after he sets down his duffel bags on Barry's living room floor. Laughing, he continues, "Okay. Okay. I lie. I lie. I did it for Barry too." The spark in Scott's eye sets off his graying temples and the weathered crow's feet of a man who has spent much of his 40-odd years outside.

As he unpacks his gear later that evening he dons his climbing helmet and asks rhetorically, "How do you get an old guy to climb hard?"

Barry chuckles with anticipation as he raises a delicate glass of Scotch whisky to his lips, sips, and then takes the bait. "I don't know, man. How?"

"You put a gun to his head." Scott says, pointing to the sticker of a black Glock nine-millimeter handgun on the right side on his blaze-red helmet. His laugh bursts from his open mouth with such force, I start laughing too.

Suddenly serious, he sets his helmet down and looks at me. "I am here to pass the alpinist torch to your generation. Mugs isn't here to do it." He punctu-ates the point with a thrust of his index finger. "Twight won't give it up even though he's through. And Barry," he waves the back of his hand at Barry, still perched on his stool. "Barry doesn't know he's done yet." He lifts his hands in front of him, pointing all 10 of his fingers at himself. "So you get me."

"You're wrong Scott about one thing." I counter, pointing at Barry with my own scotch. "I don't think Barry really is done."

"Nope," pipes in Barry, tapping his heel on the carpet and looking at the sleeping dog stretched at his feet. "If I had been born a hundred years earlier, I would have been hunting buffalo on the plains. Hunting, working for my own survival is, as near as I can tell, just like alpinism. And though it's true that I'm getting older, I still like to hunt."

The next day Barry is off early to guide a multiday ski tour. Scott and I go to climb the classic ice route, Nemesis. While leading, he suddenly exclaims, "Fuck all y'all," quoting rap music for no apparent reason.

That evening Scott bursts through the door at Barry's house and raises his hand in triumph. "Now we've downgraded that mothafucka, too. It's only two pitches. No more three-pitch route, not Nemesis! Two pitches now."

We had utilized a new, longer 80-meter rope. Most climbing ropes are 60 meters. Our ascent was no better than the hundreds that came before it, but it gives Scott something to crow about.

After I'd soloed the new route Beauty Is a Rare Thing, on Denali in 1996, Scott, whom I had not yet met, labeled me in the climbing press as "the great white hope of American alpinism." Like many of his monikers, it unfortunately stuck.

East Face of Howse Peak, Canadian Rockies: March 22, 1999

Watching Scott enjoy himself now, pouring a hot shot of coffee from his thermos, preparing to watch me lead the first hard pitch of this route, it occurs to me that he has nothing invested. He has nothing pending on success or failure.

As I move away from the belay my resentment builds. "What a bastard," I think. "He's here for the show. Now I have to perform, do I? What am I, a damn pony?" Briefly, I feel a rebellious urge to tear off my new sponsor's jacket, rappel off, and go home.

The ice rears back to vertical. I pause to whip in an ice screw at the base of a difficult section. I look up at the ice and attempt to draw in my focus with a sharp breath, tasting the frozen air. With the razor-tipped ice tools I rapidly work the ice above me. Short, sharp swings probe for the densest ice, ice strong enough to support me. Most of the frozen snow won't. Fueled by my quick flash of anger, I climb several body lengths.

Well up on the vertical ice, the burn begins – the pump caused by overgripping the tools. I struggle to place a second ice screw. To continue without protection would be to risk a bad fall onto the sloping ledge below. Hanging by my left arm I spin a screw with my right hand. Cranking, cranking it around to drive it home. I start to hyperventilate. Numbness creeps up my left arm. I abandon my efforts at the screw, quickly replace my right ice tool and then drop my left hand seeking relief. I breathe deeply, steadily now. Switching again, I return to the screw, drive it flush to the ice, and clip in the rope.

I am secure now, safe from a bad fall, but the climbing does not relent. As I climb, my emotions dissolve; my awareness focuses on just this moment.

As the early darkness of the Canadian Rockies' late winter envelopes us, Barry and I put the finishing touches on one of our "torpedo tubes." The ledges in the Rockies are too narrow and steep to take a tent; we worked out the torpedo tube style of snow cave on our first attempt on Mount Robson.

We start by carefully probing the snow drifted onto a ledge to find the deepest snow. Then we excavate from one end, creating a long, narrow snow cave parallel to the face. Our first tube, going right, ends abruptly, 15 feet deep. Going to the left, Barry ekes out a one-man tube barely sufficient to shelter his five-foot, eight-inch length. Scott happily burrows back to the end of the long cave. I follow him in. The snow tunnel is tight; I can't quite sit up. Lying on my short insulating mattress I assemble the stove and start the task of quenching our thirsts with fresh snowmelt turned to tea and soup, and eventually ramen noodles.

Scott lays his long, yellow suit-clad frame out on his long pad and disgorges a massive, six-pound synthetic sleeping bag from his pack – mine weighs two pounds, but I count on shivering half the night. Unzipping the bag he pulls out a pillow.

Recognizing my indignation he laughs as he lies back to wait for his drink. "What can I say? I'm aged and saged." He launches into a new round of laughter.

Bear, Bubba, Blanch. His fortieth birthday is in four days and a hundred people are expected to help him celebrate in his hometown of Canmore. He has spent many of those 40 years at the forefront of Canadian climbing. He has numerous friends and countless memories. Bubba was my teen idol. I kept a photo of him ice climbing taped to the inside of my high-school locker door. Someday, I plan to tell him that.

When I wake up to my alarm at 4:30 am the next morning, I find an unhappy Bubba. The wind blew into his tiny cave and drifted snow onto his down sleeping bag which is now wet and flat. Barry is chilled and shivering. But he's got the stove purring and passes me a hot pot of sugary instant coffee as soon as I sit up.

After I finish the coffee and gnaw down a Pop-Tart, I extend the length of my tie-in so I can get outside the cave to pack my bag. Slithering out, I stand and gaze up at the dark wall. The first hints of daylight illuminate tapered white streaks that cascade down the steep, black rock. The rock wall itself rises, monolithic and impenetrable: an eternity of stone.

Guess we'll be going down now, I think to myself as the sleeping bag, stove and fuel disappear into my rucksack. I don't know what Barry was thinking coming up here. I don't see where the route can go. The only possible line looks damn hard, too hard to do up here.

"My lead, eh Scott?" comes Barry's snow-muffled voice from his cave. "That pitch of snow climbing yesterday didn't count."

"Whatever you want Bubba," comes the reply.

"Where you going to go Barry?" I ask.

"I think up and left, there is a corner system. Leads up to some white stuff that might be climbable. I've seen that line come in before in my travels through these mountains. Looks hard up higher, but that'll be your lead."

I hadn't even realized there was a line on the left, but now, as I look, I can piece it together. Across the snow, up that little rock step. That doesn't look too bad. Then step left into that corner. Yeah, there is a crack in there. The corner gets steeper at the top, but it looks like it goes to the right, and as far up this wall as I can see. Maybe to the top of it.

"So Barry, what's above this wall?" I ask.

"If we can get up this first wall there is a gully that takes us up under another big triangular-shaped wall. That wall is overhanging, so from there you would most likely traverse right to the couloir that George and Joch climbed in '71." The alpine climbing brotherhood is so small Barry can refer to George Lowe and Joch Glidden by their first names.

◇◇◇◇◇◇◇◇◇◇◇◇◇◇◇◇◇◇◇◇◇◇◇◇◇◇◇◇◇◇

"Secure!" yells Barry.

"That's Canadian for off belay," I tell Scott, as we dismantle the anchor.

"Yeah? I've known that since you were in second grade," Scott replies. I think about it for a moment, and he could be right. I make an extra effort to climb slowly and carefully. I'll need the warm-up for that pitch higher up.

Scott joins me at Barry's belay. It's his lead, so he racks up and leads off, climbing quickly and with confidence. The sun shines and I give a hoot, causing him to look over. I snap the picture: yellow suit bold against the white frozen ice and black wall cleaving the deep blue sky.

Following Scott's pitch, I admire his effort. He ran it out for speed and placed gear that is solid. The climbing is steep, and getting steeper and more sustained.

I rack up for the next lead; the rack is heavy. The sun has gone, leaving us in the big winter wall's gray light.

"Up there you think, Bubba?" I ask, pointing to where the crack disappears in a mess of snow mushrooms.

"I think so, maybe up that steep snowy groove. Or if not, you could try traversing out right, but it looks thin over there."

I start, moving a few feet before placing my first piece, the beginning of the safety net that will protect me if I fall. The route above looks unlikely. The groove overhangs and is choked with heavy, snow mushrooms. As I reach the groove, I slot one tool into the crack and lean back. Overhanging snow stretches above. I reach up and gently smack one of the white orbs with the broad side of my ice axe. It breaks off and grabs at my ice axe, nearly tearing it out of my hand. It zips downwards and explodes on the wall next to the belay.

"Maybe not," I shout down. "I'm going to try right."

To the right the climbing is less than vertical as it traverses below a black rock overhang. Slowly I step to the right, kicking at the snowy bits to uncover edges beneath. The climbing unveils itself by a snow-burlesque: footholds revealed slowly as I clean off the snow.

The bulge above ends and the traverse deposits me on a small, less-than-vertical, bulletin board of hard snow. Up to my left I place my largest cam. The wall rears up to vertical. I'm standing on a kind of snow-ice, sometimes called snice. It starts as snow that is deposited on the wall during storms, then by slow melt-freeze cycles, it hardens. Sometimes it's climbable; sometimes it just looks climbable.

I reach up again and again, ripping through the snice with my pick. Ten times: nothing solid. Twenty: the pick slips through it like it's whipped cream. Shifting my feet just a bit higher I stab the pick far out to the right. It sinks in, this time with a bit of resistance and a squeak. Careful not to break the precious ice away, I lever my pick out and tap it back in with just a bit more speed, a bit more power. A high squeal confirms the steel point is set.

Just above that tool there is a gap in the ice caused by a four-inch-wide roof in the rock. This is the turning point. From here I could down climb to the last crack, the last protection, and retreat to safety. That will not be possible after this next move. I take a deep breath and go.

Carefully setting my tool under the small roof, I climb. I see the next gear placement. I breathe loudly and focus on reaching it. The ice is getting thinner and more prone to shattering under my ever-gentle taps. As I reach the crack, the smear under my feet breaks away. I struggle to lift my feet back up. I place one crampon point on an edge that had been hidden under the ice. I step my right foot out far to the side to form a secure platform.

Stemming between two tiny wrinkles in the rock, I let my ice hammer hang by its leash on my wrist and grab for the medium knifeblade piton. Reaching right I press its tip into the crack a few millimeters. I tap it gently with the side of my hand. Carefully, quickly, I grab my ice hammer and take aim. A glancing blow will send the precious piton soaring down the wall. I deliver gentle taps, each driving the pin in a few more millimeters. With a third of the piton's tip buried in the seam, I take the hammer by the end of the shaft and drive it home with a few hard, fast blows.

Above me the ice narrows again and dissipates under another small rock roof. I scrape my left foot to a higher edge, then bump the right foot up. The ice is too thin – just a half-inch thick – to take a pick. One misplaced swing and I'll send it all down leaving nothing to climb. I pause and look all around me. Trying to see everything: every feature, every lip, every fold. There is nothing else for my ice tool. With the tip of the right tool twisted in the piton crack, I carefully chip away the top edge of ice. Working at it, one little bit at a time, until I have created a tiny platform one centimeter thick and a few centimeters wide, an edge upon which I can place the pick of my tool and pull down.

Forcing my upper body in close to the wall, I lay the teeth of my axe sideways and set the pick on the edge. Working my foot higher and trying to keep my body pressed in close, I pull hard with my left arm, and push down and out with my feet. I lift the tip of my other ice hammer as high as I can and am just able to reach past the roof. The pick scrapes against featureless rock. I try again – more to the left – and my pick bounces off bare stone again. I shift my right foot farther up until I'm fully extended, stretching and reaching as far as I can. Nothing. Gently, I shift my head back, but not too far. Even such a subtle shift in weight could cause me to lose my balance, and a fall here would be unacceptable.

Tilting back, I see a tendril of ice. It looks gray, the color ice gets when it's older and has distilled itself of air bubbles. Mentally mapping the ice, I drop my head down to maximize my reach. With my arm fully extended I hold my breath and draw my wrist back. Tap. I have it. The tip of the ice hammer feels solid. I pull up.

Higher, the angle relents and easier ground leads to a stance where I build an anchor. I have only ice screws; I left every piece of rock gear on the pitch. I use all eight screws, but only one of them goes in to its full depth. With my remaining cord and some climbing rope I equalize them and tie in the ropes. I shout for the lads to start up. I look at my watch: the pitch took three hours.

Shivering, my sweat freezes on the inside of my jacket. Barry is cleaning the pitch using ascenders, rope clamps that slide up the rope but not down. I eavesdrop on his self-talk as he removes each piece of gear. "Ooh. That was a good one." And later, "Glad he didn't fall on that!"

Barry arrives and eyes the eight tied-off screws holding us all to the mountain. "Scott," he yells down. "Wha'd'ya think, eh?"

Scott ascends another body length in silence, apparently contemplating the shattered ice and scratched rock edges. He looks up with a wide grin. "I consider myself to be good at this type of climbing. And maybe I could have followed it. But I bet there are less than a dozen men in the world that could have led it!"

Later, this lead became known as "The Pitch," and in each retelling the experience has receded into the mist; simultaneously diluted and inflated. I wonder now if it was really that difficult. We named the route M-16, a play on Scott's Glock and in mockery of the popular grade of high-level difficulty, road-side, bolt-protected, mixed climbing of the time: M-8.

But all of that would come later. Now I am too cold, too hungry, too jaded by Scott's previous declarations. I want the food and water he has in his pack.

Barry takes the next and final pitch of the day, a wave of ice that steepens and turns to snow. He backs off, returns to rock on his left, then aid climbs. Soon he is up the short aid section and disappears into the snow bowl above. We follow.

The next morning our little snow cave is full of activity in the predawn blackness. We've burrowed into the top, right corner of a large rectangular snowfield, just 10 feet right of where the ice flows down and over the wall we climbed yesterday. We're getting ready to gun for the summit. While I stuff my bag into my pack, Scott unblocks the cave entrance.

The scene illuminated by his headlamp is horrific. A storm has come in overnight and we're camped on the edge of a snow version of Niagara Falls. Avalanches constantly pour from the steep headwall above, funnel down past our cave entrance, and into the gully below. Most is spindrift but some of the more clamorous sloughs hide chunks that alarm us as they fall, unhurried, thousands of feet to the glacier.

We're stalled. Scott replaces the snow block that seals the door. "Guess not," he says, his voice flat and matter of fact now. "We can't go up or down."

"Well," starts Barry, "we'll just have to wait a bit. If it improves in the next few hours we can still try for the top. If not, we'll have to go down tomorrow. We only have one more dinner."

With nothing to do, we remodel the snow cave into a comfortable three-bedroom with a central kitchen. We make the door more robust and Barry tinkers with our rock anchors to make staying tied in more comfortable.

With sleeping bags resituated, I'm now the one who can see outside. I pry back the snow block door: it's still snowing hard and the avalanches continue.

Gradually we settle into a long day of conversation. This is my third alpine route with Barry, and I learn more about him on this one afternoon than I have on all our past days of climbing together. He tells stories of Viennese lovers, near misses on his first trip to the Alps, delivering milk with his milkman uncle, getting beat up for being half native in the bad part of Calgary.

Scott's tales are even more foreign: punk concerts, hard drugs, and stunningly bad pickup lines that worked. I 'fess up to the picture in the locker, from which Scott gets a huge laugh. But my stories are much tamer. In high school I bucked 80-pound hay bales for summer work. I met my wife Anne at the outdoor recreation office my first week of college. I seduced her by bringing diet Pepsi to her late-night study sessions. Once I inadvertently passed a police car on my motorbike, and gunned it.

The last light fades as we take inventory: eight ounces of fuel, one instant soup packet, some almonds, four nutrition bars, and 18 GU packets. As the night matures I peek out to see the first flash of moonlight and a patch of stars. We decide to try for an early start and settle in to wait.

It is 4:30 am. Barry has the stove humming before anyone else is up. The moonlight has been shining off and on through my view hole, and the cave is over-flowing with confidence. We are packed before the coffee is brewed. I'm the first one out, and the first to have his heart broken. It is snowing and the avalanches have begun. We slip back into the cave and make the obvious decision: retreat.

The decision's made but as I sit, slouched against the wall, I'm haunted by "The Pitch," the crux. It was my best effort, an ideal of hard mixed terrain high in the mountains. I stay quiet as we eat the last of the hot food. I slurp down my share of soup in silence.

We've failed, I keep thinking. This is always hard to digest, and I can't deny how deeply I still want to finish the line. The crux lead is wasted, lost. I try to let go of my disappointment, but I want to finish this line and be able to stare up at it from below.

Suddenly Scott announces, "Why don't we just go up and see how it goes? If we can't deal, we'll go down. Let's not just assume it can't be done."

Barry perks up, "Yeah, I'd do that."

When they look at me, I stare back in amazement. "Are you guys sure? I mean, we're out of food, we should probably use this window to go down in."

"Let's face it Farmboy," starts Scott. "How do I put this? Okay. Barry and I have been climbing a total of what, like 40 years Bubba?"

"Something like that," Barry says, giving Scott his full attention.

"Well, correct me if I'm wrong Bubba, but neither of us have ever seen any-one climb a pitch like the one you climbed yesterday. If we go down now, you might not ever be able to repeat it. Or the ice – or whatever that was – might not form like that next year or for the next 10 years. We've got to finish this route, at least to the ridge, so that your pitch can take its place as what it is, one of the most brilliant pieces of climbing ever done."

Scott pauses, and looks at Barry. When he looks back at me he reads my pos-ture: knees up, arms crossed, forehead on my arms. "I know, I know. You hate to hear that. But you have to. Its your time now, Steve. I told you when I got here what I was here to see. What I was here to do. I'm not done yet. We have to finish this route."

I wasn't prepared for this. I want to go on, but all three of us must certainly understand that we're making a bad decision for highly questionable reasons.

I stand in the door of the snow cave and belay as Scott charges the lead. He climbs well, leading up an ice-filled gully before beginning a long traverse over steep, Andean, snow flutings. The traverse finally intersects the Lowe Couloir, which cuts deeply into the summit of Howse Peak.

The old guys want it! Barry Blanchard, two days before his 40th birthday, about to climb into the spindrift of the Lowe Couloir, high on the east face of Howse Peak. He came to regret that he didn't put his hood up. STEVE HOUSE

We make a short 30-foot rappel onto the thick ice of the gully and nestle ourselves safely against the rock wall. Barry takes the next lead, venturing out to the center of the gully. The snowfall is picking up: big, wet sticky flakes – cow pies. The flakes accumulate above and every few minutes release as a vicious avalanche.

Every time another avalanche bears down on Barry, Scott and I shout a warning. Barry leans into the ice and holds on. If he should lean out at the wrong moment and catch the full force of the snow, he'd be plucked off as easily as a peach in August. I know that what he is doing is insane, but I am proud that he's still got it in him to try this hard. Barry stretches the rope and builds an anchor as far to the side of the avalanche path as possible. Dutifully, Scott and I follow him into the maelstrom, into his madness.

We're close to the top, but the avalanches continue to pound us. I inch my hood back just enough to sneak a look at the rolling blue ice in this deep gash. Such a wild, inhospitable place, a place where long-term survival is impossible. Even our temporary residence is an extreme gamble.

We hunker down against the punishing snowfall. Bubba belays just below the ridge crest directly beneath a cornice. It juts out 40 feet from the face, sheltering us from the snow and wind. Above us lies the summit, just half a pitch away. Gusts of wind blow streamers of snow out onto the face below us.

Here we must make a decision. We could climb the remaining 40 feet out of the gully. Dealing with the snow and wind looks like it would be more difficult than the actual climbing. Then we would have to traverse the summit, descend the east ridge, traverse over another peak, climb down to a saddle, descend 3,000 feet to our skis, and ski six miles to the car. Or we can descend our route, sleep in the cave for a third night, and rappel the rest of the face in the morning.

We have one headlamp and three packets of GU each. Each GU contains 100 calories. We have no water. We left our sleeping bags in the snow cave to save weight. No words are said. I look at Barry, his whiskers etched with snow. Barry looks at Scott.

Scott breaks the silence. "So it's my turn then?" And he drills an ice screw into the ice and starts rigging the ropes for a rappel.

I feel neither the sting of defeat, nor any swell of victory. Only gathering relief as each rappel brings us closer to the safety of the snow cave. Scott is leading us down, setting the anchors and tending the ropes. Each time I look around, cornices and snow mushrooms peek out from behind cloudbanks. I harbor an uneasy feeling.

"Off rappel Barry!" I yell as I arrive at the last anchor. From within the snow cave I catch the muffled clanking of pots as Scott, the first one down, fires up the stove. As I anchor myself safely to the wall I am annoyed that Scott hasn't tied in the ends of the rappel ropes. This means if the anchor were to fail while

Barry is rappelling he would fall the length of the face: Bubba and our ropes would be gone.

I pull up the ends, tie a good knot and clip them in to the anchor. At least this way if Barry goes, Scott and I might still survive. Just as I think this, I cock my head to the gathering rumble of another avalanche. A huge powder cloud tears down the gully. In the maelstrom I see dark chunks I can't identify screaming towards the glacier like ghosts from hell. I hope one wasn't Barry.

"Barrryyy!" I shout.

The ropes still stretch up to the anchor, so he must be there. I strain to see a sign, some movement. Anything. The gully is a mass of impenetrable white.

"Baaarrryyyy!" Long seconds pass and I draw several forced breaths. Deep inside the cave Scott hasn't heard a thing. I shove my head into the cave's entrance. "Scott! Barry!" and turn around again. My lungs are screaming. "Barrrrryyyyyyyyy!"

I look up and see Bubba fumbling to place an ice screw. He has been pushed to the edge of the gully and hangs below a single remaining piton. The rest of the anchor is gone. His pack is gone – shorn from his back by the slide.

I can tell he is injured by his stiff, awkward movements. I feel nauseous, balanced on the edge of the trauma of another tragedy unfolding before me. Slowly he begins to rappel. I cling to the ends, guiding him to our sanctuary on this mammoth wall. He is white, white from the punch that packed his collar, zippers, gloves, helmet, harness – even his nose – with snow. He is white with shock and fear. Only his eyes are black.

He gropes his way onto the ledge with one leg held stiffly behind him. Reaching his harness, I clip him to an anchor and hug him as he lies there. Panic gives way to tears. Barry's clothing emits the ammonia odor of fear. I can see it in the recesses of his dark, unfocused pupils.

Scott is beside us now. He and I shuffle Bubba to the cave entrance. He kicks with his one good leg. Scott goes in first and pulls him inside by his armpits. Immediately Scott covers him with his big synthetic sleeping bag.

We have nothing to eat. We use the last of the fuel to make a hot-water bottle and a cup of tea for Barry. Once I am settled into my bag I go through the trash, pulling open used packets of GU and licking out the insides. Bubba is past the shock now; he and Scott snuggle in the sleeping bag. I listen to the weather forecast on Barry's two-way VHF radio. The barely audible forecast for tomorrow: clear and sunny. Exhausted, I fall asleep and, luxuriously, suffer no dreams.

I wake in the middle of the dark night, my stomach aching for food. I pull back the door and see many stars. The storm has passed. Without calories I am cold, so I do sit-ups in my sleeping bag to keep from freezing.

The piece of sky framed by the door slowly brightens. "Hey guys, it's getting light."

I push my sleeping bag and bivouac sack into my pack. I toss the useless stove, the trash, and my headlamp in on top. We have little left; packing is quick and simple. Scott and Barry have the one sleeping bag draped over them like a blanket.

"Did you sleep?" I ask.

"No," Scott laughs. "But Bubba did, and you were doing a fine imitation of an Oregon lumberjack for awhile." Barry grunts and sits up, his head just missing the low roof. His left leg is stretched out before him. He lifts it manually, and grunts again.

"My leg is fucked. It's really stiff." Registering my alarm he adds, "I think it will be okay once we get out to civilization. But I won't be doing any skiing out of here. Once we get out onto the broad part of the face I'll have better radio reception. I'll try to call the wardens and see if they can pick me up from the glacier with a chopper."

I help him out of the cave. Standing up with a perfunctory snarl, he quickly discovers that weighting his leg hurts.

Whenever I lead, whether it be climbing up or rappelling down, I feel the weight of responsibility for my partners and by extension the hopes and fear of those who love them. That love weighs especially heavy this morning as I begin making fall line rappels down the gully. Quickly we are out onto the glittering openness of the crux wall. The sunlight is weakly warming.

As I leave the next anchor I see Barry take out his radio to call the Canadian park wardens.

"Did you get through?" I ask as he descends to the next rappel.

"I got through, but it was really hard to understand them. I don't know how well they heard me. I did understand them to say that Catherine had been calling them concerned. It's been raining in Canmore the last few days."

The final rappel anchor is a spare ice hammer pick driven downward behind a flake. Barry is working his way down awkwardly when we hear the whump-whump of a helicopter. The radio is of no use to contact them – it's shorted out now.

A rescuer attached to the end of a 100-foot, short-haul line sails in towards the wall. He is a little too high and a little too hot. He hits the wall violently, ricocheting off.

"Uff-da," comments Scott. "That's gotta hurt.

The chopper pulls back and hovers for a moment, seemingly to get a better read on the wall. The rescuer comes in again. This time his crampons spin wildly around our heads. We all duck and the chopper pulls back a second time.

The pilot hovers again and then takes a third pass. The rescuer smacks into the wall again. This time he is a few feet lower and his crampon points perfectly pierce the knot on the webbing into which we are all clipped. Thinking quickly Barry grabs the rescuer's daisy chain and clips him into the same knotted sling that is tied to the driven pick head which serves as our anchor.

Our guest rapidly unclips from the heli's line and speaks into the helmet mike. Quiet comes back to the wall as the helicopter dives away from the wall and flies toward the highway six miles distant.

"Welcome to our world," Scott says.

Ignoring him, the rescuer asks, "So who wants to go first?"

None of us want to go; none of us wants anything to do with those sketchy aerial acrobatics. He agrees to our plan to rappel with us, and then down climb to the glacier. Then he spots our anchor: the driven pick.

"Oh, no. I've got children to go home to, eh? I'm not rappelling off that. No sir. No way."

Ten minutes later, Barry and the warden soar straight out and away from the face. Scott and I perch on the steep slope, alone in the stillness.

Scott reaches down and picks up the ropes, holding them towards me. "After you, Farmboy."

The beginning moments of the avalanche on Shishapangma that injured Conrad Anker and killed Alex Lowe and Dave Bridges. *Outside* magazine posthumously declared Alex to be "The World's Best Climber." Alex once said, "The best climber in the world is the one having the most fun." KRISTOFFER ERICKSON

CHAPTER ELEVEN

Death on Easy Ground

Twenty Miles Outside of Bozeman, Montana: October 17, 1999

A BUNDLED SECURITY GUARD checks my ID against the guest list and waves me through the gate. I drive up and park in a hayfield converted to a parking lot. A broad house sits beyond a corner of the field. Next to it a sagging grey hay-barn holds vigil next to a low-lying pavilion building.

Many people are driving up and getting out of their cars. All are dressed in black pants and suit coats or long dresses underneath formal coats. I'm wearing my best jeans and a black T-shirt. I'm shivering. I feel conspicuous. I start toward the buildings when I see Barry walking up in black cowboy boots, faded jeans and a long black western-shirt with a turquoise and silver bolo.

"Hey Barry. Hi Catherine. Look at us, the jeans brigade."

Barry chuckles softly, "Yeah. I guess so."

We start walking together. Barry's wife Catherine puts her arm around me in consolation.

I step back behind Barry and Catherine as we approach the open pavilion. Conrad Anker turns the corner, his eyes meeting mine. Conrad was caught in the same avalanche as Alex and Dave Bridges. Conrad ran to the right, Alex and Dave went straight. Conrad lived, Alex and Dave died. He and I first met in Cody, Wyoming, the time I climbed with Alex. We have not climbed together. His pupils are dark and withdrawn, his eyes glassy and rimmed with swollen pink mucus. His face is pale; red abrasions cover his gaunt cheeks. His stubbly scalp reveals several rows of puffy stitches.

With one glance we acknowledge that our membership in this society of risk-takers cuts both ways. It has sharpened my awareness, helped define my choices, and tempered my ambition. Today we are reminded of a million experiences with the finest friends who are now gone. Ropes no longer to be shared, meals not to be cooked, wine that will go uncorked.

I am happy to see Conrad. I want to embrace him. I want to plan things with him. I want to live some precious moments together before the possibility of that also is gone. He drops his eyes and ducks into the large room before I can put this thought into words.

Inside, I lose sight of Conrad as my eyes adjust to the dim light. Then I see him moving towards the front. He takes a seat next to some of the other expedition team members. They are wearing matching black North Face fleece jackets for the occasion. I turn and find a place against the back wall, and drop into sadness as the ceremony begins.

Jenni Lowe and her three sons approach the podium. The youngest is so tiny, maybe three years old. I wonder what he'll remember of Alex, if anything. The oldest, Max, will clearly remember a great deal. He describes climbing the Grand Teton with his dad less than two months ago.

Alex's father doesn't make it through his speech. His wife Dorthea, follows him off the stage. Famous climbers, expedition mates, and friends are each given their turn. After everyone has spoken, the brothers, Andy and Ted Lowe, lead us through Tom Petty's "Wildflowers." We all join in for the chorus; with each line we get braver. We sing the chorus three times. By the third time we are belting it out, our emotion unleashed.

You belong among the wildflowers,
You belong in a boat out at sea,
You belong on a very tall tower,
You belong to all the world and me.

The music stops. There is not a dry eye in the house. As the musicians step down the only sound is the echo of grief against the battered maple wood floor. I start to panic, something is wrong. Instead of remaining aloof from it, disdaining the weakness that allows it, I feel their pain and suffering. I feel my pain.

Before today my rationalizations have shielded me. Acknowledging and feeling this grief, how will it be possible for me to climb what I need to climb?

Alex made no mistakes, I think, reciting the familiar rationales: Wrong place, wrong time. Random death. Death on easy ground. Game of chance. Sobbing echoes through the room, I can still feel the wrenching pain of loss. My reasoning is failing. I turn and lurch for the door.

My exit is halted by loud footsteps crossing the stage. I look up, and there is young Max. He stops and puts his fiddle to his chin. With another fiddle and

Alex and Jenni on their front porch with their three sons (left to right): Max, Isaac, and Sam. GORDON WILTSE

Alex making the first ascent of Expanding Horizons in Hyalite Canyon, January, 1998. The route is graded M-8 R. The R indicates a runout, which means that a fall may be dangerous assuming the protection holds, and very serious or fatal if the protection fails. KRISTOFFER ERICKSON

a guitar back up, he serenades us, gently at first, then spiritedly with "Whiskey Before Breakfast" – a plucky, upbeat, bluegrass tune.

Alex's oldest son has saved me; tragedy becomes revelation. There he is, there is Alex, in Max: the same concentrated gaze; the long, limber fingers; the head bursting with stiff hair.

<><><><><><><><><><><><><><><><><><><><><>

As the plane takes off I curl up next to the window and sleep. Alex appears in my dream. So do Marija, Jože, Caroll, Julie, and Steve Mascioli. They are not in a mystical place, or a perfect place, just a room. It looks like my childhood tree house. They're all sitting, relaxed. I don't know where they are, but they seem accessible. I could speak to them if I wished, and them to me. Yet no words pass; a comfortable silence between friends.

Turbulence jolts me awake. I look out the window at the Teton Range, Alex's second home. Alex is gone; the stone fortress of those mountains remains – unchanged. I remain as well, but I am forever changed by having known Alex. I was his admirer, his friend, his partner.

I am weary of the disdainful superiority of alpinists like me who have survived, and who, chests puffed, cast knowing glances as if to say, "We are better than they were; we survived."

I'm tired of long black dresses and black jackets. My eyes are tired of crying.

Tragically, I will never again watch Alex unleash his grace and power on a frozen waterfall. Never listen to Mascioli around a campfire, describing an unclimbed wall in British Columbia, a splash of whisky in our coffee. Never watch as Jože and Marija strike off toward a Himalayan summit, as if out for a seaside stroll.

There is a certain schizophrenia to these feelings. I feel a need to break from society's structure, to move in a grand, natural environment, to measure myself, to find identity, and to prove my worth. These feelings teeter in balance with the fear of being the next one to be buried in an avalanche, to be hit by a falling stone, to fall to the bottom of a cliff, to get wedged in a crevasse, to become fatally exhausted. To die.

I close my eyes and imagine my own death over and over. I imagine it was me in Marija's, Jože's, Mugs', Julie's, Caroll's, Steve Mascioli's, or Alex's boots. That it was me exhausted, frozen in the snow, killed by rockfall, by a snow-mushroom, by an avalanche. I imagine the last breath being crushed from my body.

Luck is nothing of which to be proud. Each of these cold, tired deaths could have been – might still be – mine. Ultimately, survival in the big mountains depends upon a great measure of luck. Where is the pride in that?

Mark Twight and I at 17,400 feet on the Cassin Ridge. Behind Mark are the tracks of climbers Mark Westman and Joe Puryear from several hours earlier. We've been on the go for 56 hours and are 2,900 feet below the summit of Denali. SCOTT BACKES

CHAPTER TWELVE

Partnership

Anchorage International Airport, Alaska: June, 2000

"YOU KNOW," SAYS SCOTT BACKES as he, Mark Twight and I wait in baggage claim for his equipment, "the whole way up here I debated, incessantly, whether I'm over it or not. Last I checked, I'm not getting younger. And I haven't climbed, except in my beautiful little quarries back home in Minnesota, in a year. In fact, if it hadn't been for a particularly savage bike ride the other day, I wouldn't have come on this trip."

He pauses, shoves his hands into his pockets and draws his shoulders back. "I really wouldn't have. But when I saw you two in arrivals, I knew there was no turning back. I took a deep breath." He takes a huge breath and holds it. As the air rushes out a few moments later, he continues, "and I held it all the way down the Jetway, and here I am, walking into the breech one more time. You both know that I wouldn't have come for anyone else."

The next day a curly haired climber dressed in faded baggy jeans and sticky-rubber hiking shoes approaches us on the airport tarmac in Talkeetna. He stops right in front of us. We're busy preparing our gear to fly onto the glacier.

"So, did you hear that a couple NOLSies scooped your route? What are you guys going to do now?" He says.

Scott draws himself to his full six-foot-four height. In his mountain boots he is even bigger. This is the seventh person in 12 hours to inform us of the obviously talented National Outdoor Leadership School instructors' climb.

"Listen," Scott starts in. Mark and I fold our arms across our chests and flank the victim; I catch Mark suppressing a grin. "We're here because we care about our experience and our ethic." Scott punches towards the ground with his index finger. "We're here to climb the Slovak in a single push. We're here to do the hardest route on the mountain faster, with less equipment, and with the greatest commitment. We're willing to put ourselves in harm's way for our ideal."

Not pausing, and not releasing the man's gaze, Scott continues, pushing his finger into his own chest. "Personally, I think it's great that those guys did the second ascent. It took them eight days, right?" A small nod. "Perfect. That'll be the counterpoint to us, if we do it, because we're going to do it in two days."

Scott may feel old and out of climbing practice, but he brings a born-again passion for the task at hand. And he believes in what we can accomplish together. To Mark and I, it's still science fiction. Scott's sermon is just what we need to make the leap of faith that this is going to require. Never in the history of mountaineering has anyone ever done such a technically difficult, high, cold, long route as quickly as we are planning.

To succeed we will have to climb naked. Forget fixed lines, stocked camps, and cached gear. Forget tents. Forget sleeping bags. Forget solid food. We'll carry the clothes on our backs, one insulated parka each, and two stoves to keep us hydrated for 48 hours of nonstop climbing. After the first 12 hours we won't have enough gear to descend the way we came; we'll be committed to completing the climb. We each understand that if one of us is injured and can't continue, the others will have to leave him to die. And if it's me who must be left behind, I will have to love Scott and Mark enough to let them go.

<><><><><><><><><><><><><><><><><><><><>

The previous June, Mark and I met here in Talkeetna, the launching pad for most Denali expeditions. We flew in and followed Denali's normal route to the 14,000-foot camp in three days. After a day's rest we climbed wind-polished snow up the West Rib route to the summit.

Along the way we were recruited by the National Park Service to help recover equipment left at 18,000 feet as part of an earlier rescue effort. Back at base camp, resting and retooling for an attempt on the Slovak, Mark asks the ranger for a favor of his own: a radiophone call to his girlfriend.

A long time later he comes back and sits on his pack with his elbows on his knees pressing his forehead into his palms. His hat drops to the snow. I lean sideways, but can't see his eyes. I have just finished digging out our camp and the stove is purring under a large pot of snow

"Everything okay Mark? Lisa?" I ask.

"Yeah. Lisa. She's in Hawaii." He pauses. "With an old boyfriend."

I poke at the snow starting to melt in the pot. "Are you going to Hawaii too?" My gut twists and I breathe to release the tension. "You can go."

"We were having that conversation and the radiophone didn't work too well."

"Look, I don't know what's going on, but you should fly out and call her. You can get a plane in here tonight. If you decide to leave after that, send word back to base camp and I'll pack up your stuff and fly out." I'm scared, because I want to climb, but I also know that Mark will be worthless as a partner if he's distracted in any way. He looks up and absentmindedly runs his hand across his shaggy crew cut.

An hour later he boards a ski-equipped Cessna and flies to Talkeetna. The next afternoon he gets off a returning plane, smiling, freshly showered and carrying a cold take-out pizza. That night, as we eat the pizza, it starts to rain. One week later, never having left the tent, the sky clears and we're grateful just to fly out.

∞∞∞∞∞∞∞∞∞∞∞∞∞∞∞∞∞∞∞∞

This year, Mark, Scott and I start with the obligatory acclimatization on the West Buttress Route. The park service recruits us again: a 62-year-old climber with cracked ribs and the onset of pneumonia needs to be evacuated from the 17,200-foot camp.

Back in the tent that night, after helping to make the rescue in eight hours round trip, Mark asks, "Why do I enjoy doing that? Why do I like being good at it?"

I look at him, locking eyes, and expecting him to see what I see. When he doesn't, I answer, "Because it further justifies your elitist attitude."

The next day I am seven minutes behind Mark to the summit up the West Buttress Route. Scott is another 53 minutes behind me. We return to base camp to resupply and spend a few days listening to light snowfall rattle the tents. Between snow showers we plug powered speakers into Mark's mini-disc player. Mark blasts '80s punk, mixed with vehement Henry Rollins and the loud rock of Tool. We carve chairs out of the snow and insulate them with sleeping pads.

Mark and I cackle as Scott lambastes a slightly overweight mountaineer starting up the West Buttress. "Instead of measuring your granola out into little premarked baggies, spending hours threading orange flagging around little sticks of bamboo to mark the route you're sharing with a thousand other people, you should have been training!"

High pressure builds and we point our skis up the east fork of the Kahiltna Glacier. Under crystal-blue skies we camp hard against the base of the Cassin Ridge for protection from the massive ice-cliffs of Big Bertha, the large serac band in the center of the South Face. The Slovak Direct takes the steep wall immediately right of the iconic Cassin Route.

That night we study a route map made by Adam Blažej after he and two partners made the first ascent in 1984. They were supported by fixed ropes and a sister party of three climbers who met them on the summit and helped them

127

descend. They spent 11 days opening the route and a mere 167 words describing it in the 1985 *American Alpine Journal*. Their sentences are cryptic and understated. "Finding bivouac sites caused us great problems." "We wore out new crampons and ice axes." "We got to the summit at 2 am."

We pack two stoves, with 22 ounces of fuel and a titanium pot for each. Synthetic belay parkas for Mark and me, down for Scott. Fifty packets of GU per man. Two ropes and a rack of rock and ice protection. When we add the nine quarts of water we'll start with, the total weight distributed among the three of us is only 55 pounds. On our second day at camp we race up the first 1,000 feet in 90 minutes to test our speed.

We return to camp and that night I prepare a last supper: rotelli pasta heavy with reindeer sausage and dehydrated tomatoes. For dessert I want to provide something bitter to go with the sweet mugs of cocoa. So I read out loud from Yukio Mishima's *Sun and Steel*:

> *"Pain, I came to feel, might well prove to be the sole proof of the persistence of consciousness within the flesh, the sole physical expression of consciousness. As my body acquired muscle, and in turn strength, there was gradually born within me the tendency towards positive acceptance of pain, and my interest in physical suffering deepened."*

Mishima committed *seppuku*, ritual suicide, the same year he wrote that. In two sentences he had described our need to climb without knowing the context. We were here to prove the existence of our consciousness.

To do that we need to be ready for true partnership: Scott, Mark and I will have to truly and fully believe that we can do this. Mark and Scott's egos will need to acknowledge my technical prowess. Scott and I will need to accommodate Mark's powerful will.

Seattle-Tacoma International Airport, Washington: March 1, 1998, (28 months earlier)

Mark Twight is smaller than I expect. He stands at the edge of the boarding area, and I first recognize him by his climber's pack. As I get nearer I notice the square cut of his chin. I approach to the aqua-blue shimmer of his eyes, which greet me with equal recognition.

Mark is among the best, and best-known, alpine climbers in the world. When I was a senior in high school I read his article, "The Rise and Fall of the American Alpinist," in which he argued that the destitute state of American alpinism stemmed from failures of training and will. Americans sucked in the big mountains because they didn't train in the Canadian Rockies, they didn't climb with Canadian or European partners, and they didn't attempt big alpine style routes in the Himalaya.

Now, 10 years later, I wonder if I have subconsciously molded my life in an effort to disprove Mark's thesis. I am about to meet one of my avatars. I worry that I might not be able to meet his gaze.

We're meeting here to fly to Alaska hoping to climb new routes during late winter. We're expecting to find ice plastered across the massive granite walls of the Ruth Gorge. On the flight I show pictures of where I think we might look. Mark hands them back across the aisle and I notice his blue eyes slip to the floor with trepidation.

"Another fallible hero," I think. "Another man with faults and fears, just like me." Since I first read his writing he has made an honest effort to set his bulwark of ideas upon a solid foundation of action. He has left his punk hair cut behind and now looks like a Marine in a recruitment commercial. But not so boyish, more like that same Marine after 15 years in the field: jaw set by hardship, face leathered by sun, hair freckled gray.

We join forces with Mark's long-time friend, Jonny Blitz, and climb a difficult new route on the south face of Mount Bradley. On the tenth day of the trip Mark backs off from leading the crux pitch. It is a crucial moment. I know I can climb the fragile drop of icicle that falls 30 feet and ends, hanging in space. But I need to address the moment gracefully, not the climbing, but taking over the lead. I want to leave Mark's ego, and the possibility that we might climb together in the future, intact.

When Mark returns to the belay, I ask for the rack. He looks at me for a moment, bends his head and hands it over without a word. I grab it, a little too quickly, and take off. I place two pieces of gear in a crack behind the icicle, stand on tiptoe and stick the pick of my ice hammer into it. I pull up once, then twice. My arms are burning. I make a third pull up, and step a foot towards the rock wall to try to take some weight off my arms. I hold my body there – toe against the rock, one arm fully flexed – and swing the other tool. The icicle makes a sharp tearing sound, and breaks. I ride it down, feeling a little jolt as the first piece of gear rips out. The second – and the only – piece remaining between me and the belay holds. I dangle at the end of the rope, my ass kissing the ledge.

Without pause I climb back to the cam and twist my picks into the crack behind the broken-off ice. At the top of the crack I place two more pieces of gear, lean out, and strike at the icicle. It holds.

Mark had been right to come down. Up higher – though the climbing is less difficult – the cracks pinch down and disappear. The granite is austerely polished. I climb 25 feet with no protection, risking serious injury. Night is coming on when I complete the pitch and rappel back to the ledge Mark and Jonny have been flattening for our bivouac.

"I'm sorry about that," I start as soon as I land. "That was too dangerous to be doing up here." Mark's furrowed brow softens, and Jonny looks at him, still knocking snow off the ledge with his boots.

Finally Mark chuckles softly. "Yeah, that's what I thought. And Blitz and I were just talking about how risk like that isn't yours to take. If one man goes down, we all go down."

"I know," I reply uncomfortably.

The next day we complete the route, and return to the same bivy at 2 am. As we sit in our sleeping bags, waiting for the stove to melt snow, green and purple flashes split the sky. Wordlessly we watch the northern lights for an hour before fatigue forces our eyelids shut and we sleep.

The Start of the Slovak Direct Route, Denali's South Face, Alaska: June 24, 2000

At 6 am we leave the tent, climbing solo – an opening act of trust that seeds confidence. By 8 am we have passed the Slovak's second bivouac. We stop to belay and I take both ropes and tie in to lead. We plan to take turns, each leading six pitches. At 11 am I belay near the Slovak's third bivy. We've done in five hours what took them three days. Our belief in what we're attempting is fortified. Scott takes over the lead and climbs transparent water ice that cascades down a brilliant white granite corner. The sun warms us. Scott swings his tools into the steep corner, pulls up, and motors on. We're hauling ass.

Near the top of the first icefield Scott crosses the bergschrund, the end of the icefield. I know from the topo map that this was their fourth bivy. As Scott climbs past the 'schrund 200 feet above us, Mark and I reach a platform. It's the bivy ledge cut out of the steep snow by Mahoney and Gilmore, the NOLS instructors and guides whose ascent had been rubbed in our noses in Talkeetna. To find such a ledge a month after it was cut is remarkable. Mark and I simultaneously recognize the opportunity. We've been climbing eight hours without pause and here is the perfect chance to rest and recharge ourselves before heading into the long night.

I stand on the flat ledge, and take a deep breath. "Scott!" I yell. Scott is on steep ice, limbs splayed in a six-foot-four yellow X against the wall. He can't turn his head to see us.

"Yeah?" he answers.

"Come back. We should stop here. There is a ledge."

Scott doesn't respond. Mark plants his ice tool in the frozen snowdrift that occupies half of the platform, stands up and draws a big breath. "Scott. Come back. We'll brew here."

Scott climbs back down two body lengths of steep ice and steps onto the downhill edge of the bergschrund. Though he is far away, I see him turn towards us and immediately recognize his aggressive stance.

"God damn you mother-fuckers. God damn you." He pauses for a breath.

Our ascent – done in 60 hours – was the third ascent. The first was done by a three-man team fixing ropes and being supported by another three-man team for the descent. It was completed in 11 days in 1984. The second ascent, and first alpine style ascent, was made a month prior to our climb by Kevin Mahoney and Ben Gilmore in seven days. The ledges chopped by Kevin and Ben were of great advantage to us. MARK TWIGHT

"It's my block. My lead. My decision where we fucking stop and I say we keep going. I said it by climbing past that ledge already. We are moving too well to stop. I follow your decisions when you lead. God damn it."

Mark and I look at one another, stunned. Mark knows Scott far better than I, and to my relief he picks up the discussion with Scott. "Scott. You're right. It is your call. I know it's before the time we'd talked about stopping. But there is this easy ledge here. Seems like we should use it."

Scott lays into another round of curses as he turns in and starts climbing down to us. By the time Scott reaches the ledge, I am finished clearing the new snow off. I carefully empty my pack as Scott clambers down onto the ledge and starts pitching in, scraping the remaining snow away with his spiked boots. Putting together the two stoves, I kneel on my backpack, fill the pots with clean snow, and spark the white gas to life.

After we've all seated ourselves on our packs, Scott breaks the silence. "I'm sorry, guys. I'm sorry. You're right. I was feeling so good. You two fuckers are tough acts to follow, and I've been dragging ass this whole trip. Just when I was feeling strong, feeling good, leading, you rein me in."

Mark and I say nothing, but we both glance at each other, and then look at Scott in acceptance. The stoves let out their guttural, jet-engine growl.

"Tell you what. Tell you what." Scott lifts his arms wide, his face breaking into smile again, reclaiming his charm. "This will forever be known as the incident on the first icefield. Naming it is letting it go, right? But later, when we're in that nursing home someday, we'll tell the story every damn day. Deal?"

"Deal," we say in unison.

∘◇◇◇◇◇◇◇◇◇◇◇◇◇◇◇◇◇◇◇◇◇◇◇◇◇◇∘

Three pitches above the ledge and 15 hours into the route, Mark gets to start his first block of leading. He casts himself up grainy rock and thin smears of ice as the soft rays of evening illuminate the north face of Mount Hunter, siren of the range.

At 1 am we reach another prechopped ledge. It's cold, but I sit and doze a little as Mark runs the stoves to make more water. Scott starts leading at 3:30am — hour 21. It's my block but I was sleeping, so Scott picked up the rack and started. I doze a few more precious minutes as Mark belays.

"I'm glad to have gotten off of that without getting hurt," Scott says as Mark and I reach the hastily chopped stance. The topo shows 100-degree ice above. Ice never gets steeper than vertical, 90 degrees, so we're all interested to see what this pitch is like. In the half-light of 5 am, I know what I have to do: climb well, climb quickly, and not fall.

Taking the ropes from Scott, I climb off of the belay. With each swing I drill

132

the ice tools hard into the cold waxy ice, a body-wide frozen passageway up flawless golden granite. I put in a screw beneath a roof of ice. This must be the 100 degree ice I think. I breathe through pursed lips until I'm in my focused place. As I climb, I do each move before I've thought about it. I forget every move before I've completed it.

I stack my picks side by side in delicate, thin ice. My left foot steps out onto the granite wall, bracing me. Ten feet above my last protection I press my front points into a tiny rock seam and pull around the roof with one arm. Locked off there, my body tense, I pull my right tool from under the roof and replace it high. Weighting this tool, I kick my legs free and pull over the dangling tentacles of the roof.

On the next pitch I lead until a dead-end – a steep flat wall – rears above. The ice has petered out. I belay Scott and Mark to my stance. They offer the gear quietly and I rerack it quickly.

"You're on belay Steve," Scott says before I have time to look up from organizing the ice screws and nuts and pitons. I climb up 10 feet, place a good stopper in a crack, and lower 15 feet down to my left to gain a ramp. The topo shows this to be ice, but the ice is gone now. The protection is very sparse and the exposure – 1,000 feet of overhanging rock below– is absolute. I belay again, and when Mark arrives before Scott, he takes over belaying Scott. I pull off my gloves and breathe on my numb fingers. Vaguely I register the sunrise on Mount Hunter. Wordlessly Mark takes what gear he has and puts it on my harness.

The next pitch starts with steep climbing right above the belay; I know it will be the final piece of this crux section. With butterflies in my stomach, I reach up, twist my picks into a crack, and swing my right heel up high and out to the side. Needing the sensitivity of bare skin, I pull off my gloves with my teeth and stab them into my jacket for safekeeping. I get myself up onto a one-inch edge. My fingers are completely numb. I press them against the hot flesh of my neck to bring back sensation. I place a cam in the rock, replace my gloves, and resume climbing.

The next 100 feet pass in a trance. The moves get harder and harder, the protection gets sparser and sparser, and I hardly notice. My feet stand confidently on ripples in the granite's grainy surface. My tools bite assuredly into the back of a closed-off crack. And then, suddenly and unexpectedly, both feet cut loose, loading my tools. I gasp and pull myself back on. Carefully, I climb the final 25 feet to the top.

Belaying on an easy snow slope, I slump my shaking body against the anchor. My mind is wrecked from stress. The topo promises that the hardest pitches are behind us. This snow ramp should take us to an icefield, which skirts almost the entire last rock band to the right. Then two moderate mixed pitches to 17,000 feet. From there it's all hiking to the summit. Steep, exposed, dangerous hiking, but certainly not 5.9 climbing with numb hands, cramponed boots, and no gear.

No more of that. I think. Now I can coast. Mark will still be strong, and I can draft for a while now.

It's hour 33. Morning comes and as Mark leads off, fog rolls over us. "Is the high-pressure over?" I wonder. The clouds spit a little snow. I hang against the one ice screw belay as Scott feeds out the rope.

I hear a hollow *klunk* sound and I glance up. I had placed both my axes in the ice off to the side of our belay. One of them has half fallen and is lying on its side, stuck in the new snow. It seems fine, and I'm too tired to stand up and clip it in. I lay my helmeted temple against the ice, close my eyes and the world fades away. Then a *swoosh*, and I listen to the receding clatter of my ice tool falling 5,000 feet to the glacier below us.

I lift my head and reach for the other axe, knowing that to lose that might be fatal. We carry no spares.

"I used that hammer on every route I've done since '96," I say to nobody, feeling a tinge of remorse. I can't tell if Scott is listening. "At least it was KIA. I won't have to retire it when I don't trust it anymore. It never let me down. Hopefully it won't matter. And you guys are leading the rest of this route. I did my part."

Several pitches later we are lost in a frozen sea. The fog has thickened and laps at the broken rocks and ice. I can see less than a rope length. Mark down climbs towards to us. "Dead end," he confirms.

"Let's rap down a few pitches, we have to go farther right," someone says. The aural hallucinations buzz and rise in pitch, then disappear, blending gently with the conversation.

"Big Bertha's over there," I say, knowing that I don't want to get underneath any serac bands.

Scott drills a V-thread, two intersecting ice-screw holes through which we thread our ropes. Three rappels later Scott takes over and leads up to the right. He places four pieces of gear in an extremely easy 30-degree ice pitch and takes 20 minutes to build an anchor. I've never seen anyone so wasted.

We both dread leading ourselves, so stupidly we allow Scott to start another pitch before I say to Mark, "He's too fried to keep leading."

Mark checks his watch. "He's been on this pitch for almost half an hour." He says, "Scott could solo this in five minutes if he was fresh. We all could." When I get to the belay, I take one of Scott's tools and ask him for the lead ends of the ropes.

"What?" Scott asks.

Again Mark absorbs Scott's indignation. "You were 40 minutes on that pitch. You could solo it in nothing flat if you were fresh. Steve is taking over. We should let the fastest guy lead."

For a time we'd eloped, the three of us, into a bubble of bonded perfection. All that is dissolving in the ammonia and lactate poisoning our muscles and the

Starting into the last hard pitch on the Slovak Direct route. At this point we have been climbing for 30 hours, with two breaks but no sleep except when we inadvertently dozed off at a belay. MARK TWIGHT

thickening of our blood. Mark's right. It's time to be smart, not proud. A nasty gale whips off Big Bertha, striping snow into my face as I start to climb.

The Alaskan night is too frigid to stop now, but we're too far gone not to. I set up a belay beneath an overhanging boulder and bring Scott and Mark up.

"We should break here. Wait for the sun," I suggest.

For an hour Mark and I chop hard at the ice. My arms have never known an hour of chopping on top of 40-odd hours of climbing. Somehow they still swing the tool, sending a few cubes down the face. Scott watches, eyes glazed, occasionally tossing a glancing blow at the turquoise ice. We sit with our backs to the rock. After 10 minutes the first of the stoves hisses away the last of its fuel. It's hour 48.

Mark reaches over and turns the other one off. "I can't listen to that again."

I twist left to regard him and see that we have reverted into separate entities now. We are turtles in our separate shells. I am reminded of Greg Childs' comment about climbing K2: "Up here, where we need each other most, it is every man for himself."

On the other side of the ledge, Scott sits straight-legged, head bowed, hands tucked between his thighs holding his bottle of energy drink: a warm, chocolaty, 500-calorie quart.

"Mark, you want that?" I point at Scott's bottle. Like shipwreck survivors, we divvy up the dying man's ration. Scott may be freezing to death, and he's too wasted to eat and drink – the one thing that might bring him back.

"No." He reaches over, takes Scott's bottle and hands it to me.

I look at my watch, 6 am. The sun will start to warm us soon, but the cold, for now, penetrates deeply. I should drink it all now, while the liquid is still warm. In 20 minutes it will be frozen. I feel good and I'll need it, I rationalize to myself, because I'm going to get us off this thing alive.

I down the first half of the bottle easily. Stretched by my own ration that I already drank, my stomach bloats to accommodate my greedy feeding. I force the last of it down. Immediately, the pressure in my gut starts to feel worse. With a familiar hiccup, and a deep heave, I vomit up the precious calories.

"Are you okay?" Mark's voice is feeble.

Without turning toward him, I wipe my chin with my mittened hand and reply, "Yeah, I'm just defining my consciousness. It's just like Mishima said. Painful."

I return to my quiet place, where the thoughts drain away. Twisting, I look at Mark's azure eyes, open wide, his face hollow. I turn back, knowing that Mark's thoughts have gone down a dark, dark hole. Scott, on the far end of our small ledge, seems to be sleeping, hibernating, checked out. I hope he can find the strength to continue.

I tuck my chin into my chest and start to drift into comfortable blackness. Cold penetrates from my feet and into my legs. I am freezing to death and I don't care. I'm counting on the sun to resurrect me. I need to sleep for just a moment. Just one moment.

The sun touches me. As I wait to get warm, I turn to look at Mark. He is half in sun, half in shade. Scott is still shrouded, his eyes open but unseeing, his face desiccated and dark. Are we all too far gone? I wonder.

Scott suddenly leans forward and starts to tighten the laces on his boots. Mark stands up behind me.

"Time to go, then," I say to myself as I turn to pack the one stove that still contains fuel. I stand stiffly. Mark is focused now, determinedly tying into the ends of both ropes to lead. Like a boxer standing at the eight count Scott turns, pushes himself up with his arms, and sways slightly as he stands erect. I put Mark on belay. Wordlessly, he climbs off.

"This is it," Scott says, with a slight waver to his usually forceful voice. "Put up, shut up, and maybe die trying." He laughs. Scott is back, or as back as he can be. The sunrise, though surely beautiful, inspires no poetics, just thoughts of survival.

Following the sixtieth odd pitch of the route, I am able to marvel at how good the climbing still is: cleanly fractured granite, firm ice. We reach Mark quickly, where he belays us from four tied-off pitons. At the end of the next pitch he keeps tugging on the rope.

"What about the anchor?" I yell.

"Leave it. We're done." He shouts back.

We move, still roped together, up the sun lit slope, blunt front points hacking loudly. My light clothing finally feels warm enough. After several hundred feet, Mark stops at a rock outcropping and pulls the ropes up. Unceremoniously we leave everything we will no longer need at 17,200 feet: our rack of pitons, ice screws, rock gear and carabiners, one rope, all three helmets. With a moment's hesitation, I leave my wind shell, desperate to lose the eight ounces, gambling that I won't need it on the descent. As much as I hate to leave this trash, it is the price of survival.

Traversing left into the Cassin Ridge route at 17,400 feet, we find nice tracks. Two climbers shout to us from several hundred feet above. We stop to revel in the relatively flat, safe ground. Its hour 56 and mentally we can relax a little. I kneel in the snow and down an energy gel and a couple mouthfuls of cold water. Scott musters enough energy to snap a picture.

"It's my block to the top," Mark says and he takes the first step.

I follow Mark as he follows the tracks. I stay close at first, but then drop back slightly to pace Scott. We have an 11,000-foot descent to our skis and then another 11 miles to our stoves, food, tents and sleeping bags and maybe 14 hours to get there before the killing cold comes again. I don't know if Scott can survive another unprotected night; fatigue claims him, step-by-step, bit-by-bit. I will survive and Mark still looks strong

We are so far past the duration of effort that any of us has previously known; the amount of work to keep climbing blind-sides me. To stop is to fall asleep. To fall asleep now could be fatal.

Flowers sprout from behind rocks. I hear someone nearby stop and sing me a song. They're out of key. I pause, raise a hand, and push them out of the way, not bothering to watch their 8,000-foot fall. I look up and see that Mark is farther ahead.

My concentration comes back to the step in front of me. Scott paces me now, though I'm in front.

"I will live. I will bring Scott back alive." I adopt this as my mantra. Drilling each syllable with a cramponed step. I know this mountain the best of all of us. I try to focus through my hazy consciousness. As I take each step I look to my left and right and check my altimeter. I figure that I know exactly where we are.

I pick up the pace slightly, and where Mark pauses, I pass him. At almost 20,000 feet, the ridge doglegs right. From here I set off to the west. Setting a course that will take us most directly to Pig Hill, the final hill on the normal route, 300 feet below the summit. This is the most direct way down, to life, to survival.

"I will live. I will bring Scott back alive."

Mark stops. "What are you doing?"

"Getting us back. This will take us to the West Buttress, to the base of Pig Hill. This is the fastest way down."

"No, we should stay in the tracks," Mark says. Scott agrees. I relent to their opinion, but as I plod ahead, my thoughts return to what is most paramount: survival. "I will live. I will bring Scott back alive."

I think of the many, many miles still to go. I imagine how we will pass through the camps of many climbers. How we must not accept their aid. We must continue to base camp, to our own food, stove fuel, sleeping bags, and tents.

"I'm going across, whether you come with me or not," I proclaim.

Mark and Scott relent, just as I'd hoped. Mark takes over and breaks trail for a bit. Fresh snow over rock makes the going difficult, and the 8,000-foot drop of the southwest face yawns to our left. I stop to watch Mark and Scott struggle. One of my small gifts is that I'm fast and secure on this kind of terrain. They stumble frighteningly. I've made a mistake.

"I'm sorry, staying in the tracks would have been easier," I say to Mark.

Scott catches up. "What the fuck are we doing over here?"

"I thought it would be a faster way to the normal route, the easy descent." I turn back around, leading them forward. I stomp out the best tracks I can.

As the sixtieth hour dissolves we pull over a small cornice and onto Pig Hill. The summit is a mere hundred yards away. I feel responsible to make sure no one goes there. We have to get down. All the way. No time for summit niceties.

The crux pitch of The Gift (That Keeps On Giving) on Mount Bradley. Mark Twight started up this pitch and decided it was too dangerous. I led through, taking a leader fall in the process. The experience initiated a close partnership and friendship that lasts to this day. MARK TWIGHT

"Alive," I think as I look back to make sure that Mark and Scott both clear the cornice and come onto the easy slope. It is now impossible for us to fall.

◇◇◇◇◇◇◇◇◇◇◇◇◇◇◇◇◇◇◇◇◇◇◇◇◇◇◇◇

I have to get on a shuttle bus a few hours after we land in Talkeetna. Scott falls asleep on a picnic table while I stuff still-wet gear into duffels. The shuttle comes and I hug each of them in turn, unsure of what to say.

We had come down off the Slovak Direct faster than we had come off the summit three weeks ago. Two hours, 40 minutes from where we turned that cornice on Pig Hill to the 14,200-foot camp. Word of our climb arrived in camp before we did, thanks to the climbers we had seen ahead of us on the upper Cassin.

The climbing ranger on duty, Meg Perdue, and her volunteer patrol of women mountaineers and rescuers invited us in. We are men, and we were weak. So we accepted. Stupidly, I drooled on my jacket while watching one of the women make a grilled cheese sandwich. They filled our water bottles with hot cocoa. They listened patiently as we tried to explain what we had just lived through. We limited our descriptions to facts because we didn't yet fully comprehend the human side of what we had experienced.

With the bus waiting, I turn silently and step on board. That night a red-eye flight takes me to Seattle and Anne is at the airport to meet me.

"How was your trip?" She asks cheerfully. I hug her. She always looked good in cutoff jeans.

"It was great," I enthuse. I want to tell her what I had felt up there. How the three of us had worked together, experiencing Mishima's proof – not just of our own consciousness, but of each others'. How we went even one step further. How at moments our individual egos dissolved to where we climbed as if we were one six-eyed, six-armed, three-brained organism. I was beginning to understand what had happened.

I want to tell her about our mistakes. I felt bitter about not staying in the track; I wish we had gone to the actual summit. I thought I might be able to laugh about "The Incident on the First Icefield." I thought I could describe the look in Mark's eyes when the stove sputtered and died. Instead I give her a thumbnail sketch: holding close to the safety of physical facts. Times taken for each block, number of GU packets consumed, the grades of the pitches we climbed.

"I got As in all my classes last quarter," she says.

"Great."

"And I paid this month's rent. But you need to get some deposits from your summer clients, because we don't have enough to cover July right now and it's due next week."

"Okay. I don't think that will be a problem. I leave for Chamonix the day after tomorrow, right?"

I spend the next 10 weeks guiding nearly every day. Teaching self-arrest skills to honeymooners, introducing never-evers to the wonders of ice climbing, leading rope teams to a few of the grand summits of the Alps. Scott called Mark on the phone a week after they returned home. They laughed and told stories. Mark published one of his typically caustic articles in *Climbing Magazine*. He burned a music CD, printed extensive liner notes for it, and titled it, "Justification for an Elitist Attitude." He sent it out to all our friends.

Anne read Mark's article and was furious when he wrote, "...I'm an elitist prick and I think posers have polluted mountaineering...They make the summit, not the style, the yardstick of success." I agreed, but Anne had been to climb Denali as an apprentice guide and found that the cold air left her coughing. The heavy loads required by the prescribed style crushed her small frame. She identified with those same climbers Mark derided. When she came to Chamonix at the end of the season, I was unprepared for her wrath.

"You think you, Mark and Scott are the only ones worthy of being climbers? Just 'cause you're good enough to do that stupid, dangerous route?"

"Well..." I stutter impotently.

"You're all a bunch of narcissistic assholes."

"Come on," I protest, grabbing the article and skimming a few lines. "Mark is playing these verbs to his advantage." I read, "...there's no climbing on the West Buttress (route on Denali). Folks call it what their egos need to hear."

"You see," I say, "he's working it, working you, for an effect. Look, if you don't climb Denali, what do you do? Mountaineer Denali? Hike Denali? Traveling on a glacier, walking across ridges wearing crampons where a trip, if you were unroped, could send you to your death. That is not the domain of hiking."

"What do you think, then?" she asks.

"I think we did a great climb. I think we did something that has never been done before. I think that what I experienced up there, with Mark and Scott, has changed me forever. And for the better." I pause, and almost as an afterthought I add, "I didn't know that kind of connection was possible with another human being."

After a moment Anne gets up slowly, takes her coat, and leaves the room.

Rolando Garibotti 12 hours into our 25-hour ascent of the Infinite Spur. The fastest time before our ascent was seven days. This accomplishment stirred more admiration and comment than the considerably more difficult ascent of the Slovak Direct route the year before. STEVE HOUSE

CHAPTER THIRTEEN

Evolution: Beyond the Americas

14,000 Feet on the Infinite Spur, Mount Forakar, Alaska: June 9, 2001

I CRANK IN ANOTHER ICE SCREW, clip in the rope, and continue across the calf-pumping slope. The front points of my crampons bounce against the polished ice. I kick three, four times. The points finally stick and I step up with burning muscles.

Angling upward, I crest a ridge littered with many little summits. I scramble happily to the far side where it's sunny and less steep. The pump begins to empty from my legs as I fervently kick steps up and across the snow. The inspiration for George Lowe and Michael Kennedy naming this route the Infinite Spur after its first ascent in 1977 is quite obvious. They belayed 90 pitches over 11 days, and averaged 14 hours of climbing a day. I shiver at the thought of climbing with a fully-loaded pack.

My pack started out weighing 12 pounds. Between Rolo and I, we're carrying a stove, a quart of fuel, a small titanium pot, 40 GU energy gels each, eight packages of instant soup, some halvah, a map, compass, altimeter, GPS, radio, one 8.8 mm rope, some ice screws and rock gear, my emergency tarp, and our Polarguard parkas.

We've been climbing 12 hours. We're past the technical crux, but that is little consolation at the moment because I can't find any protection. Resigned, I climb a 150 feet to where I can flip the rope around a cornice. Now if one of us falls the rope may catch on the cornice between us and keep us from falling to the glacier 5,000 feet below. It's not a guarantee, but it's better than nothing.

My watch ticks off our thirteenth hour of climbing when I stumble upon a small flat spot chopped into the crest of the ridge. A pair of Canadians who climbed the route a month earlier must have made this platform for their tent. Grateful for the rest I sit down and belay Rolo.

I greet him as he steps onto the ledge. "I think we should brew and rest here for a bit. Take advantage of this spot."

Rolo coils up the rope, lapping the rope over his head so fast that it's a blur. This is Rolo in a snapshot: of Argentine parents, born in Italy, and married to an American. Part international man of mystery and part roadrunner. Ladies swoon in his presence. Before that, I didn't know what a swoon was. In 20 seconds he has the 200-foot rope coiled and places it on the snow as insulation for his oft-coveted derrière and sits down. I kneel and pull out the stove as Rolo farms some clean-looking snow to melt into water.

Three hours later the cold in my arms wakes me. I open my eyes and see Rolo turn, searching for a more comfortable position. He's awake, so I sit up and light the stove for a hot pot of soup before we push on toward the summit.

We've spent almost four hours at Rob and Eamonn's ledge when Rolo starts leading the final pitches. The ice is less steep than we climbed earlier, but we are tired – the effect of pushing hard lower on the route. Rolo continues to lead. Four pitches stretch to six. We are near the snowy ridge when I take the lead. Within 100 feet I'm kicking steps up the soft snow of the easy crest.

Thirty minutes later Rolo's self-proclaimed allergy to snow climbing starts to show itself. We have different paces: mine like the tortoise, slow and methodical. His more like the hare.

Frustrated by these differences, I shout down the ridge, "Let's unrope. Okay?"

From a 150 feet away he answers with a faint, "What?"

"Un! Rope!"

I finish coiling the rope as Rolo catches me and pauses. I go ahead, punching steps towards the top.

Gaining altitude, my pace slows. Fifteen thousand, and then 16,000 feet pass. I count steps to push back against the boredom. I count to 200 before taking a 30-second break. The snow has the look of a white tortoise shell: bumpy and polished smooth. These conditions often cover crevasses with thin bridges of wind-packed snow. I walk on, looking for shelter from the cold northerly that's started blowing. I find a scoop that breaks the wind and sit on my pack to wait for Rolo.

When Rolo arrives we walk together. We roll across the east summit onto a bright moonscape. We can't tell which hump is the true summit, so we keep trudging uphill.

The light plays among the many hillocks and false summits. I reach the last bump and turn and watch my partner work his way through the landscape of light. The only colors are white and blue. The isolation here is complete; years could pass without anyone standing here. I throw my rucksack on the summit.

I would have never attempted to lead this route, Barely Legal, had it not been for the support and enthusiasm of Alex Lowe. This was the route's second ascent. Shoeshone River, Wyoming. BRAD JOHNSON/PEAKS AND PLACES PHOTOGRAPHY

Myself, Barry Blanchard and Joe Josephson drying out after an attempt on the Emperor Face. Barry and Jojo are two of the most influential climbers to ever swing ice tools in Canada. Barry opened numerous hard alpine routes and waterfall pitches throughout the world in the '80s and '90s. Jojo, a U.S. citizen living in Canada at the time, brought an intense and obsessive energy to climbing steep, sustained pitches of ever-thinner waterfall ice which ultimately ushered in the era of climbing steep, bare rock with ice tools and crampons – now commonly known as mixed climbing. Mount Robson, British Columbia. STEVE HOUSE COLLECTION

Joe Josephson and I following a pitch Barry dubbed "the traverse of the stubbies" in reference to the short ice screws needed to protect it. This was the first difficult pitch of our ill-fated second attempt on Mount Robson's Emperor Face. British Columbia. BARRY BLANCHARD

A view of the east face of Howse Peak the day Scott Backes, Barry Blanchard, and I climbed the route, which we named M-16. In 2002 Will Gadd, Scott Semple, and Kevin Mahoney climbed a route in the same vicinity continuing to the summit. They named their route Howse of Cards, a veiled parry to our choice of route name which Barry exploited by writing, "M-16 – twice as hard as M-8." The original, and true, meaning of M-16 we kept to ourselves. Howse Peak, Alberta. BARRY BLANCHARD

Scott Backes leading below the section that became known as "The Pitch," which goes from the top of the wide ice flow above Scott, traverses right, under the snow mushrooms, and then climbs straight up gray, partially visible ice into the steep black rock below the horizon line. Howse Peak, Alberta. STEVE HOUSE

Scott Backes and I approach the east face of Howse Peak. Our intended line is the dramatic waterfall right of center. The large waterfall to the left was unclimbed at this time, but was ascended by two strong young Canadians while we were engaged on M-16. Alberta. BARRY BLANCHARD

I lead though the crux of the first of three consecutive difficult pitches on the Slovak Direct route. The topo showed this section as having "100-degree" ice, which we were interested to see. We had been awake for 25 hours and climbing most of that time. Denali, Alaska. MARK TWIGHT

Denali from just below the summit of Mount Foraker. Visible, from left to right, are the Father and Sons Wall, the Washburn Wall, the West Buttress, the West Rib route, the Slovak Direct route, and Mascioli's Pillar. I have climbed each of these routes at least once between 1993 and 2000. Alaska. STEVE HOUSE

Marko Prezelj and I bivied at 20,000 feet on the British-Sherpa route on Nuptse. In the morning we ascended to 22,000 feet in stormy conditions and then decided to return to base camp. In the race to descend before night fell, Marko captured this stunning image of Ama Dablam. Himalaya, Nepal. MARKO PREZELJ

I took this self-portrait on the summit of Cho Oyu, the world's sixth highest mountain, on September 27, 2001. I climbed from base camp to summit to base camp in 27 hours, breaking trail in boot-top to knee-deep snow for the last 3,000 feet. Mount Everest, Lhotse, and Nuptse are visible behind me. Himalaya, border of Nepal and China. STEVE HOUSE

The seldom-climbed, 25,660-foot Masherbrum viewed from the north. A joint Pakistani-American expedition completed its first ascent and put Willi Unsoeld and George Bell on the summit. The route ascended the heavily glaciated, and now extremely hazardous, south face in 1960. Karakoram, Pakistan. MARKO PREZELJ

Hajji Ghulam Rasool: guide, cook, and friend. We were traveling towards the glaciated, 18,000-foot Gondogoro Pass from our base camp north of Masherbrum. It was snowing and would be dark before we found that night's campsite. Still, Rasool was smiling and laughing. Karakoram, Pakistan. MARKO PREZELJ

Marko Prezelj following the first difficult pitch on North Twin. This was an exceptionally high-quality pitch of climbing on perfect rock and set the tone for what was to come. Alberta. STEVE HOUSE

The pitch above the crux section of the Lowe-Jones route goes up a perfect limestone crack to the roof above me. I climbed out to the left towards the horizontal snow mushroom. The quality of the climbing on this difficult route was truly superb. North Twin, Alberta. MARKO PREZELJ

The last hard pitch before the "three-butt-cheek bivy." With all my weight on my front points and my pelvis braced against the rock, I'm trying to set my pick into a thin seam. North Twin, Alberta. MARKO PREZELJ

The fourth day of our North Twin epic was tough. Marko had to lead everything because I had lost one boot shell. We had no water since the night before, and the weather was deteriorating. You can see the snow blowing down the rock as the climbing remained difficult to the very end. Alberta. STEVE HOUSE

Marko leads the last section up to where we exited to a long 50-degree ice slope. We climbed that slope in another 13 pitches to attain the bivy below the summit cornice. North Twin, Alberta. STEVE HOUSE

With only one boot shell, I follow one of the many pitches of moderate ice to the summit. If I had had my boot we could have climbed these 13 rope lengths in a few hours. Instead it took us most of the day. North Twin, Alberta. MARKO PREZELJ

K7 with its summit shrouded from view. The difficult climbing near the summit consisted of climbing through the steep sunlit rocks just below the summit cloud. The pinnacle to the left was appropriately nicknamed the "Mo-fo" by Conrad Anker and remains unclimbed as of 2009. Karakoram, Pakistan. MARKO PREZELJ

Looking down the crux pitch of K7 during my successful ascent. I have aid climbed the thin cracks below me to get to this point, where a short section of ice climbing leads to a rightwards traverse. The rope is feeding out of my small pack sitting on a snow ledge below me. Karakoram, Pakistan. STEVE HOUSE

As the sun casts a pink light across the Rupal Face on September 2, 2005, Vince Anderson speeds across a dangerous gully. You can see where the previous days' avalanches have stripped off the snow behind him revealing gray ice. Nanga Parbat, Pakistan. STEVE HOUSE

Vince Anderson leading enjoyable mixed climbing at 18,000 feet just before noon on the second day. At this point we've gained over 6,000 feet since we left base camp and we have almost 8,000 feet remaining to reach the summit. On most big-wall climbs we would be at the top after that much vertical gain, or at the bottom with that much to go. In our case on the Rupal Face we are just approaching the middle. Nanga Parbat, Pakistan. STEVE HOUSE

Though incredibly exposed, we were very lucky to find a place we could set up the tent and sleep flat. We slept in our harnesses and clipped into the rope, along with the tent and everything in it. Nanga Parbat, Pakistan. STEVE HOUSE

The Rupal Face rises 15,000 feet above base camp in Latoba Meadows and 13,500 feet above the bergschrund at the base of the wall. It is the world's ninth highest mountain at 26,660 feet and is the western most 8,000-meter peak. Nanga Parbat, Pakistan. STEVE HOUSE

Kneeling on it to keep the wind from stealing it away, I can see no human sign anywhere. The nondescript dome of compact snow offers a 360-degree view of the Alaska Range. This is the fifth highest point in North America and the second highest point in the United States.

Across from us is Mount Hunter, the Alaska Range's third highest peak. When you land at the glacier airstrip, Hunter dominates the view. From this perspective it looks small; its 10-mile breadth far more impressive than it's one-mile vertical rise. Beyond Hunter, dozens of peaks scatter in the near distance. I've either climbed or tried to climb every one of them: Mount Huntington, Peak 11,300, Mount Dickey, Mount Barille, Mount Dan Beard, the Moose's Tooth, the Eye Tooth, Broken Tooth, mounts Wake, Bradley, and Johnston.

Reigning over everything is Denali. The name means "the Great One." And great she is. My eye is drawn to the improbably big and steep south face that Mark, Scott and I climbed last year. The Slovak Direct soars up the biggest, hardest wall on the mountain, going straight to the highest point on the continent. That's proud, I think. I stand up and Rolo backs down a few steps to snap a summit photo. I forget to smile.

Base Camp, Southeast Fork of the Kahiltna Glacier, Alaska: June 11, 2001

The rattling, tent-shaking roar fights its way through my dreamless sleep. Each ferocious beat knocks me further and further from sleep. Every time the visceral thump starts to fade I swim back down, back into slumber. A few blissful moments pass and I'm shaken awake again.

Looking at the inside of my tent with slitted eyes, I feel the oppressive heat of mid-day. The noise has faded, but then it starts to grow in strength and power, until it vibrates right over the tent.

The Infinite Spur comes back to me in bright flashes of memory: Front points dulled by the blanched granite of the lower route. Spinning in ice screws at warp speed while my calf muscles burned. My heart racing as I stretch the rope between Rolo and me. A stiff wind sending us scurrying across Mount Foraker's 17,400-foot summit just after dawn. Being confronted by Denali's south face from the summit. The burning quadriceps muscles as we descended the long Sultana Ridge. Looking across infinite green expanses of Alaskan tundra jeweled with a million glittering lakes. The south face of Denali, so big and so sheer, dominating everything. The Slovak Direct Route eclipsing every other route I've done.

I unzip the arc of the tent door as the noise recedes, this time toward Mount Hunter. A heavy blanket of cloud hangs bright white a few hundred feet above the glacier. A large black National Guard Pave Hawk helicopter banks at the upper reaches of the cirque and lumbers down the valley towards base camp. A dozen walls, built of sawn blocks of snow to protect the tents from base camp's frequent winds, sag like melted cheese. I turn as a cloud of steam comes out of the tarp Rolo pitched as our cooking space. His sleeping bag dries on the roof of his tent.

I reach for a water bottle and sit back down on my own sleeping bag. The down bag releases a breath of stale air from weeks of sleeping in the same clothes. Draining the bottle, I feel hungry and wonder what Rolo is cooking.

"Pizza ready?" I ask, stepping into the tent.

Rolo turns from the stove and smiles. "Gosh. No, pizza is sold out. Today's special is ramen noodles."

"That was yesterday's special."

"Yes. And tomorrow's I think." Rolo laughs, handing me a bowl. The soup is hot and tastes good.

"We done good, eh?" I say. I've been trying to teach him some western colloquialisms.

"Done good?" He asks. I nod.

"Yes. But I found the route, how do you say, banal?" he struggles with the wording.

"Too easy. I know. I thought there would be more hard climbing. It certainly must be hard with a big pack."

"Yes. I can't imagine. It would be so difficult!" Rolo agrees and I slurp down the hot noodles.

"That was something else," I continue. "The view from the summit. I mean the south face of Denali really stands out." Rotor wash shakes the cooking tarp as the helicopter circles again, and I reach for the center pole to keep it from blowing down.

"Yes. I'd say you guys did the plum line there, no? I mean really. That is the best line I saw, no?"

"I thought the Infinite would be as good," I say, blowing cool air across my food. "The line is as good. It's almost as much vertical relief, but the climbing certainly wasn't as hard."

"Do you think I'm a bad man to say I'm disappointed?" Rolo asks.

I laugh at his honesty. "No. No. I don't. But some people probably will. Will you think I'm a bad man to say I think we've climbed out the Alaska Range?"

"Yes! There are many routes, no?"

"But not so big and beautiful and difficult as the Slovak," I conclude.

"Yes, but the smaller mountains contain much beauty, no?"

"That's true, but I think we should try that route on the south face of Nuptse in the Himalaya. That looks good. Just as good as the Slovak."

"I would like that," Rolo replies.

I pause on the summit of Mount Foraker. Though Foraker is the fifth highest summit in North America and the second highest mountain in the U.S., it goes years between ascents. Behind me, the massive south face of Denali catches the first of the day's light. ROLANDO GARIBOTTI

The phone rings as I finish clearing the dinner dishes. "Hello?"

"Farmboy!" followed by laughter.

"Mr. Backes. How are you?" I drop into the armchair next to the crackling wood stove, relaxing in preparation for a conversation with Scott. Conversations with him are almost always intense.

"Good. It's winter in Minnesota. There's ice in the quarries. I went out with Dahlberg last weekend. But I called to hear about Cho Oyu."

I tell him about climbing from base camp to the summit in one day, and meeting a Norwegian climber near the top. He was using supplemental oxygen and moving fast, and then periodically dropping to the snow to rest. As I approached he would jump up and sprint ahead 50 or 60 feet, then flop down again like a dead fish. He raced me to the summit and then insisted on me taking 30 or 40 pictures of him with the flags of all his various sponsors. Scott laughs at the story.

"Hey, nice cover shot!" The new *Climbing Magazine* has just come out. A profile of me is the feature article, and I'm on the cover, climbing a vertical icicle, sticking my tongue out to catch a tiny snow avalanche.

"Yeah. That's a little weird."

"I thought they did a good job though. And what do you expect? You can't do all these routes, change the rules of alpine climbing, and go unnoticed."

"No, it's good. The deal with Patagonia has really solidified, and what I make from working with them on product development should pay for one expedition a year. It's not like I can quit guiding or anything, but it sure is nice to have an additional line of cash flow."

"Well, I'm sure you will figure it out. I wanted to tell you, nice job on the Infinite. Twenty-five hours! You guys were hauling ass."

"Yeah, that's weird. Everyone is blown away by that, but to both Rolo and me the route was such a disappointment. It was too easy, Scott. I expected, and hoped, to have another Slovak Direct experience. But it wasn't the same."

"Funny you should say that because that's what I want to talk to you about." Scott's tone deepens. "Steve, here's the deal. I know it was a year and a half ago, but what happened up there, on the Slovak, that was magical. You know that right? That synergy was unlike anything any of us experienced before and I want to apologize for that."

"Apologize?" I'm confused.

"I'm sorry. But I'm not sorry, too. See, it took Mark and I ten years of climbing together and living through a lot with each other. And not just in climbing, but in our lives. I was forty-two on that route. Mark was thirty-eight. And we had been building toward that place for a long time. Because of who you are and what you have been through you could mesh with it and contribute to the strength of the whole. I'm sorry because you were what, twenty-nine?"

"Yeah, twenty-nine."

"I love Rolo. He's the prototype, the man. He can rock climb better than any of us. But we both know what happened; you were two separate egos on that route. And it sounds like that route was too easy for you. The stress level wasn't high enough to require you to come together in that synergistic way. But that's almost beside the point because the fact is that you guys did the route in twenty-five hours, taking six days off the fastest time. People are going to understand that, probably more than they understood the Slovak in sixty hours."

"Come on Scott. There are maybe fifty people who understand what we're doing."

"Fifty?" Scott laughs. "That many, huh? I think a dozen. In the whole world, maybe two dozen because you never know about the fuckin' Euros."

"I don't care about that, you know me."

"I do know you and I've seen you in action and that's why I wanted to warn you," Scott says.

"Warn me about what?"

"That the Slovak won't happen again any time soon. That's what I am sorry about, that you were exposed to it – to what partnership can be – so young. And now Mark and I are both done climbing. You have to find a new partner, or partners. You have to be very open; keep a beginner's mind. You'll know them when they come. And Barry is done too, or is he going to Nuptse now?"

"He's going. We're going with that Slovenian guy, Marko Prezelj and Stephen Koch. Rolo and I met them both in Alaska. They seemed nice. Marko's hilarious, and so experienced. I don't know about Stephen. He's nice, or maybe he's just polite. I can't tell yet. I really don't know him."

"Stephen's okay. I like Stephen. You guys will be fine. Maybe you and Barry can find your zone up there on Nuptse."

"I hope so." I hang up a few minutes later and stare into the fire with the phone in my lap. Rolo has decided not to go to Nuptse. Barry's coming, and his wife Catherine too, but since breaking his leg on M-16, Barry seems less keen. He already has made an off-hand comment about "heading into the fray one last time."

Bivouac at 23,000 Feet, on a New Route on the South Face of Nuptse, Nepal: May 18, 2002

I climb the last few steps to the cracked granite slab that Marko has just crossed. Barry and Stephen follow 10 minutes behind me. As I start across I hear Marko kick a boot into the ice repeatedly to make a step for himself.

"*Čakaj, čakaj!*" Wait, wait! he yells. I pause and look up. He takes out a

173

Barry Blanchard soloing moderate technical ground during an acclimatization foray on the south face of Nuptse. The stunning west face of Makalu rises behind. MARKO PREZELJ

small video camera and makes some adjustments. "Okay." I look back at my feet, place my crampon points in the horizontal fracture in the white granite and start across.

On the other side I climb past Marko to the crest of the ridge, stop and turn to wait for him. We've been pacing each other all morning, interrupted only by occasional stops for him to shoot video and photos of me clearing an ice bulge, or the sun blasting over a nearby peak, radiating across the dark blue sky.

Barry nears the rock traverse and plants one tool firmly in the ice. Turning his left foot sideways he uses the side points of his crampons to chew out a platform wide enough to stand on with one foot. Marko stands and makes an adjustment to the camera.

Barry clears his throat and considers the rock traverse. "Could use a rope here," he says.

"No. It is good on the crack. Step on the crack," instructs Marko as he kneels to the viewfinder. "Okay. Go."

Barry doesn't move and I sense that this might take awhile. I turn to the ridge and start climbing in search of a bivouac where we can spend the night and gain some valuable acclimatization. I churn upward, gaining height. The first opportunity to climb during an expedition is always cathartic. Where the angle of the ridge slackens the snow deepens. I wish Marko was here to share in the trail-breaking.

After an hour of climbing, the ridge abuts a steep ice tower and I need a rope, and a partner, to continue. I sit on my pack and take out a chapatti I dressed with peanut butter earlier this morning. I am washing down my lunch when I hear Marko approaching. From the sounds of it he has been climbing at top speed to catch up, and as he crests the slope he stops a dozen feet below me.

Pausing for a couple breaths he shouts, "You should wait for me!" I look at him for a moment. I understand something about his language and culture. His direct, commanding way of speaking doesn't offend me.

"It is good for camera on this ridge," he starts again. This time I interrupt him.

"Marko, I came to climb."

Marko looks at me for a moment and takes the last steps to my stance. He removes his pack and sets it in the snow. He takes out a camera case, removes the video camera from around his neck where it has hung all morning and puts it away. I stand and take out our climbing rope and put away my thermos.

"Good," says Marko, stepping into his harness. "Now we climb."

Bivouac at 23,000 Feet, on a New Route on the South Face of Nuptse, Nepal: May 18, 2002

"Steve, you okay? You look a little green," Barry says.

The three of us are squeezed into a tiny two-person bivouac tent. Barry lies half outside the door we have enlarged with a vestibule. Marko is wedged on one side of Barry's legs. I'm on the other. I have just emptied a pot of soup and handed it to Barry. The driving pellets of snow on the tent sound like rice slowly being dumped on a linoleum floor.

"I don't know." I sit up. "I do feel a little nauseous."

A moment later, it hits me: a wave of vomit pushes up my esophagus and my cheeks bulge like Dizzy Gillespie blowing a high note. Panicked, I reach for the nearest container, which happens to be Marko's partially full pee bottle. I have an instant to decide: lock lips with the pee bottle, or spray vomit across our down sleeping bags. I choose the bottle, which surges as I fill it. It nearly overflows, but I gain control and catch a few drops with my sleeve.

"Oh shit!" Barry exclaims, holding out the pot in case another wave hits me. I hand him the pee bottle, take the pot, and brace myself, but my stomach settles slowly.

Marko laughs. "Nice. Nice."

Barry too starts to chuckle. "Great catch Farmboy!"

I lie back down, my head scraping the frosted tent wall and sending a rain of cold droplets onto my face. "Drank the soup too fast. I always do that. Can't eat so much up here."

The next morning the winds have increased. "Looks bad," Barry says, zipping the door shut. "Can't see fifty feet. Maybe we should wait an hour and see what the trend is."

"Black-side, down-side, up-side coming," I say, mimicking our base camp cook's ever-pessimistic forecast.

In the afternoon Marko and I climb away from the tent, front pointing on steepening ice. The blizzard seems to be abating. We still don't have much visibility, but it has stopped snowing. Having gone as high as possible without belaying, we turn in an ice screw and hang the ropes and rack in a stuff sack and descend back to the tent. Barry has already decided not to attempt the summit, but has offered his services as high-camp cook and moral support.

"How's it look?" he asks as we step back down onto our tent platform.

"Can't see much, but its nice climbing." I crawl through the door to the back corner of the tent and get inside my bag. It seems peaceful without the wind shaking the tent. A few odd drops of snow skitter off the nylon of our shelter as Marko follows me in.

Once situated in his corner with hands tucked between his flexed knees Marko says, "Now we wait. If no good weather tomorrow, I think down. Stove gas finished."

"Yeah," replies Barry. "We've got one full canister. I think I can get you guys sent off tomorrow morning with a good meal and lukewarm water for the thermos, but no tea or soup tonight. Cold rations from here on out."

George Lowe on the first ascent of the Infinite Spur in 1977. George is on the ridge leading back to the hanging glacier and easier upper slopes. This photograph was taken very close to the same spot as the photograph on page 171, only 24 years earlier. MICHAEL KENNEDY

Michael Kennedy on the first of 11 days spent climbing and descending the Infinite Spur during the first ascent. June 27, 1977. GEORGE LOWE

I look at my watch; it's 2 am. The tent wall's staccato vibration keeps me awake, the alarm will go off in an hour. I doze between wind gusts and when the alarm finally sings, I shift onto my back and speak to the tent, knowing that Marko and Barry are awake.

"Looks like it's down side for us."

"Black side now up side," says Barry.

"Oh well," I reply.

As dawn breaks the tent shakes harder. Barry brews a pot of coffee that we share before stuffing our sleeping bags. In the cramped space only one person at a time can put his boots on. Marko goes first.

Edging towards the door he says, "I go for ropes, no?"

"Okay," I reply. After he leaves it is too easy to lounge in the disappointment of not climbing Nuptse.

"No magic this time, eh Farmboy?"

"Yeah. That's the way it goes."

"You know, I think this is it for me. I'm done with big mountains. It's too dangerous, and Catherine and I want to start a family. I'm forty-four, and I'm happy to have done what I did."

"I understand. You know, it was too bad about Stephen leaving with that tweaked knee. But I really like Marko. I'm glad I got to know him better. I think we'll climb together again."

"I think that'd be mega. You guys get on well. I see the spark," Barry replies.

"I don't feel any spark quite yet, but these things take time."

"You'll get there. I see the spark."

The east face of Masherbrum catches the morning's first light. MARKO PREZELJ

CHAPTER FOURTEEN

Filling the Void

Base Camp, Mandu Glacier, Masherbrum, Pakistan: July 1, 2003

THE SATELLITE PHONE BEEPS and I quickly pick it off the battered metal table, push view and read the text message aloud, "Snow on and off." Marko and Matic laugh.

"That's it," I repeat, scrolling down to see if I missed part of the message. "Snow on and off."

"Shit!" exclaims Marko. "This is real shit. Every forecast is same. 'Snow on and off.' This is real bad joke now."

Taking advantage of the newly affordable, portable satellite phones, I have arranged for a meteorologist in the United States to text weather forecasts to us every other day. For two weeks the forecasts have not varied. Unfortunately for us, they have been accurate.

I stand and unzip the mess tent door and look towards Masherbrum. Clouds hide its steep slopes. We've seen the peak only three times since we arrived in base camp five weeks ago and during our various acclimatization forays, we've triggered a total of seven snow avalanches.

◇◇◇◇◇◇◇◇◇◇◇◇◇◇◇◇◇◇◇◇◇◇◇◇◇◇

Stepping into the mess tent the next morning, I hear Matic speaking to Marko in Slovene. "I'm done. Finished. If you two want to go up, it's no problem for me. There is only one week left, but anyway, I think the snow conditions are too dangerous to try."

I sit next to Matic. We've just started to get to know each other, Marko being the link between us. "You sure?" I ask.

"Ya, ya. I am sure. Go if you want, if the weather is good."

The next morning Marko glances at his watch, 10 am. Time for the weather forecast. I try not to stare at the phone. I stand up, walk to the mess tent door, and step outside. I can see the bottom flanks of the mountain today: bright white with fresh snow except for spots of blue that have been scoured clean by recent ice avalanches.

I hear the phone beep and a moment later Marko reads, "Today: snow on and off. Tomorrow through Thursday: three days of clearing. Ending with moderate amounts of precipitation with little wind."

A pause, then Marko looks up. "Okay. We go."

"Yes," I reply. "We go."

That afternoon we lay out supplies: food, fuel, a small tent, sleeping bags, mattresses, one stove and pot, two lighters, two ropes, a rack, photos of the mountain from all sides should we need to descend another way, goggles, Polarguard parkas and mittens, and a dozen other small items like film and lip balm.

We each pack our share before retiring to our individual tents. I write in my journal, musing on the despondent state of my marriage of eight years. As I struggle to transition to climbing bigger mountains – ramping up my commitment to train harder and work harder to pay for the longer, more expensive expeditions – my relationship with Anne has grown difficult. I am a goal-oriented achiever, which has left little energy for my marriage.

Marko calls home, talking to his young wife, Katja and his two boys: Bor who is four years old and Tim who is nine. Katja is a trained chemical engineer, but the current job market in Slovenia is so dismal that it is best for family finances if she stays home to raise the boys. Marko is immune from homesickness. When I question him on this he answers, "When I am on expedition, I am on expedition. When I am home, I am home. End of story."

The next morning we breakfast in the dark and strike across the glacier as the first hint of color enters the eastern sky.

"What do you think of this snow slope?" I ask four hours later. Five minutes earlier I had triggered our eighth avalanche of the expedition. It buried me up to my knees. We had thought that today would be cloudy, but the Karakoram sun bears down, heating the snow pack. The increasing temperature weakens the bonds holding the snow to the mountain. Before me is a long narrow snow slope angling sharply to the right. What we cannot see, but know is there, is an 800-foot high cliff of vertical ice below us. We could see it from base camp, and even a small slide, like the one I just triggered, could sweep us over that cliff to certain death.

"I think it's too much. I have had enough," says Marko.

Breathing a sigh of relief, I agree and add, "The slope ahead is even more dangerous."

I had been waiting for Marko to call it, curious where he would draw the line. I had already decided that I would not cross the next slope in these conditions and am relieved that he has independently reached the same conclusion. I stare at the striking pillar of Masherbrum's north face. It's a fantastic line, one of the best in the big mountains. It's as big as the south face of Nuptse, and a purer line than the Slovak Direct. Masherbrum's summit has only been reached five times since its first ascent 40 years ago.

Resentment looms. I wish the conditions were better; my desire to climb burns hot. From what I know of Marko, I think he feels the same. Neither of us speaks, recognizing that voicing such desires in these fragile moments can invite a bad decision. I am here to climb, not to die. Hero or martyr: in death they are both the same.

"Okay. Let's go." I turn and we start back.

Islamabad International Airport, Pakistan: July 24, 2003

Two weeks later we ride together to the red brick Islamabad International Airport and I say goodbye to Marko and Matic as a dozen blue-shirted porters squabble to carry their expedition luggage to the terminal.

"Okay. See you next time," Marko says. "I like the idea of going to Canada in the spring." We speak in Slovene, enjoying the fact that no one around us can understand our conversation.

"That'd be easy. Just get yourself to Seattle or Calgary, and I'll take care of the rest. There are some really good mountains in the Canadian Rockies. Very Himalayan for small mountains." I give him a slap on the back as we disengage from a firm hug.

"Matic."

"Štef.

"It was good, no?" I ask. "Of course, the weather was bad, but to be in the mountains together, it was good. Good luck building your house in the spring." Matic smiles.

"Thanks. Lucky Trails."

"Lucky Trails." Matic intones the familiar Slovene climber's farewell.

From the airport I direct the taxi to the Ministry of Tourism for a trekking permit. I am not anxious to go home to Anne. I wonder if our lack of intimacy is a symptom of the cumulative effects of time apart, or of my single-minded ambition. I struggle to make sense of my feelings. I do know that the mountains hold a much stronger draw than going home to face the dilemma of my relationship.

That afternoon I start back to the Charakusa Valley. The Karakoram Highway leaves Islamabad threading through plots of red-clay farmland. Refugee camps from the ongoing wars in Afghanistan dot the countryside. The edges of the road are crowded with dirty boys selling roasted ears of corn to hungry drivers. Small groups of women ferry hand-cut grass baled with a hank of rope looped across their foreheads. Some have loads so large their feet are barely visible.

I listen to the stuttering rhythm of the driver and his assistant and wonder what they are talking about. Then I wonder what I would talk about had I company. This makes me sad and homesick. The feeling sits there in my gut sloshing heavily back and forth as the mini-van accelerates out of the corners and swerves between the potholes.

Eventually my thoughts turn to the place I'm traveling to. It becomes difficult to feel sorry for myself. Without a partner to pursue what Mark, Scott and I experienced on the Slovak Direct, it seems logical that I might find the same sensation, the same wholeness within myself. Climbing is the only vehicle I have to achieve that odd sensation of both emptiness and fullness where I no longer feel alone. My thoughts turn to Anne and I wonder if I am running away, or doing what is necessary to achieve something great, to transcend. One question nags at me as we drive through the night: How will I know the difference?

Charakusa Valley, Pakistan: July 28, 2003

It rains as I walk up the glacier with 12 men from the village of Hushe. We pick our way across the ice, weaving in and out of the rocks. The snow is long melted, the surface gray from embedded rock dust, and violently blue where sheets of water stream into the nearest crevasse. The porters have hung sheets of plastic over their loads. The leading edge of the plastic ends at their foreheads, and rainwater drips into their faces.

At noon the rain relents as we hop across huge white boulders that sometimes shift with our weight. We cross through tall grass that soaks our pants and ends in a large sandy plain threaded through with a braid of one-hop streams and dotted with house-size boulders. At the far end of the plain we cross a torrent of milky glacier runoff and reach a small nook of grass. On the left, spring water flows from thick banks of moss into a stream that trickles down and out to fine gravel banks dashed with small purple and pallid-yellow wildflowers. There, between the stream and the glacier, we make base camp.

"Is good?" asks Rasool, understanding full well the beauty of the place.

"Why not?" I reply, turning his favorite reply to my frequent requests back on him.

Rasool's beard is gray around the mouth, and his wiry dark hair has thinned since our first expedition together four years ago. He is quick with a joke and easy with his laughter. Last winter he finally saved $2,500 and was able to make the Hajj, the pilgrimage to Mecca and Medina, which Islam asks of all Muslims who have the means. His fellow Baltis, the people of Baltistan easily recognized by their gilgiti, a thick wool beret rolled tight around the edges, all call him Hajji Rasool. I detect a new respect and seriousness in their tone.

I pay the porters 1,350 rupees each – about $30 for two long days of work, which seems fair given Pakistan's average annual income of only $300. They fold the money once and tuck it into the button up pockets of their shalwar qameez, the traditional Pakistan dress. As they depart, each one shakes my hand, thanks me, and wishes me luck.

<><><><><><><><><><><><><><><><><><><><><><>

At 2 am, three days later, I wake and lean forward to light the stove sitting in the snow next to me. Half the hemisphere is filled with stars; their pin-pricks of light washed out by an unseen full moon. Behind me, the sky is filled with the wall I have probed with binoculars these past two days. The base of the un-named, unclimbed mountain is wide and swept by an ice face that starts off moderately, but gets steep before it narrows and turns to dry rock. The rock is checked with crack systems and chimneys, some holding ice. The face concludes on the mountain's northeast shoulder, which is capped by a tower of granite rising to an exacting needlepoint. I first saw this mountain a few weeks ago while hiking out with Marko and Matic from our Masherbrum expedition. If I climb it, I will name it Hajji Brakk in honor of Rasool's pilgrimage.

At 3:01 am I start and within 15 minutes I am climbing the ice wall by the light of my headlamp. The ice is brittle and fractures into thin-angled slivers, like a broken mirror, they skid and whir down the face. My head plays games with me; I see my body sliding against the ice, making a zipping sound and then going airborne in an unwitnessed blur of color.

I try to stop these movies running in my mind, but then decide to let them play. Perhaps when they play out I can be finished with them forever. The climbing steepens and I focus: I swing my ice tool from the shoulder, tune into any possible looseness in my crampons, notice any fracturing in the ice supporting me. I climb; how I enjoy the movement of climbing.

When I reach the base of the rock wall I chop a step in the ice and place a screw. I check my watch: 6:30. As I reach for a second ice screw a powerful crack shatters the stillness. In that instant I feel naked, exposed to falling rock or ice. The remains of the cornice disintegrates violently 30 feet to my right and disappears down the face, strafing the slope I just climbed.

That falling cornice came down the icy chimney I intended to climb. I reverse the ice screw and climb further up and to the left. After 100 feet I stop and repeat the process with the step and the ice screw. I add a second screw and equalize them with a short sling before tying the end of the rope to the anchor and clipping myself in with another sling. There is another, safer, but more difficult looking chimney here.

I hang my pack on one screw and flake loops of rope back and forth across it. Giving myself about 20 feet of slack, I tie a clove-hitch knot and clip it into a locking carabiner attached to my harness. With this as a self-belay, I am ready to start climbing. As I go I will place gear, clipping the rope into that gear. When I have climbed 20 feet, I will pull up some slack, tie another clove hitch in a second locking 'biner and untie the first one. This system is light and simple, but means that any fall would be at least 20 feet. I slip a spare ice hammer into its holster, check that my gear is organized, and start to climb.

The entrance to the chimney above is clogged by a snow mushroom. I climb to it, place a screw below it, and clip in my rope. The mushroom is larger than I am, and I know from experience that it is much, much heavier than me. Dislodging it would crush me, or possibly load my self-belay system to, or beyond, its breaking point.

I climb the wall to its left. It starts off well, but the holds quickly become small, unstable and barely useable. I can't lean on or climb the mushroom without risking its collapse. I look down at my feet and unbidden, the movie starts again: a 10-foot, ankle-shattering fall; the ensuing retreat to the bivy, 20-odd rappels sliding on my bum; the glacier crossing to base camp crawling on my knees. I down climb to the ice screw.

After a short pause I start up the right side. It's steeper here but an angling crack provides secure purchase for my ice tools. I press my left foot onto a bad rock edge, which crumbles under the pressure. I climb up a few moves, feel unstable, and come back down.

"Commit. Commit. You can do this." I exhale sharply into a puff of frost and start the moves again. I get one move higher before the video of my potential fall and the consequences of a mistake replays. I climb down again.

At the anchor I look down the ice field, streaked with vivid blues and chalky whites. I reposition my feet and ice chips rattle away and are quickly silenced by gravity. I think about descending. In less than five minutes I could have those two screws out, make a V-thread and be rappelling. My stomach growls at the thought of a hot lunch on the safety of the glacier. Should I give up now without demonstrating to myself that the climbing is really too hard?

"What do I need?" I ask myself. Do I need to fall off? Do I need to push beyond what I can do in order to learn what I can't do? It would be stupid to fall up here, belayed to a clove hitch on that 8-millimeter half rope. No matter how much you can live inside your own head right now, no matter how skilled

The view looking down one of four difficult pitches I soloed on Hajji Brakk, the unclimbed 20,000 foot peak in Pakistan that I made the first ascent of alone and in a single day. STEVE HOUSE

you are at distracting yourself from exertion and discomfort with fantasies, you won't be able to divorce yourself from the real pain of a serious injury. No daydream will stop the blood flowing from your skull once it's cracked open. Do you have an answer to that? Of course not. You knew all of that when you came up here; so what's changed? Nothing. Nothing has changed. Just up or down. What's it going to be? Up or down?

I look up at the snow mushroom. Bad luck, I think. But then that mushroom is probably always there and will be there long after I'm gone. I need to get some gear in to keep me from falling onto the ice slab if I pitch off. I reach for the crack again and climb a few moves. Cranked up on my tools I peer into the crack, it's full of dust, but it just might take a piton. I pick the thinnest pin off my rack and slip it into the crack, using the tip to brush away some of the dirt. It slots in tightly after a quarter inch.

Breathing hard, I shift my feet and try to relax my arms. I shake out my left hand first, then my right. I make a short move and hold on tightly with my left arm while I take the hammer in my right hand and tap on the slim titanium piton. *Tink, tink, tink.* It works its way in and I make each blow a little stronger. The pitch of the sound rises, and finally, *taunk, taunk, taunk,* and it's in solidly. I pull a sling from around my neck and shoulder and quickly clip the rope to the piton.

After 200 feet I find a good horizontal crack where I nest four pieces of gear for a solid, multidirectional anchor. I rappel down to clean the pitch then reclimb it with a self-belay from my toprope, carrying the pack to the anchor.

Back on lead, I scratch around the shallow cracks and corners above me like a dentist probing for flaws in enamel. The sounds are similar. There are no useable holds, so I down climb five feet to a place where I can stem: pressing my right and left feet against opposite walls. Extending, I can slot my tools into a second crack system.

Two hours later I surmount a chockstone and pull onto a foot-wide flow of ice. My pant leg is torn and my eyes encrusted in dirt. I have used all my rock gear. I feel tired and bruised as I mechanically clean the pitch, dropping my spare ice hammer in the process. The way to the peak's shoulder is clear now. The climbing is not over, but the crux is behind me. My mind has played no more movies and I enjoy the drag of fatigue on my arms and shoulders. I feel the snow, ice and rock under my tools and crampons without having to search for the sensation. I swing my pick where I need to, kick my crampons where I want to, and know when I'm at the end of my rope without looking.

At 1:30 pm I anchor my rope to a horn of solid granite and rappel back down to clean the last pitch and retrieve my pack.

Back on the shoulder I sit and reward myself with two GU packets and an extra swig of water. Looking out, the Charakusa Glacier flows away to my left.

I count eight unclimbed summits. One is a striking granite tower that looks exactly like a dog's bottom canine. A cumulus cloud drifts from the south and casts me in shadow. "Tick, tock. Tick, tock," I whisper to myself.

My crampons grate noisily on the coarse-grained rock as I hoist myself onto an edge and use my knees to gather my feet underneath me. I hold onto both sides of the tapering rock fin as I stand up. I reach, standing on my toes, and touch the pinnacled summit at 4:48 pm.

I take my first 360-degree view of the day mechanically: K6 and K7, both across the valley from me, and each with a single ascent. The massive trapezoid of Chogolisa, where the great Hermann Buhl died falling through a cornice in 1957. K2, the world's second highest peak, looms massively: a huge, white Egyptian pyramid. Muztagh Tower, its near vertical black profile offers a striking contrast to neighboring K2. Masherbrum looks absolutely massive, it's east face clearly overhanging; perhaps this is the steepest wall on any of the world's highest summits. Nanga Parbat hangs like a cloud on the southern horizon, distinguished by its immensity. I sit in the sun, soaking up the possibilities, knowing that in 10 lifetimes I could not climb all these mountains.

I take four pictures, three of the mountains, and one of myself. My altimeter reads 19,980 feet. I set a single, small wired nut in a crack and clip in one carabiner, the first of many rappel anchors. Three single-point rock anchors later, I reach ice where I can rappel from simple V-threads. As I drill my third V-thread darkness falls, slowing my pace. After six more rappels I'm tired, my arms are going numb from the pressure of the pack straps. When I throw the ropes, they don't slither effortlessly down, they hang up and I have to work, retossing the ropes several times for each rappel. I finally leave the rope hanging from my harness and down climb.

Twenty minutes later my headlamp dies. Moonlight doesn't reach this north face, so I continue by a kind of icy mountain braille, pushing through the pain of cramping calves and the dull, hungry ache of my belly.

I cross the bergschrund, the finish line, and look at my watch. It's 10:05 pm, 19 hours since I started climbing. I hold the camera in front of my face and force my eyes open for a self-portrait. The flash blinds me for a few moments. I let gravity lead me, staggering, to my bivouac.

K7 Base Camp, Charakusa Valley, Pakistan: August 4, 2003

On the morning of my 33 birthday, Rasool makes pancakes and fries two eggs overeasy. All that's missing is bacon and coffee. For lunch, I open one of my two bottles of Coke. I read until midnight. Rain drums on the tent as I drift to sleep.

After breakfast the next day the clouds begin to clear. "Rasool. You want to go onto the glacier? To look?" I ask.

"Why not?" He says with a wide grin displaying stubby teeth worn by decades of eating local stone ground flour. Twenty minutes later he emerges with gaiters covering his boots and holding an ice axe.

"This very good." He says tapping an index finger on his old and slightly rusty axe.

"Yes. Very nice." I realize he's excited for a little adventure. After two hours all we've seen is clouds and some Ibex tracks in the snow. We turn around and the wind pushes us from behind. Wet, dark rock appears at the base of K7.

Winds silently rip clouds from the granite walls and needles, revealing more towers and summits. These prove to be tiny horns on massive walls as the next gust tears back yet another layer. The mountain grows bigger and bigger. Without noticing, I've stopped, gawking at the spectacle unfolding before me. The wind shreds the final cloud from K7's summit and my eye is drawn to a line of steep waterfalls dead in front of me.

I snap two photos and take off my pack to get the binoculars. Yes, it would go. The ice doesn't touch, but there is a climbable ramp from the right to get to the thicker ice. Here is a mountain I have to climb, I think. A mountain in which to lose myself.

The next day I leave base camp in the dark. In my isolated halo of light, I imagine my impending glory – this will be the climb of the century. I fantasize about my Piolet d'Or acceptance speech, ranting about how the award is politicized, bashing less deserving climbs and climbers, exalting my solipsistic conquest.

When I get within a few hundred feet of the base, I can hear the sound of gushing water. The ice is melting fast. My vain fantasies vaporize when a great sheet of ice peels off the rock thousands of feet above. It floats for a moment before striking the wall and shattering into a million pieces. Walking back to base camp, I wonder if I'm experiencing good luck, or bad.

As I retreat to base camp I see a line of weakness in the rock that might be easy enough to solo. After lunch I pack for another attempt: rock-climbing shoes, two slings, five nuts, nine pitons, and one ice screw plus a puffy parka, a couple pairs of gloves, a bivy sack, a stove and pot, and a bit of food this time. I think I can get to the summit in 30 hours, and back in about 20.

A few puffy cumulous clouds drift in from the south, otherwise the sky is clear. The pressure is down one millibar; nothing to be alarmed about. My plan is to leave at first light, have a brew stop and a nap in the afternoon, then climb the ridge by the light of the full moon. I'm counting on clear skies and no wind. If any component of this plan is missing, I'll rappel down.

Seeing the ice line disintegrate has checked the imagined glory misguiding me to push myself ever further. It doesn't take much figuring to predict how that would end. I will cut the rotten pit out of my motivation during today's meditation. What I need now is no pressure. No other of any kind – no awards, no cares for sponsors, no responsibility for anyone.

I start climbing in the predawn gray. The ice disappears where the rock steepens and I change to rock-climbing shoes. The climbing gets steeper with each passage and suddenly I'm on terrain too hard to be soloing. I've read that a samurai endeavors to make every decision within the space of seven breaths. By the sixth breath I have an anchor placed and am rappelling down.

I walk out onto the glacier to gain perspective and toss my gear on a large flat rock. Following a hunch, I take the rope and a bit of climbing gear and walk to the right side of the cliff. Water-polished rock carries me into a chimney where I find the first human sign I've seen in two weeks: an old piton. Two hundred feet higher I find old ropes bleached by the sun. I continue and the climbing stays moderate. Three hours later I've climbed 1,500 feet above the glacier.

I've found it: the key to the mountain! The terrain above is ice and mixed ice and rock, climbing that plays to my strengths.

Someone has attempted the peak by this rock chimney before, but this is not the same route taken on the peak's one and only ascent. In 1984 eight Japanese university students placed 450 pitons and bolts and fixed 8,000 feet of rope over 40 days to gain the summit.

In base camp Rasool cooks a delicious curry. "Eat," he admonishes. "Climber must be very strong. Very good eat."

I sleep until the sun's heat forces me out of the tent the next morning. Packing is easy. I know exactly what I need, and more importantly, what I do not need. I replace a couple of nuts abandoned on yesterday's retreat and increase my ice screw count to two. I stuff a bivy sack, an old pair of down pants and my lime-green DAS Parka into my backpack. It all weighs 11 pounds. This is usually the point where I dump it all back out and go through each item checking that each has multiple uses, that every item is essential. Nothing weighs more than a few ounces, but ounces make pounds. And pounds, as they say, make pain. This time I put the pack in my vestibule and retire for an afternoon nap.

By noon the next day I have regained my earlier highpoint, switched back to boots, and started up the icefields above the rock barrier. The climbing winds wonderfully back and forth through strips of ice under a serac and between exposed fins of yellow granite. It starts to snow lightly.

I climb into a section of vertical ice. Where it begins to overhang it gets chalky and soft. I traverse right, struggling to set a solid right foot to move onto. I swing too hard from nervousness and my tool gets stuck and I feel the first burn of a pump. I make large moves between sure, precise swings. The angle slackens, the exposure here is incredible, and I spot a jutting serac above and to the right of me.

The visibility is dropping and its snowing like it means it now. I climb towards the serac. As I get closer, I see a hollow beneath the cantilevered ice roof. I continue 100 feet past the natural cave, but decide to return to it and take my good luck where I can.

A slip of spindrift, a mini-avalanche of newly fallen snow, hisses past me as I step into the hollow. I move to the back and place a screw in the wall. I clip myself into it and scrape a flat spot with my boot. The light fades as I deploy the ultralight, five-ounce bivy sack that Todd Bibler made for me, promising that it would last only five bivies. I've counted over 20 bivies when a burst of spindrift launches off the lip and the wind kicks it into my face. I look up and notice that the light is fading. The thickening storm clouds hide the setting sun.

Four hours later I awake to my wristwatch alarm. With cold fingers I fumble the watch, dropping it in the snow. The beam of my headlamp is full of cloud and snow. The green bivy sack is hidden under a white blanket.

Too cold to sleep, I'm gone at first light. I don't want to descend the way I came. It's too dangerous due to the large snowfield that could avalanche with the new storm snow. I work my way up a faint ridge of steep snow above the bivy cave. This exertion warms me from the thighs out. I traverse towards steep waterfall ice I'd seen the day before and start my rappels.

It's raining as I step onto the glacier late that afternoon. Failure is often bitter. But I am elated with the challenge that lies ahead of me, satisfied by what I've learned, and filled with the knowledge that I will spend the coming year training for and dreaming about climbing K7.

I lost my outer boot shell on the climb and had to attach my crampon directly to my taped up inner boot. Unable to use my skis, we had to escape across the Columbia Icefield after completing the climb. MARKO PREZELJ

CHAPTER FIFTEEN

Trust

North Face of North Twin Tower, Canadian Rockies: April 4, 2004

"Off belay Marko!" I shout, my voice carrying through the calm winter air.

As I rappel, Marko is digging a bivouac out of the snow drifted against the vertical black wall. Reaching the ledge, I clip into a long tether and coil the remaining rope.

"This will be good, no?" Marko asks, as he pries off a large block of wind-hardened snow.

"Yeah, great spot." I kick the block off the edge with the broad side of my boot. "And great view of Mount Alberta, too." The snow block turns on edge and cartwheels down the steep slope, going 500 feet to the glacier below us.

"Yes. Really nice." He switches to Slovene. "This is a proper beast." He points the shovel blade at the soaring black wall above us.

Beast implies a wild dog; I see a seven-headed hydra. "Ya, proper beast," I say.

Today we have traveled 16 miles through the post-equinox Canadian wil-derness. We crossed the frozen braids of the Athabasca River, then skied past lynx tracks, through a spruce forest, and eventually crested and dropped into Woolley Creek. We traveled through deep snow in the creek bed, our passage eased by an old ski track left a month ago by French climbers.

After a two-hour climb to Woolley Shoulder, the five-miles distant north face of North Twin dominated the surrounding view. The brooding black wall accentuates its steepness and suits my own dark mood.

A month ago I left behind my home, my wife of nine years, and our beloved avalanche-search dog. I bought an '84 Ford van, packed my most important belongings, and said good-bye. Forever.

At 25, when I wed Anne on a rainy November day, I believed true love to be self-sustaining. I don't understand why my thesis failed, but staring at 4,000 feet of black limestone reminds me that these mountains may be my solace and my curse. Purpose has its price, but it wasn't just the time apart; I've always needed that. In the last six months, I realized that with Anne I am no longer capable of the intimacy I seek. Our failure to communicate our needs to one another buried us under years of resentment and judgment. I know, from climbing, that a deep connection between people is possible and that is what I want in a relationship.

In the morning I ascend the rope as the sky's pink tint gives way to clear blue. Tying back into the ropes, I lead through a roof to a fine, thin drytooling crack. I belay on a sloping ledge and snap photos of a jubilant Marko between moments of pack hauling and belaying.

Marko leads a short tricky pitch to a small snow-covered icefield. Speeding up the icefield we enter a deep six-foot wide chimney. Climbing three pitches in this gash, the only sound is our occasional shouts bouncing off the chimney walls and echoing from the overhanging wall above.

I had just turned four in August, 1974 when George Lowe and Chris Jones completed the first route on this forbidding wall. Climbing historians now recognize that this may have been the most difficult alpine route in the world at the time. When I was 15, David Cheesmond and Barry Blanchard opened an even more difficult route on the great pillar surging up the center right of the wall. In the 30 years since the first ascent, and the 19 since the second, no one else has climbed the face.

To this point we haven't been on either of these two routes, but when we reach the headwall we find monolithic stone rearing up into square-cut overhanging roofs. We had hoped to forge an independent line through this central part of the wall. It is painfully clear now that we are too lightly equipped for the time consuming and slow aid climbing that would be required. We zag left. Traversing across the large low-angle snow band that skirts the base of the headwall, we arrive at the crack systems of the Lowe-Jones route. I continue left 100 feet, intrigued by a line of ice dangling with promise.

Marko is having none of it. "What are you doing? Come back!" he shouts. Minutes later I am belaying as Marko, a 5.13 rock climber, expertly leads above the ledge and reaches a belay as night falls.

As Marko prepares to descend back to the snow band, I start to dig our second night's bivouac. We've cut out every luxury to ensure that there is only one loaded pack to carry. The leader climbs with a small pack containing a belay parka, a few snacks, and some water. The second climbs with the bivy gear: one sleeping bag to share, two thin closed-cell foam mattresses, a 5-foot by 8-foot tarp for shelter, GU gel and energy bars, the stove and fuel, and a few evening meals of dried potatoes preseasoned with instant soup. One large Cadbury's chocolate bar and a bit of instant coffee made it into the food bag as a last minute concession to luxury.

After drinking his morning brew, Marko ascends the fixed climbing rope in the slow jerky motions of a cold morning. I run the stove to melt more snow for myself. When he reaches the anchor I shut down the burner and pick up the pot. Bits of ice bump into my nose as I drink down the metallic-tasting water.

"On belay Steve," yells Marko. I shove the empty pot into the backpack, grab the already-cold stove, spin off the fuel canister, and quickly dump it in the pack.

The rope snaps tight against my harness; Marko urging me to get going.

"Climbing!" I shoulder the pack and place my front points carefully onto an exposed edge of rock and start climbing.

Hours later my hips are numb from hanging in my harness at the belay stance. Over two hours ago Marko led off, up and to the right, and disappeared around a corner. Occasionally I hear metallic banging as he places a piton. Every few minutes the rope pays out a few inches. I shiver in a sudden chill and do hanging squats against the stone to warm myself. Somewhere above, Marko progresses another few inches.

The still air is suddenly torn by Marko's voice, "Off belaaaayyyy."

Relieved, I put on the pack, remove the two pieces of gear from the anchor, and wait. When the rope comes tight. He yells again, "On belay!"

I shout back with a long "Okay," and take out the last piece.

Still wearing my big parka, I start to climb. I move up around the corner and see the ropes going sharply right across a small horizontal ledge system. The rock bulges above the ledge, a polished shield. With little to hold onto, I balance on my feet and carefully shuffle across, keeping the weight of the pack as close as I can to the rock.

Finally, I arrive at the point where the ropes stretch up the past-vertical stone. Here a tiny seam splits a small six-inch overhang and widens slightly. Above that roof, just within reach, the seam opened enough to accept our smallest piton. I hook the pick of my tool into the hole of the piton, match my other ice tool on top of that and pull myself up.

"Nicely done, Marko," I say, gasping.

"It was the only option. No?"

He's right, there was no option but to climb that tiny seam-turned-crack. The fissure continues above Marko's belay to a triangular roof with deep, good-looking cracks, which lead out the roof's left side to another vertical headwall. That should bring us to what I hope will be a ledge. It's past noon already and darkness will surely catch us there, if not before.

"This is for you," Marko says, handing me the neatly organized gear. I hurriedly finish reracking. My crampons scrape for purchase as I climb toward the triangular roof. There is a block, three or four feet tall and several feet wide, perched under the roof, seemingly cemented to the wall by the traces of snow winter storms have blown into the outlining cracks.

I place a good piece of protection a foot beneath it. I can plainly see that if the rock comes out it will fall directly onto the ropes and probably cut them before landing on Marko at his belay stance 40 feet directly below. Tethered to the vertical wall, he would only be able to move a foot to either side to evade the missile. Carefully, I stem, placing one cramponed boot on either side of the block. At the crest of the roof I move left, past the deadly block.

"Five meters!" Marko yells. I climb a few more feet and stop to build an anchor. I can see a fixed piton 10 feet above me that confirms that we are still on the path of the Lowe-Jones route.

I belay as Marko climbs gingerly past the block under the roof. When he's above it he gives it a tentative kick. *Chunk.* The block makes a hollow sound. Marko rears his foot back to strike again with slightly more force. The block silently tips through the air and skids down the slab, right where the belay had been. Then it flies; spinning, whirring, and with a loud, echoing *thwack*, it impacts the slope near where we bivied last night.

"Ooooh," Marko says, as he considers what might have been.

<hr />

It's nearly dark. Lines of white snow reveal the flat edges in the black rock: the crucial footholds. I keep climbing, hoping for salvation in the form of a ledge large enough to sleep on.

"No go!" I yell down to Marko and start back to the crack six feet below me. I've been unable to find a better bivy site than the tiny ledge where Marko now stands 150 feet below. I place five pieces of gear, fix one rope, and descend to Marko's marginal stance.

As I start down the rope, I hear the dull hacking of Marko chopping frozen rubble with his ice axe. In the yellow glow of his headlamp, I see that the ledge he works to flatten is two or three feet across and triangular. One person might sit comfortably, leaning against the rock with his feet stuck in a suspended backpack for support.

"Not so good," I say, eyeing the ledge that is, at best, three butt-cheeks wide.

"Eh. It is okay," Marko replies. "We will survive."

Marko's attitude is unflappable. He's right I think, surveying the ledge. For two it will be difficult. Though we will survive, neither of us will sleep.

We cook half the remaining dried potatoes flavored with the big half of the

Marko cooking our meal on the "three-butt-cheek ledge" that we shared on our third bivy. To find snow and ice to melt for water I ascended 50 feet to another small ledge and loaded snow into my empty backpack, hence all the equipment clipped in behind Marko. STEVE HOUSE

last cube of butter. Marko finishes the cashews at my urging. I store the stove and pot in a hanging stuff sack as Marko clips the sleeping pads to the anchor. Anything dropped from here will be gone, swallowed by blackness.

I retrieve the one bit of extra clothing that we have allowed ourselves: dry socks. With dry socks we can sleep with warm toes, and by stuffing my damp pair next to my inner most layers of clothing they will be dry in the morning.

Sitting on the foam mattress pad, I unlace my outer boot. I'm wearing double boots composed of an insulating foam inner boot and a protective and supportive outer. I wonder for a moment if I should clip it in. I have rigged a thin blue piece of cord on the back of the boot for this purpose, but I notice that it has a small nick in it, cut part way through while climbing. I place it between me and the wall and press against it. Marko stands and carefully begins to put the stove together.

With the inner boot off I wiggle my toes into dry socks and feel the cooling night air through the Capilene fabric. I loosen the laces on the inner boot and slide it onto my foot. Reaching behind me I retrieve the outer boot. With nothing better to take hold of I slip my index finger into the small damaged loop I threaded into the back of the boot. Putting the outer boot over the toe of the inner boot, I pull the shell onto my foot with the loop of cord.

The loop of cord goes suddenly slack on my finger. The boot stutters and floats quietly in my headlamp for a moment before it plunges into the dark, and is gone.

Silence. All I see is the weak cast of light illuminating the space in front of me where moments ago my boot was. It's gone. There is no way to retrieve it. Even if we did have enough gear to leave rappel anchors all the way down the wall we would never find it.

The ramifications cascade: We can't go down, so we must go up. I have no boot, so I cannot wear a crampon. Without a crampon I can't climb. Without a boot I can't ski. Without skis it will be a very, very difficult walk out. We are over 20 miles in a straight line from the closest road. Most of those miles are covered in crevassed icecaps and glaciers, or steep mountain walls. By the calendar it's early spring, but our environment remains in full winter; the daily high temperature doesn't exceed 20 degrees. At night it's easily zero. We have three ounces of dried potatoes, half a stick of butter, six energy gels, four energy bars, and some freeze-dried coffee. We have 12 ounces of fuel, enough to produce two gallons of cold water. The weather has been clear for two days, but that will surely end soon. We carry no radio, no communications device of any kind. We won't be reported overdue for three more days. All of this is calculated in an instant.

"Argh!" I let go an animal scream of anger. It is completely unsatisfying. "Fuck!" No better.

I look at Marko. He is quietly staring at me, jaw slack with disbelief. "What happened?" he asks flatly.

I hold up the broken bit of cord still wrapped around my finger for him to see and throw it after the lost boot. "Fuck! Fuck! Fuck! Fuck! Fuck! Fuck! I am so stupid!" I still don't feel any better. I take a few deep breaths and carefully change socks on my left foot. I keep my boot clipped into the well-inspected laces.

As I finish, Marko hands me the stove, and says, "I will leave my socks on."

〰〰〰〰〰〰〰〰〰〰〰〰〰〰〰〰〰〰〰〰

Snow spills onto my face and I jerk awake. I wipe it off with a gloved hand, suddenly remembering where I am. I'm slipping off the ledge, so I snug my tie-in a little tighter. I lean forward to change the pressure point on my numb right leg and let Marko shift toward the wall in his continuous fight to stay on the ledge. I look at my watch: 12:22 am. Marko has slept fitfully the last hour, his head resting on my shoulder. This is bad, I think. Though the night sky is clear, the wind blowing near the summit indicates the good weather is ending.

Marko grunts awake and sits erect. I flip on my light, take my half-booted feet out of the backpack, and stand up. Futilely I try to close the gap between the tarp and the wall that is allowing the snow to dump onto us.

Sitting down I pull the tarp back over our heads and groggily reflect on our situation. I am suddenly aware of how much Marko and I need each other to survive. We have to finish climbing this wall and cross the Columbia Icefield back to a road. Our futures depend on one another.

An hour after dawn I am hanging at a belay, thirsty, as Marko finishes a long traverse. We were unable to start the stove in the now-constant snowfall so we have no water today. From a stance 180 feet to my left and 10 feet below me, Marko pauses a few minutes to build an anchor before calling out, "Off belay."

Nervously I break down my anchor, knowing that the traverse will be difficult to follow. Before we left this morning I went through our small trash bag and salvaged three plastic bags, the kind you put apples in at the grocery store. I placed all three of those, plus one gallon-sized, heavy-duty Ziploc bag over my socked foot before donning the inner boot. After that I wrapped the inner boot with athletic tape, the sole component of our first aid/repair kit. I hope that the plastic will keep my socks dry and that the tape will reinforce the fragile fabric of the inner boot.

Carrying the pack full of bivy gear, I gingerly start the traverse. The inner boot works surprisingly well on the inch-deep square edges. I wasn't able to fasten my crampon to the inner boot, but I can feel the rock's texture underfoot, almost like a rock shoe.

As I continue, the holds become smaller. Soon, I'm balanced on tiny edges. My left front point is securely edged on a small feature. But my right bootless foot pads desperately at the nearly smooth slab. Off to the side I reach an edge

The morning after our bivy under the summit cornice. Our tarp doesn't quite meet the ice wall on the right. We had been too tired to redig a narrower trench. The gap allowed snow to blow onto us throughout the unpleasant night. MARKO PREZELJ

that I hook with my heel to keep in balance. With no other option I pull on my ice tools, which are set delicately on small edges. Suddenly I'm off, my stomach flips as I drop down and across the face. The small steel nut set in a crack above me starts to arrest my swinging fall, and then pings out and I accelerate across the wall.

The swing spins and batters me. I slam my helmet into the stone and bruise my shoulder. When I stop, I take a quick inventory: I held onto my ice axes, and seem unhurt.

"Good thing that was me," I say to myself, borrowing an old tough-guy mantra. "Someone else might have been hurt."

"You okay?" shouts Marko.

I look up to answer him and see a cut on one of the two climbing ropes ten feet above me. Quickly I scramble to get back on the rock and remove my weight from the damaged rope. I can see the white core of the rope through the outer sheath. The rope is cut half-through; I look down at the glacier 3,000 vertical feet below.

I face upward and shout, "I'm okay." No time for explanations. Marko will know everything when I get to the stance. I still have the good second rope belaying me.

"Shit," he says as I climb the last few feet of the pitch. "The rope is cut."

" I know," I answer.

"Fuck. How did you do that?" I stay silent, letting him figure it out as I reach to clip myself in. I assume that when I fell, the rope was sliced by a sharp edge of rock.

"We will have to lead only on these ends." He indicates the ends to which he's tied. Since one of my ends is nearly cut, it is no longer strong enough to protect against a leader fall.

"Yes," I say. "Where now? Pendulum to that ice?"

"Yes, that should be the exit."

"I hope so."

That night we dig a trench against the back of the summit cornice. It's about four-and-half feet wide and seven feet long. Marko and I stretch the tarp tight across the trench. We dug it too wide and one side is open to the wind. A gust christens our grave-like trench with a frosting of snow. I kneel on one foam mattress and roll out the second mattress for Marko. We've successfully become the third party to climb the wall and done a variation to the '74 route, but there is no room for self-congratulation in this grim bivouac. Marko's eyes shimmer in the reflected light of the flame as he huddles to cook the last of our food.

Stolen moments of exhausted death-like sleep stretch into minutes before my slowly freezing flesh pulls me back to consciousness. My feet go numb and I do sit-ups. Marko keeps his back turned as each repetition pumps cold air into the sleeping bag we share, draped over us like a blanket. I doze again, visions of ropes cutting replay in my dreams.

At first light I sit up. I shake the snow off the stuff sack protecting the stove and start preparations to make a pot of hot, sweet coffee. As the stove purrs I have the map out. Being as careful as I can in my hungry, dehydrated, half-frozen state, I count millimeters. I'm calculating the UTM grid coordinates for points I have plotted for our escape across the Columbia Icefield. Without a boot, there is no use in returning to our skis stashed at the bottom of the face. Our only option is to traverse the Columbia Icefield to the Banff-Jasper Highway.

Tiny bubbles form at the bottom of the pot and the stove sputters and dies. We have one last eight-ounce gas canister for the possibility of another bivouac. I mix the last dehydrated coffee and sugar and pass the pot to Marko. He props himself on his elbow, nodding as he takes the pot. He slurps the hot liquid with satisfaction.

Pulling the GPS unit out of my inside pocket where I'm keeping it warm, I enter 10-digit strings of numbers. Two of these number strings delineate one waypoint. When I have eight waypoints programmed the GPS shows the straight-line distance as 28 kilometers, nearly 18 miles, away.

◇◇◇◇◇◇◇◇◇◇◇◇◇◇◇◇◇◇◇◇◇◇◇◇◇◇◇◇◇◇

In a near whiteout, I break trail with my face glued to the yellow and black GPS trying to keep an eye out for swales indicating hidden crevasses. I want to repay Marko for leading all 14 pitches above the bivy where I lost my boot. Several of them had been quite hard, with serious fall potential. Wordlessly we each recognize that I should lead due to my familiarity with GPS navigation. The GPS counts every meter.

I bend and scoop some snow into my mouth, sucking out a small amount of water. I walk holding my hands in front of me for reference. I wear a crampon on the left foot and my right foot flexes comfortably in its inner boot. I tried to lash my crampon onto it with accessory cord, but after an hour, and a half-dozen stops to reattach it, I've given up. My toes are dry though; the plastic bags have worked. My back aches because without a boot one leg is two inches shorter than the other: a small price to pay for being alive. I try to concentrate, not taking my eyes off the yellow and black GPS.

Many long anxious miles later, with heavy legs, we descend from the shoulder of Snow Dome in the late afternoon. We have to find the nearby pass where the Athabasca Glacier slips down between Snow Dome and Mount Andromeda, but the GPS heading is leading us into a zone of ever-larger crevasses. I have no choice but to take us back to the right, away from the Athabasca Glacier.

I veer off the heading and we rapidly lose elevation. I check my altimeter:

204

Holding the GPS in my left hand I lead through the whiteout. The flat light made walking very difficult and my back began to ache due to the missing outer boot making one leg several inches shorter than the other. MARKO PREZELJ

As the second day ends, Marko leads the first pitch of the upper headwall of North Twin. The next night would prove to be a critical moment in our adventure together. STEVE HOUSE

9,500 feet. To miss the 9,100-foot pass will take us down the Saskatchewan Glacier, which could add 10 miles onto an already long day.

As I walk, the whiteout conditions lessen and the surface of the snow becomes more distinct. Tiny shadows begin to reveal tiny wind-whipped crests of snow. Dropping my hand carrying the GPS I see a horizon for the first time today. A dozen more strides and I see the pass just a few hundred yards off to my left. I let out a whoop and glance back at Marko. He lifts his head and stops.

"That's it!" I yell back. I think I see him smile under the red hood of his parka.

◇◇◇◇◇◇◇◇◇◇◇◇◇◇◇◇◇◇◇◇◇◇◇◇◇◇◇◇◇

Stumbling out of the lower icefall of the Athabasca Glacier, we spot a small group of people skiing up the glacier toward us. Marko, who is ahead, veers toward them to take advantage of the track they're making. As we come closer they stop and huddle together on the flat glacier.

When he is 20 feet away, one of them calls out, "Where are you coming from?" The tone sounds somewhat incredulous. A raw wind is raking up the valley carrying pellet snowflakes that blast against our clothes and our faces.

"North Twin," Marko says, and keeps walking.

"Where?"

"North Twin." Now Marko sounds annoyed with this interruption.

"Where are your skis?"

Coming up even with the group he replies, "We left them there." He turns slightly and pushes the point of his ice axe back towards the black clouds we've just descended from.

"We climbed the North Face." Marko still hasn't stopped walking and is past them, stepping into their ski track. They crane their heads around to watch him go as I approach. Feeling the need to fill in some of the details, I slow my pace.

"We climbed the north face of North Twin and had to descend across the icefield. We've been out five days," I say.

The group turns towards me. I am struck by how clean they look; they seem garishly overdressed. Too much crisp, primary-colored Gore-Tex and fashionable goggles that surely fog up. "We haven't eaten all day and want to get to the road before dark."

They say nothing in reply, and huddle in on themselves, so I resume full walking speed. Then one of them says loudly, "North face of North Twin?" He pauses, and then swivels towards me. "Who are you guys?"

"Nobody," I say. "Just two guys."

The K7 massif taken from the summit of Hajji Brakk; K7 is the right of the two spires in the center, the snow covered peak to the left is K7-West which Marko Prezelj, Vince Anderson and I made a first ascent of in 2007.
STEVE HOUSE

CHAPTER SIXTEEN

K7 is My Universe

Charakusa Valley, Pakistan: June 26, 2004

LATE IN THE DAY THE RAIN STOPS and the clouds perform their slow, alpine striptease. Two-dozen peaks, ranging from thin soaring rock spires to hulking alpine massifs, emerge to ring our small grassy base camp. I can feel my teammates' excitement at seeing this valley for the first time: cameras click, fingers point.

Last summer I visited this Karakoram valley twice – once coming from Masherbrum and again two weeks later when I soloed the virgin 20,000-foot peak I named Hajji Brakk. After that climb, I made four attempts to climb the most compelling objective in the valley: K7.

K7 is the most strikingly beautiful and complex mountain I've ever set foot on. A team of Japanese university students made its first ascent in 1984 via the southwest ridge. The only subsequent attempts were by a small team of Americans, led by Conrad Anker, and an adventurous group of Brits. It was the beginning of the British route that provided the key to the upper mountain.

By the fourth attempt I had refined my systems and my strategy. My pack weighed eight pounds, and I moved with complete confidence – not in success – but in knowing that I could deal with any situation. Though I failed to reach the summit, I realized I possess both the desire and the ability to climb K7 alone by a route of my own discovery. When I left the Charakusa Valley I knew I would return to complete my solo of K7, and I knew whom I wanted to bring with me.

By late winter I had commitments from a solid group of alpinists: Marko would come from Slovenia, plus Jeff Hollenbaugh, Bruce Miller, Doug Chabot and Steve Swenson from home. Pooling our money, we drew permits for K7 along with the unclimbed peaks of Kapura and K6 West. The five of them planned to attempt different objectives with different partners, depending on weather, conditions and individual interests. I planned to acclimate with the group, and then resume my solo project on K7. I trained long, hard and carefully through the winter and spring, eagerly anticipating the coming summer's trip.

◇◇◇◇◇◇◇◇◇◇◇◇◇◇◇◇◇◇◇◇◇◇◇◇◇◇◇◇◇

For the past two weeks the weather has been poor, but I remain ready. My teammates make various plans; they pack and repack, even change their objectives. I stay focused on soloing K7. I have little to pack. My agonizing is not over my gear or my goal; I am tortured by the weather.

Everything I am at the moment, everything I want, revolves around climbing K7. During drizzly afternoons I try not to play the life-isn't-fair game. A two-year-old screams inside my head: mine, mine, mine! I want it! In calm moments, I ask myself pragmatically what I will do if the weather and the conditions prevent me from climbing.

I have one rule for my soloing: never climb alone because I don't have a partner. Soloing must be a journey into a solitary, egoless universe. Whether my efforts result in something my fellow climbers perceive as success or failure is irrelevant. Success, when achieved, is deceptive – for there lies praise, closure, achievement. Failure is the more valuable fruit, borne as it is from the knurled vine of process. Taking up crampons and ice axes after failure forces me to own my shortcomings, learn from them, and to capitalize on the strengths that I found.

With partners I have pitched and belayed my way up some of the biggest walls in the world. In all those thousands of pitches I've fallen only once. What security did the rope really bring? It provided us the confidence to try, to act. By joining together we became stronger because we fought together, because we fought for one another. At the moment of greatest commitment, when we had to climb up and off the mountain to survive, the rope became true partnership.

But I don't want that this time; I can't handle it right now. Since the Slovak Direct four years ago I have not been able to replicate that connection of pure partnership. Subsequent partners have let me down. They did not stay by me or they did not let me in. Marko is a prime candidate now. On North Twin we worked well together, but for some reason the mysterious bond was not formed. One, or both, of us is not ready.

I should have more carefully heeded Scott Backes' warning. I must take my time. Adopt a beginner's approach to climbing; prepare myself for the partner that will once again provide that magical synergy.

◇◇◇◇◇◇◇◇◇◇◇◇◇◇◇◇◇◇◇◇◇◇◇◇◇◇◇◇◇◇◇

In the afternoon there is a bump in the barometer. I depart, climbing through the first rockband of ledgy granite. Leaving the moldering fixed ropes left by the Brits, I switch from rock shoes to boots, and scramble 1,000 feet before making a bivy. I use my ice axe to scratch out a body-length flat spot in the tilted gravel. To ensure I don't roll off, I perch a few large rocks on the downhill edge. Then I roll out my sleeping mat and start the stove to melt snow. A few feet away the edge of a small glacier sweeps up, steepening until it's lost in the thinning mist roiling through the rocky ramparts surrounding me.

Starting at 3 am, I retrace the route I discovered the year before. Past the small bivy cave that marks my previous high point, I pull onto the ridge, a wind-whipped whirl of snow just inches wide at over 20,000 feet. Here my route joins the Japanese route and I continue treading carefully through knee-deep snow on moderate terrain.

After climbing nine-and-a-half hours, with 700 feet to the summit, I am stopped in my tracks. An impenetrable bastion of rock guards the summit ridge. I stare at it, looking for a way to climb it.

I tenuously continue along the left side of the ridge; it steepens. I cling to the sharpened edge, plunging my tools into the snow to gain ground. The snow approaches vertical and becomes too dangerous, too insecure. I retreat and rig my rope to rappel down the right side. I make three raps, searching for a route around this obstacle. At the end of the fourth rappel, I see no possible route and climb back to the ridge crest.

I pause to eat and drink, trying to imagine how and where the Japanese climbers went. They probably stayed close to the ridge; maybe they placed bolts here, for aid climbing. But I can't find any sign of their passage.

I start again, and stay just underneath the right tip of the ridge top. I climb under the curled lip of the cornice; like ducking under a frozen wave. After 50 feet I exit and surmount a big boulder. In the wall above is a bolt.

The bolt is in smooth rock near a 10-inch wide ice runnel that ends atop a 40-foot thin crack the Japanese must have aid climbed. I can't get off the far side of the boulder, so I retrace my route under the cornice and climb down the way I rappelled earlier. After 100 feet, I traverse toward the granite bastion and ascend an ice couloir to the base of the 40-foot crack.

After five feet in the crack the wall steepens and I get spooked. The exposure is tremendous; a fall from here would send me thousands of feet. I place a piton, tie a sling to my harness and clip myself to it. Reaching higher, I place a nut and clip another sling to that. I add another piece of gear in the narrow crack and attach myself to it with a third sling. I place a fourth piece of gear up high, reach down, and unclip myself from the lowest piece and clip that same sling into the new gear. As soon as I'm clipped into three pieces again, I knock out the bottom piton. Leapfrogging, I progress slowly.

After an hour I clip the first bolt. This is where the ice starts and the climbing – for me – becomes easy. I don't even clip into the second bolt as I climb past. The young Japanese must have been new to ice climbing, but good at rock climbing. I hurry, knowing that darkness is coming.

The ice ends under a large, horizontal roof of granite. A foot-size ledge continues to the right. I brush away snow to find handholds. I find tattered remnants of the fixed rope last used in 1984. Unwilling to trust the old rope I continue across, free soloing. As the traverse continues the ledge gets wider until I step onto a snowy shoulder.

Climbing to the top of the shoulder, I look up and see a narrow ridge leading to a short snowfield, which in turn leads to the summit. The way is clear, but I have just two hours before dark and the summit looms three or four hours above me. I can't get there today. To stay out overnight is to forfeit fingers and toes, possibly to die. Accepting this, I fix an anchor and begin descending 7,000 tedious and dangerous feet in the dark.

◇◇◇◇◇◇◇◇◇◇◇◇◇◇◇◇◇◇◇◇◇◇◇◇◇◇◇

Back in base camp failure gnaws at me. And this time I use the word failure decisively. I did not summit K7, and I pushed too far. I had difficulty descending the complex gullies and snowfields in the dark. I was too cold to stop and rest, and one bad decision would have had dreadful consequences. That I escaped does not justify taking so many chances. I need to rein in the risk.

I wish I had summitted and so ended this baleful obsession. I hate that I must go up there again. I am angry that I train so hard for these routes but am unable to climb them. I berate myself for squandering my opportunity to be a professional alpinist; with all this time and support, I am still unable to do the big climbs, the groundbreaking climbs.

At night I lie in my tent, eyes closed, questioning: Where is the line, what risks are acceptable? What price am I willing to pay? Maybe a partner? Should I invite Marko to climb with me? What happened to my relationship with myself? Why am I so isolated from the rest of the world? In soloing did I travel so far within myself that I am unable to return to normality?

In the dark of early morning I wake to the realization that to complete this cycle I must follow the path before me. I am committed. Like the Slovak Direct with Mark and Scott, North Twin with Marko, I must climb up and off K7 to move on, to survive. Anger cedes to frustration. In the daylight my angst has receded; I laugh with my mates again.

◇◇◇◇◇◇◇◇◇◇◇◇◇◇◇◇◇◇◇◇◇◇◇◇◇◇◇

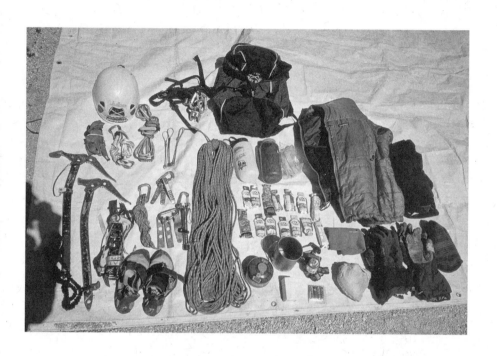

This is the equipment I used on my second to last attempt on K7. When packed, this kit totaled seven pounds. On the successful attempt I eliminated the left-most bundle of slings below my helmet. STEVE HOUSE

At the high point of my sixth attempt on K7, I was above 22,000 feet and the summit of K7 was visible. I was turned back by the oncoming night, the fading light of the sunset is visible behind me. STEVE HOUSE

K7 is my universe. This pitch, my world. The movement, the yellow rock edges toward which I direct my crampons, the crack in which I cam my pick. This is my moment.

I climb past that first bolt 7,000 feet up the mountain. Above a white granite wall I swing my ice tools into old, dirty-white, iron-hard ice. When I lever the shaft of the axe upward, the ice creaks and cracks and sometimes breaks. This time the weather is with me. I started before dusk yesterday and climbed the well-rehearsed lower mountain in the dark, leaving the warmest daytime hours to get past this difficult rock tower below the summit.

The sun is just kissing the western horizon when I stand on the summit. Deep orange rays are broken and scattered by the chaotic skyline of jagged clouds and rugged summits. I feel nothing because, suddenly, there is nothing to feel. My breathing slows. My movements cease. For several quiet minutes I take in everything between myself and the horizon.

K7 lies at the top of the mighty Charakusa Glacier. The peaks of the Kara-koram – K2 and her brethren – lay before me, holding court over the world. I study this view to understand what I have done and where I am. Night is approaching. As I promised Rasool, I take a photo of myself with the Pakistani flag he gave me. Then I dig out my headlamp, flip it on, and start down in the gathering darkness.

I down climb the summit snowfield and traverse back across the stegosau-rus's icy spine to where I am forced to begin rappelling. I pull a steel piton out of my pocket, something I scavenged from the Japanese climbers. I find a diagonal crack in the granite and drive in the piton. I attach a carabiner, one of only 20 I carry, clip in my skinny rope, meant to hold just thrice my body weight, and rappel into the night. I move ceaselessly for the next 14 hours, down climbing wherever I can to save gear and rappelling where I must.

It is midmorning when I walk into base camp. I have climbed K7 alone, by a new route, and in a single 41-hour, 45-minute push. I am exhausted, dizzy as I collapse on the offered stool. Rasool unlaces my boots while our liaison officer, Captain Amin, mixes a large pitcher of Tang. I eat only a little and fall into my tent for that first sleep, the dreamless, unconscious sleep of exhaustion. At dusk I get up and eat again. That night I sleep like a man at peace.

I stood on the summit of Nanga Parbat a few minutes before 6 pm on September 6, 2005. I had first seen this mountain while riding the roof of a bus in 1990. I was 19 years old on June 30, 1990, when I wrote, "The road becomes smoother and I become more tired, all but Henrik and I have gone below. I fall asleep, but a jolt in the road makes me realize how uncomfortable I really am. I get up to shift my position. Before me is a big mountain. At first I see only the base. Then I look up. I quake and shiver with excitement, happiness, and relief. Before me is Nanga Parbat. I am awake now and I am fixed upon Nanga Parbat. Rising out of the barren, dusty Himalayan foothills. Here is a mountain! I first dreamed of trying to climb it over two years ago. Now it is real. I am here. It is already a part of me. I fear it and respect it. I desperately want to stand on its summit. Not to conquer it, but to experience it. I am quite determined to experience it. I will experience as much of this mountain as I can." VINCE ANDERSON

CHAPTER SEVENTEEN

Return to Nanga Parbat

Approximately 26,000 feet on Nanga Parbat, Pakistan: September 6, 2005

Since we left the summit I feel like I could cry. Turning sideways to the slope, I lean back on my uphill leg to lever my downhill crampon out of the snow. I tip forward, my downhill foot plunging ahead, my crampons screech across the rock, catch and settle in place. I hold the skinny six-millimeter rope coiled sloppily around one hand. Vince is tied to the other end; we move down together.

He stops, twisting to look over his shoulder. "Did you see that?" he asks. "It's like," Vince breathes, "another guy."

"Oh yeah. I know." I gasp for four breaths. "The ghosts. Hallucinations."

"Yeah, like someone is following us." One, two, three breaths. Vince is breathing hard too. "I see them." Two breaths. "Then they're gone."

"Hallucinations." I tell him. "I've seen that. Before. Up this high. Keep going."

I gulp for air and force my uphill leg to follow lamely, dragging a little. I lean back again and plunge my foot weakly down the slope. To my right the sun is setting, but I can't see it; we've come off the ridge and the western horizon is no longer visible. Emotion continues to well up in my throat. It tastes like lemonade. After the 1990 expedition, then last year's attempt with Bruce, I have finally climbed Nanga Parbat.

"Let's stop," I say. A step in the rocks offers respite from the exposure. Vince stops and kneels, coughing. He takes noisy, sloppy breaths.

"Put on. DAS parkas. And puff-pants," I gasp and stop for more breaths. I kneel, and lean against the back of my mittened hand. My fingers quickly chill against the freezing rock. My head falls forward, and I see two snowflakes, tiny perfect snowflakes on the toe of my boot. Each one is thin and frail – a cold, bluish-white brazed to the black of my boot.

"And headlamps," I continue. "Will be. Dark soon."

"Yeah. Okay."

Neither of us moves except to heave breaths in and out. I take the pack off, awkwardly setting it in front of me. Breathing. In and out. The pack's fabric cracks noisily, stiff from the cold. I clumsily work the plastic toggle, too afraid to take off my mittens. I hand Vince his parka and pants. I loosen the buckle of my harness. With great effort I stand, the harness drops to my ankles. I zip on my insulated pants, take my parka out of the pack, and put it on too. More breaths. In and out.

Bending to pick up the harness, I have to stop and catch my breath again. I rebuckle the harness over my clothes. I have to take a mitten off to thread the webbing through the steel buckle. The pads of my fingers quickly go numb where they touch the steel and I ball my fingers into a fist and shove them quickly back into the mitten. I work the fingers, flexing them against my palm until the feeling comes back. I hyperventilate through pursed lips as the pain from the cold surges up my arm. I swing the hand a few times and the pain retreats, leaving plain, cold flesh.

I have six inches of clothing on all over my body making me feel fat and clumsy. Drunk on altitude. I'm light-headed and dizzy, but oddly in control.

It's almost dark. I kneel to rub the snowflakes off the toe of my boot. I feel them burning into my toe. I brush them away with my blunt mitten, but they stay. I slap at them with the back of the mitten. Still they remain. I take out my headlamp and put the battery pack inside my jacket and stretch the headband over my hat. My chest heaves in and out.

The Pool Wall, Ouray, Colorado: January 10, 2005, (eight months before)

It's a cold, clear day. Vince Anderson and I are taking a day off from climbing ice near his home to climb bare rock, to feel the stone with our bare fingertips.

"Did we meet in Alaska the first time? Or on that rock-guide exam in New Hampshire in 1997?" I ask.

"I think it was in Alaska, '93 or '94. I remember seeing you there for sure in '95. You and Eli were about to do your route on the Father and Sons Wall."

"Hmmm. I remember seeing you with Rodrigo guiding on the West Buttress. But I have no idea which year that was," I say as I start climbing. The rock is coarse and clean to the touch.

I climb the pitch and lower back to the ledge. Then he asks, "You and Bruce going back to Nanga Parbat?" Vince has known Bruce since his own college days in Boulder.

I unlace my rock shoes. "I want to go back, but Bruce and Michelle want to have a baby. I'm not sure we're the best team for that route anyway."

"What about Marko?" Vince asks, handing me my shoes and socks.

"It's interesting, there is another Slovenian guy going to try the Rupal Face this year. Tomaž Humar."

"Oh, that guy? That guy sounds like a kook." My eyes follow Vince's gaze across the valley to where buffalo are grazing in a field, fenced in and raised like cattle.

"Yeah. He is. But he's huge in Slovenia, a regular celebrity. His recent expeditions have been more reality-TV than alpinism." Vince laughs, obviously familiar with Humar's heavily-reported attempt on Dhauligiri's South Face in 1999. "Anyway, Marko doesn't want to be on the same mountain as Tomaž. He thinks the media will turn it into a competition."

I stand and put on my jacket as Vince ties in to take a turn on the climb. "I've thought about going by myself, but the logistics are immense. I don't know how I could get my pack as light as I had it for K7. It's really big, almost 14,000 feet of relief and ends really high, 26,600."

Vince tightens the laces of his rock shoes and stands up. "You'd need a rope to rappel the face and all the anchors for that." I continue, "It'd be heavy, thirty pounds. Probably too heavy to carry alone."

A wind comes up. I look back over at the buffalo. They are facing away from the wind and nuzzling through the snow to get the new shoots of grass starting to come up. Vince prepares to climb.

As he's about to step off the ledge, I look at him. "What about you? You interested in something like that?"

"Me? Well yeah. I'm interested. I don't have as much experience as you do. But..." he trails off, leaving the thought on the ground as he steps onto the vertical rock face.

I pull in the rope to give him a safe belay. "Think about it. Maybe Nanga Parbat isn't the best place to start, but I've had a real hard time finding good partners lately. People who want to do the same things. You know?"

He doesn't answer, he has climbed above me already. When he lowers to the ledge, the invitation, though neither accepted or rejected, remains open.

Grenoble, France: February 25, 2005

Six weeks later I stand on a broad stage with 15 climbers from six countries and try not to squint at the bright hot lights. Heavy in my hands is a three-inch square crystal trophy. On it is engraved: Prix du Public 2005, Montagnes Magazine, 25 Fevrier 2005. I have just received this award from the 1,400 audience members who voted my solo of K7 as the climb they considered the best of

2004. As the announcer excitedly fires away in French about my audience choice award, a television cameraman pans across and pauses on my face.

The Piolet d'Or – Golden Ice Axe – is the climbing world's pre-eminent and longest running prize. The Oscar of climbing, it was created in 1991 by the Groupe de Haute Montagne, an invitation-only alpine club based in France, and the French outdoors magazine, Montagnes. Their intention was to create an award for "the year's most important alpine performance."

Recently the Golden Ice Axe has been awarded to highly publicized climbs, while a number of excellent ascents done with little self-promotion have been conspicuously ignored. The secretive nomination process chooses six climbs a year. The climbers of these routes are invited to present their ascent to a jury, which is headed each year by a different prominent climber.

Historically, North Americans have been overlooked in the nomination process. I am the second to be nominated in the Piolet's 16-year history, and that came only after two British climbers removed themselves from contention. The British climbers suggested to the editors of Montagne that there were two ascents more deserving of nomination, both done by Americans: my K7 climb and an ascent of Great Trango Tower by Josh Wharton and Kelly Cordes. I was surprised when they chose me. Six months ago, in a widely circulated editorial, I castigated the Piolet d'Or regarding the 2004 winners, writing:

"This (the 2004 award) accomplishes two things. Most sadly, it publicizes an ascent that was accomplished using a style that made the ascent irrelevant to contemporary alpine climbing. Secondly, it demonstrates to me, and to others, that the present Piolet d'Or award is so badly out of touch with alpinism that the award itself has become irrelevant."

The winners that year were two Russian climbers who fixed ropes on Nuptse, a sister peak of Everest. They had gone back three successive seasons, fixing ropes and leaving them for the next season's attempt. After their ascent they rappelled the ropes, leaving them all in place, along with all of their tents, food, fuel, and equipment that they didn't need on the descent.

This year five of the six nominees made their ascents in alpine style, climbing only with one or two climbing ropes, moving the camps or bivouacs with them as they ascend, and taking everything with them off the mountain. The remaining nominee, a large Russian team, climbed expedition style. The 11 Russians had ascended the north wall of Jannu, a mountain of similar height to Nuptse. They unabashedly admitted that they had abandoned 77 sixty-meter-long sections of rope – a total of 15,400 feet of rope – fixed along their route, along with all of their camps and their remaining supplies.

As I weighed the crystal audience choice award in my hand, I wondered if the jury would have the strength and vision to award the Piolet d'Or to a climb done in good style. Or were they under pressure from the primary sponsor of the event, which this year, was Russian.

This image of Vince Anderson captures well the pain and relief we felt. We hurt too much to feel exaltation, though I do remember thinking, "we've done it, we've actually climbed Nanga Parbat," and then quickly looking around to check if there was some higher point. STEVE HOUSE

Vince and I face into the sunset before heading down off the summit of Nanga Parbat. STEVE HOUSE

When the announcer presented the Russian team with the Piolet d'Or, I felt let down, though I had suspected they would win. The Russians pumped the Golden Ice Axe high above their heads. A hundred flashes went off in our eyes. They jumped and proudly slapped one another on the back. I was ashamed to stand next to them. I stepped back and walked behind the row of men. With all eyes on the Russians, I left the stage.

Approximately 26,000 Feet on Nanga Parbat, Pakistan: September 6, 2005

We kneel in the snow 700 feet below the summit of Nanga Parbat facing one another. It is dark now, but I still haven't turned on my headlamp. I reach up and place my hand on Vince's shoulder. Leaning in I put my face just inches from his. Our foreheads almost touch each other, but not quite. In Vince I have found a true partner, the thought of him getting hurt is terrifying.

"This is it, man." I breathe two breaths. "We've done it. We've climbed the Rupal Face." The steam of Vince's breathing shrouds my own face and in the darkness I cannot see his eyes, even this close.

"But none of that matters. Unless we get down." More breaths. The steam from our breathing crystallizes, swirls and disappears in the darkness. "Let's go slow. Be safe."

"Okay," Vince responds. Two more breaths.

"And get down," I say.

I push my fist against a rock, stand up and pause to catch my breath and get my balance. I switch on my light and Vince starts down; we follow the tracks we made in the snow this morning.

As we edge toward the lip of the Rupal Face I see a few tiny specks of light in the valley: cooking fires from the mortarless stone shacks that are roofed with whole young trees, rocks and dirt – the small summer herding villages in the upper Rupal Valley. From here, it is over 13,000 feet to the glacier at the bottom of the wall. Vince descends first. I wrap the rope around my waist and brace myself against a rock. If he falls I'll catch him, or get pulled off trying.

Vince down climbs to the end of the rope. He gives a tug – breath is too precious to shout – and I start climbing. Black rocks jut through the snow. I turn in and kick my crampons for a secure step. In the dark below me, Vince makes a similar effort at a belay. If I fall, he will have a harder time catching me because I would fall down past him and be falling rapidly by the time the rope became tight. I can't fall.

"How you doin'?" Vince asks as I approach.

"Okay. You?"

"Fine. Maybe we should. Start rappelling now," he suggests between breaths.

"Yeah?" I shine my headlamp down the slope; it is a long way down. Rappelling would be safer, but slower. "Okay."

"There is a rock horn here," Vince says. I take off my pack, pass a sling to Vince and rack the ice screws and a little rock gear onto my harness. I put the remaining six slings over my shoulder while Vince threads the rope through the sling we're leaving. With the rope threaded, I coil up the ends and throw the wad down into the darkness. The ropes jerk and sail down, making a soft noise in the snow below us.

"Okay?" Vince asks. He has prepared to rappel.

"Okay." He starts down, moving jerkily.

His light disappears beneath a squat tower and with it a quiet stillness descends upon me. I click off my light and the clouds of breath vanish in the darkness. The sky is full of starlight. We are completely beyond the reach of mankind. No helicopter could aid us here, or find us. We might as well be on one of those stars.

I breathe out forcefully and fill my lungs strongly, and then release the breath, trying to release the day's tension.

"Steve!" Vince's call is strangely directionless.

"Yeah?"

"It's not that hard." I wait for him to take more breaths. "Climb down."

"Okay!" My climbing down will save us one sling, one rappel anchor. That might prove important later. "You got the rope?" I yell.

"What?" echoes back up the cliff.

"You. Have. The. Rope?" I repeat.

"Okay."

I toss the sling, with the rope through it, down the slope. It goes a few feet, and hangs up on a snow step. I plunge my ice axe into the snow and climb downwards. Reaching the step with the rope on it, I brush it away with my crampon; annoyed that Vince hasn't started pulling in the rope yet. The rope tumbles and then slithers down out of sight.

The track turns to the left and traverses. I climb across onto a small narrow ridge protruding from the wall, the top of the large gully we ascended this morning.

"Where is the rope?" I ask.

"You had it," Vince replies.

"No. I thought you did."

"Nooo," he drawls, the implication dawns slowly. Without the rope we will die; there is far too much steep ground to down climb.

"Shit." I start to laugh but instead I choke and start coughing. In 1990, Mark Twight, Barry Blanchard, Ward Robinson, and Kevin Doyle were descending this very face in a storm, at night, and in their depleted state they dropped both their ropes in the very same situation. I start back across the slope to look for the rope.

At the end of the traverse I shine my headlamp past the steps. Twenty feet away, the rope is caught several times around a dark knob of rock sticking out of the snow a mere three inches. Being careful not to dislodge snowballs that might send the rope down the wall, I climb down to the rope and hook it with one axe. I tie a knot in it, clip it to my harness and climb back to Vince.

Breathing hard across the traverse, I look up as Vince snaps a picture. The flash startles me.

"There's a horn here," he says. I pass the rope to him and he pulls it towards him, threading it through a sling. "You go," he says. "You've got the gear." I clip in to the rope and rappel down.

I am finishing the second hole of a V-thread when Vince arrives. He kicks a step and swings one axe into the ice. He thrusts one end of the rope towards me. I stuff it into the hole and using a small metal hook, I snag the tip of the rope and pull it through. I hand the end to Vince and step back. Half sitting in the snow I click off my headlamp to conserve the battery. Vince slowly pulls the rope through the hole to its middle. I rig my rappel device as Vince throws the rope down the slope.

After many rappels I shine my light down the cliff and see the reflective tape sewn into our tent flash back at me. Almost home. One more rappel.

Vince arrives and I already have a sling around a large rock horn. He pulls the ropes and I feed the ends through the sling.

"You go," I say. "Last one."

I hand Vince the rope and collapse in the snow as he prepares to descend. Once he is down, I watch his light struggle toward the tent 40 feet away. His slow progress reminds me how strung out we are. I pick up the rope and rappel to its end. I move quickly, feeling a surge of energy in being so close to the tent. I rush to reach the snow and am soon doubled over by lack of oxygen; my pounding head hurts.

I sit in the snow, still attached to the rappel rope. "Slow breaths," I tell myself, "slow." I inhale deeply, trying to regain a steady rhythm. We are still above 24,000 feet and the altitude is debilitating when I go too hard, too fast.

I unhook my rappel device and try pulling the rope. The rope offers resistance for a few feet and then stops. I stand up straight, wrap the cord around my hand and pull hard, trying to be careful – If the rope suddenly lets go I don't want to be thrown down the steep slope below me. I tie the rope to my harness and take a few steps downhill to take some stretch out of it. I drive both my ice axes in the snow as anchors and holding tightly to them, I bounce my weight down on the rope. Nothing. I fall to the slope, breathing hard.

I sigh. I don't know if I have the strength to deal with this. I put my rappel device back on the rope, tie a knot below it, and start to climb. I have to free the rope. We need it to get down. Frustration cries small and deep inside me. I ignore it; I have no choice.

I down climb a section of Nanga Parbat moments before we nearly lost our rope. VINCE ANDERSON

At the top of the chimney, I find the rope twisted around a block of rough rock. I free it and rappel again from the same anchor, careful to keep the rope clear of that obstacle. At the bottom, I pull the rope and it cleanly piles itself into the snow at my feet.

In front of the tent I kneel in the snow and loosely coil the rope to bring it inside with me. Vince has his headlamp off and I make no sound except the rustling sounds of my clothing and my loud semi-rhythmic breathing. I can hear the stove lightly purring as I reach for the zipper to let myself in.

Vince is lying with his back against the side of the tent with the sleeping bag draped across him. His feet stick out, his boot shells are off, and I can see his bare wrists where his hands are tucked between his legs for warmth. He looks peaceful except for the abrupt rise and rapid fall of his chest. I sit in the tent and unlace my own boots, being careful not to tip the stove. My movements wake him and I notice the water is hot. I shut the stove off to save fuel.

I reach outside the tent and weakly bang my boots together to get some snow off. Looking down, I see the pair of snowflakes still frozen to the toe of my boot. I reach down to brush them with my thumb. When they don't rub off I finally realize that they're ice crystals – something more permanent. Like Vince and I, they are perfectly paired. We've achieved an enduring partnership, attained a place on this mountain.

It's good when your partner is still able to make a joke, even at 25,000 feet. STEVE HOUSE

CHAPTER EIGHTEEN

Success on Nanga Parbat

Rupal Face Descent – 24,000 Feet on Nanga Parbat, Pakistan: September 7, 2005, 10 am

We're late. Vince coils the ropes as I wiggle a pencil eraser-sized brass nut into a split in the greasy gray rock. When the sun hit the tent I woke and started the stove. I kept falling asleep while it ran but eventually we had one quart of water to wash down our breakfast of one GU each, and another quart to take with us. We struck the tent and packed what we have left: a couple more GUs, a single-serving packet of dehydrated bean soup, and one almost full fuel canister.

Now at 10 am, we're just leaving camp. My limbs are thick and heavy. My brain is filled with altitude sludge and my thoughts won't coalesce into words, just ill-defined impressions and feelings. One thought, however, is crystal clear: we need to get down off this mountain, now.

I clip our two ropes – now tied together to enable longer 165-foot rappels – into the single-point anchor and rig my rappel device as Vince tosses the ropes. I start backing up to the edge of the cliff. A thousand feet of rappelling should get us to the Merkyl Icefield. With a drag of my foot I push the last bit of rope over the edge when I suddenly drop, but manage to catch myself right at the edge.

"Whoa!" Vince shouts.

Instinctively I stand up as Vince leans forward to inspect the nut. "That's not good," he says.

"What."

"Ahh. The nut shifted as you started. Give me the nuts, I'll place a back-up."

Six rappels after Vince added the extra nut to the anchor the wide expanse of the Merkyl Icefield seems close. As I start the seventh rappel, I tell Vince, "I think that maybe we could just jump to it." At the end of the ninth rappel we're standing on the snowfield and Vince answers, "Guess we couldn't have jumped for it."

"Yeah, that was a long ways," I agree. "We'd better be careful. I don't think we're thinking too well." Vince nods and ties a loop in the end of one rope, clips it to his harness, and we start walking down together, Vince dragging the joined ropes.

"Now we're on the 1970 route, the Messner route. Down here and just right of that snowy point we have to rappel down an ice cliff." The directions I give are redundant. But they help us keep our bearings, reassuring us that we are returning to the world of the living.

"Right," says Vince, as we walk side by side down the snowfield, coughing only occasionally, our crampons driving in a few reassuring inches with each step. Dropping over 1,000 feet has already made me feel better.

Rupal Face Ascent – 11,500 Feet on Nanga Parbat, Pakistan: September 1, 2005, 4 am

As I walk into the dimly lit mess tent, Vince, hidden in shadow, presses the play button on our little stereo. The opening stanzas of "The Ride of the Valkyries" blasts full volume into the darkness. Charging out of base camp at dawn, we climb unroped for 5,000 feet to our first bivy. Early in the afternoon we scoop snow off the lower lip of the bergschrund, pitch our two-pound tent and crawl inside to rest; safe from the accelerating whiz of falling stones and the relentless heat of the sun.

We wake at midnight to climb while the loose stones remain frozen to the mountain above us. I imagine millions of them perched above and across the massive wall, waiting for the sun's rays to melt the thin layer of ice that holds them temporarily in place. Vince lashes a coiled rope under his pack lid as I start soloing across the steep slope above the bivy.

I traverse left, ice tools swinging easily, boots kicking effortlessly. I am gliding, buoyed by hope mixed with the ever-present fear of failure. I wonder about Vince. Though our friendship spans 10 years, we have not climbed more than a day route together. I am tense about having committed to an unknown partner. Flatland friendship is based on what we tell each other – much of it unverifiable. Each creates the image we want to project, who we think the other would want us to be.

The gully steepens; the ice is thinner than last year when I climbed these pitches with Bruce. Up here there is no hiding. Climbing partners can be as, or more, intimate than spouses. Over the next few days I will come to know Vince as few know him. Climbing big mountains exposes us. For this we must go, try, discover. After an hour of kicking and swinging, the ice ends in a small bowl of snow cut from the rock. I pull up against the left wall to a deep crack in the solid rock and build an anchor.

Vince steps up next to me and begins to rack for leading as I remove the rope from his pack and stack it carefully across my boots. Once tied in, he starts climbing, carrying the lead pack that, though small, still weighs 20 pounds. He reaches the base of the ice, stops, and places an ice screw. His headlamp casts a circular pool of white light around him.

As I watch him work, I am reassured by his attitude. His anxieties are correctly focused on things beyond our control – weather, rockfall – not on doubts about himself. "I don't have the experience you have," he told me when we spent several weeks climbing in Canada to test our compatibility for this venture, "but I can keep going for a really long time." I thought that was a fine answer, finally, to the question I posed him that day at the Pool Wall in Ouray last January.

Vince hacks at the ice several times. "This ice is shit," he says.

"Yeah? It was like that last year. I went up the right flow, even though it looks thinner, the ice was better."

"Okay," he replies. We've talked over these details a hundred times in the last months. I shared everything I learned about the Rupal Face on my attempt with Bruce; breaking it down into pieces so that Vince could digest what would be required each step of the way.

Our surroundings emerge as the sky slips from black to gray. Vince's halo of light recedes before the pervasive soft light of early dawn. The details of the pitch become sharper and I see that the frozen cascade is more anemic than last year. Vince ascends to where the ice narrows and nearly disappears and the wall becomes vertical. I led this difficult and dangerous pitch last year. The ice was too soft to hold a screw, and the rock too broken to take good rock protection. Afterwards Bruce told me that only two of the pieces of gear would have held a leader fall.

Vince still has no gear in. I can hear him panting as he complains, "This pack. Ugh." He sweeps away a few inches of dry, icy snow that sounds like millions of grains of broken glass tinkling down past my stance.

"Is that good?" I shout as he wiggles a cam into some unseen crack in the rock.

"It's okay." He takes the nuts off his rack and fiddles with three before one slots in. It makes a hollow rattle as he jerks sharply down on the nut to test it. With both pieces clipped he starts clearing the snice. He climbs a few tentative moves upwards, the pack pulling him off balance.

"God damn...Ugh. I'm coming down."

"What?"

"I can't lead this with the pack!" he yells. "I'm pumped!"

"Okay." I lean back against my anchor to check the progress of the sunrise. We're in the worst possible place for the warming of the day. Thousands of acres of potentially loose rocks are perched to fall down this ice gully we are climbing. From the top of this pitch we have three easier pitches – two of them we can solo if we really need the speed – before we'll be safe from the rockfall.

I lower Vince to the belay and before he has clipped himself in, I grab the gear and rack up to try the pitch without the pack.

"Ready?" He nods and I'm off, inhaling as deeply as I can, I regain the two pieces he set.

"This gear sucks," I say. "I can't believe you lowered on that."

"Maybe it shifted when I started down."

"Maybe?" I reorient the cam so it seems a little stronger and continue climbing.

I approach an icicle the thickness of my arm that hangs down 10 feet from a black rock roof and pools into a flat plate of blue ice. I place a screw in the ice pool and thread a sling around the icicle, and clip both pieces into my rope.

"This is the hard part," I think, remembering exactly which small fissure I cammed the pick of my ice hammer into 13 months ago.

"How is it?" Vince shouts up.

"Desperate!" I reply. I know that he understands that to mean that I love the tension, the effort, the climbing.

"Don't rush," I remind myself. Deliberately I torque a pick into the rock, test it with a tug, and step up on clear ice. *Whrrrrr*. The first rock sails overhead as the sun's rays touch the upper wall. I press on my right toe and am about to reach up when the ice I'm standing on breaks and I swing against the wall. Very carefully, I reach out and press my crampon point onto a rock edge uncovered by the broken ice. I release the right tool with a gentle, slow wiggle and place it into ice up higher.

At the belay, I remember exactly which piece of gear went where. I tie in and start to haul the smaller pack while Vince prepares to follow.

"Climbing!"

"Okay!" I quickly tie off the pack and let it hang halfway up the frozen waterfall while Vince climbs. When he pauses to take out the first two pieces of gear, I start pulling the pack up hand-over-hand.

"Up rope," Vince calls. I tie the pack back in and take up the slack in Vince's belay. Five minutes later he arrives at the stance winded, the smaller pack still dangling below. While he ties himself in, I pull it up and put it on with the rope still tied to it.

"Belay me," I say as I unclip, grab my tools and start climbing.

After I've gone 20 feet I hear Vince say, "You're on." At that moment a stone eggbeaters past me through the air.

Vince leading up beautiful ice strips on the flawless morning of the third day. STEVE HOUSE

"I'm going!" I find a pace just below my anaerobic threshold and hold it there: my chest is heaving and my legs pump steadily.

"Twenty feet!" Vince yells. I run out the rope, place an ice screw, clip it, and glance down. Vince has already started climbing. Wordlessly we motor toward the safety of the second bivy just a few hundred feet away.

Rupal Face Descent – 23,000 Feet on Nanga Parbat, Pakistan: September 7, 2005, 1:30 pm

Descending the Merkyl Icefield, we near the top of an ice cliff. An old, polypropylene three-strand rope appears out of the snow and angles down to the right. We follow it until it becomes too steep to walk. I turn in and front point down to where it is attached to an ice screw.

Vince stops and kneels, breathing heavily but more smoothly now. Still coughing, but with less pain in his face than before.

"What do ya say? Do we use this old screw?" I ask.

"Well. It is fixed. I don't see why not."

We've been independent of any outside help for seven days, and I'm not ready to start relying on others' relics now.

"We don't need it. I'm drilling a thread." Vince waits patiently as a fog rolls over us in patches.

After the third rappel we can't see 20 feet. Swallowing pride in the interest of expediency, I clip the next fixed ice screw I see. We need to go fast now, and the fastest thing is to use what's available. I'm haunted by past minor transgressions such as accepting food and shelter from the NPS Rangers at the 14,200-foot camp after the Slovak Direct. The lack of visibility is unnerving, but the moist air feels luxurious on the ragged tissues of my throat. This time I rig our rappel from the fixed screw and it brings us to another snow slope which angles sharply to the right. I sit in the snow with my pack on as Vince comes down.

"What's up?"

"I think this is near where Bruce and I joined the Messner route last year. And if I'm right then we need to be off to the left. The crest of the rib that the route follows is on the left."

"Looks like it goes down to the right here." Vince is skeptical.

"I know. But I think that leads to a really big ice cliff and we'd be screwed."

I pause and Vince pulls the ropes. "Whatever you think. I'll trust your judgment here."

"I think to the left. If I'm right we should find more fixed crap: ropes, maybe some kind of anchors, within the next few hundred feet. The old Messner route Camp Three is nearby, if we find that we should bivy and hope for clearer weather in the morning." I stand and start angling to the left.

I down climb facing in even though the climbing isn't steep. The fog is disorienting: visibility is almost zero. It's like climbing inside a cotton ball. No up, or down, no shadows. Just the reassuring feeling of my boots in the snow and my hands on my axes. I move down and across the slope.

I feel a subtle change in the slope angle. To get some depth perception, I scrape my foot across the snow surface, my eyes tracing the track to where it suddenly ends. I kick loose a block of snow and watch it roll twice and be swallowed in the cloud and snow and whiteness. I know the far side drops sharply away: I'm on the crest of the ridge.

"This is it!" I shout into the cold damp wall of wind. I don't know if Vince can hear me. I can't see him and he does not reply. Facing in I continue down, gliding my hand along the ridge crest like a banister. I ache. My legs move on autopilot as my mind molds the rhythm of the wind into the crescendo of a warm Gregorian chant. The pitch rises and falls, the tone deepens. I spot an abandoned piece of fixed rope that confirms we are on route.

Rupal Face Ascent – 17,770 Feet on Nanga Parbat, Pakistan: September 3, 2005, 3 am

Our second camp is safely above the greatest threat of rockfall, so we sleep late and don't get up until 3 am. Soloing by headlamp, we each climb in our individual circles of cool, white light. We follow a small ridge and prepare to cross a dangerous avalanche path. Yesterday we watched tons of snow and ice, loosened by the sun, plummet down this gully. Any one of the avalanches would have crushed a small office building, not to mention a couple of puny climbers.

In the cold darkness the gully is quiet. I pause to listen as my breath slows and I prepare to sprint across to minimize my exposure. I look out to the vivid, warm orange edge of the earth, ragged with the teeth of the Karakoram Range to the north. K2's great pyramid stands tall next to Broad Peak and all seven of the Gasherbrum peaks, Masherbrum and Chogolisa. The K7 and K6 groups frame a parade of subservient mountains marching east across the glowing Indian frontier.

I sprint just before the sun's rays light up the summit 7,000 feet above. Vince watches me cross safely and starts his own ragged, vertical sprint. Once he's joined me, I punch on ahead, searching for a sustainable rhythm. I'm distracted from the monotony by the pink light bathing the white ice wall to which we cling and the buttresses of dark stone checked through with bits of ice and mushrooms of snow.

The valley below remains shrouded in darkness; no cooking fires or lights of any kind are visible. We are already a vertical mile above the churning river, swimming upward in the sublime glow of dawn. I stop to take pictures of Vince coming up below. He grinds steadily upward, closing the gap between us as I scan the horizon. Much of the sky is filled with the mountain above, looking out I can see China and India and south to the Punjab plain of Pakistan.

The day grows warmer, and I am slowed by burning thighs; step, breathe, step, breathe. Gradually the ice steepens and becomes more strenuous until a rib of rock emerges. I climb up its right flank for 30 feet until I need the security of the rope to continue.

I balance on the rocky crest, standing on a small ledge and secure myself to a man-sized horn. I take the pack off. Vince arrives and I remove the rope from his pack and prepare the climbing gear. He clips off his pack, dumping it with a heavy sigh. Vince racks the gear onto his harness, and I flake the rope before handing him some energy gel and a water bag. He squirts the gel into his mouth and takes three large gulps.

He leads through a steep rock barrier to threads of ice gracefully formed by seeping patches of snow. Climbing great alpine walls is more about adventure than the quest for the "good" moves on solid rock that climbers rave about. But this pitch is fun. Under a bright-blue sky I edge my crampons on small wrinkles in refreshingly hard stone, following Vince up the delicate smears of ice.

As Vince leads pitch after pitch, puffs of cloud form against the wall. The climbing is moderate, but hard enough to keep the rope on. He leads a full 165-foot-rope length, places an ice screw, clips the rope in, and we climb together in running-belay fashion. He can do this for five rope lengths because we have five ice screws. I try to do the calculations in my head between steps. "Five times one-sixty-five. Okay five times five is twenty-five, five times sixty is three hundred. Eight hundred and twenty-five feet of climbing between leader changes."

I start my second five-rope lengths of leads – my 825 – as clouds build around us. Between steps my mind wanders. "The end of this block will put us at thirty-three hundred feet of climbing so far today. Is my math right?" And I start again. "Five times five is twenty-five..."

It's dark by the time I finish the fifth pitch. At the anchor Vince gnaws on a half-frozen Snickers bar. My calves burned up, then felt fine, then the burning came on again. So many cycles of pain and relief that I can't remember. Vince is climbing at a snail's pace. I hurt, that I know.

"We've gotta bivy," Vince says as he struggles to cross the last 10 feet to my next belay stance. "I'm wasted."

"Me too. I think we have to go up a bit more and then right. We should get onto that hanging glacier. I just hope we can find an easy bivy."

"No shit!" as he drills his ice tool home with a grunt.

I put my headlamp on over my helmet. It's about to get dark and we've been climbing without more than a few moments rest for 16 hours. "Your lead. You want it?"

"I don't think so."

"Okay." I've done this before, kept climbing at the end of a long day when I didn't want to climb more. I press my cool gloved hands into my face and take a breath. I wish I had some water, but we finished that an hour ago. I know I can physically go beyond this place. I have to. We have to. No choice but to be careful and do it. I exhale and reach for my ice axes.

Two pitches later, I traverse steep ice in the dark toward a fin of snow. I climb that to a block of solid rock and place a good nut in a finger-width crack. The climbing is steep; I'm on my arms, which are fried from the day's thousands of swings. I am dizzy, but somehow my body robotically continues. I drag my pick in the crack until it catches and climb to the right. I reach up and swing. It takes four swings to get the pick solidly lodged. Each swing is progressively weaker.

I step one foot out to the right; the pack drags me off balance. My feet hurt. I make another move, somehow, and another, and I'm standing on a solid shelf of ice. I put in a screw before the retching starts.

I drool and hack, my body heaving. Nothing comes up. The stomach pain is otherworldly, transcendent. I think I might faint. "Is this what it takes?" I ask myself. With no answer, I grip the ice screw with one hand and my ice axe with the other, bracing for the next wave.

Vince's voice calls through the darkness. "You okay?"

I can't speak. I try to breathe, strings of saliva slap against my chin and my nose is suddenly heavy with snot. I double over, and retch again. Some bile dribbles from my mouth.

Breathe, breathe, breathe. I force my chest open and my posture straight. Pull it together. I finish the pitch by climbing the ice rib. As I place an anchor I can see the maw of a huge crevasse splitting the chin of the hanging glacier: a perfect bivy site, just one pitch of moderate ice away. I look at my watch, midnight. We will be able to pitch our tent on flat snow, sheltered by the overhanging roof of the serac.

Rupal Face Descent – 19,700 Feet on Nanga Parbat, Pakistan: September 7, 2005, 3 pm

The fixed rope, bleached white by untold years hanging in the sun, disappears again into a slope of blue ice. I clip our rope to it, a half-hearted attempt to protect Vince and I from a catastrophic fall, and back down, slowly now. Vince is moving faster on the easier slope above and has no way to know that I've slowed. Because of the difference in our pace, the rope pools around my feet. I try to hold it out of the way with one hand and continue backing toward the dark apparition of a rock tower that I hope marks the gully of the lower Messner route.

The tower is round and broken down, but near its flank we find a large frozen coil of fixed rope and a sling of pitons. We're on route. This old rope is useless, but the pitons are a goldmine. We've left most of our rack above. All we have left is a couple of nuts and one ice screw. As long as we have that one screw we can drill V-threads from which to rappel. But it's a frustrating and tiring chore; each V-thread takes 10 minutes of concentrated effort.

As Vince arrives at the stance I take a medium-size piton from the sling and hammer it into a crack. I clip one of my last carabiners into it and rig the rappel.

"Nice to score some pins," Vince says as he pulls a headlamp out of his jacket pocket in the descending dusk.

"For sure." I lean my weight onto the rope. Instead of the hard reassurance of an anchor, I sit back and then slowly keep moving. I jump up. "Whoa!"

"Shit." Says Vince looking at the half-dislodged piton I had just placed. The rock was just frozen together without being solid. In a rush of adrenaline I spin in the ice screw to make another V-thread.

Two rappels later the adrenaline has faded and I'm laboring to make another V-thread. Vince flips off his light and stands next to me. The fog thins and reveals a thick crop of stars. Below us in the valley, we see five large fires burning.

"Hey. Looks like there's a party going on down there," Vince says.

"For us, I'm sure," I say. The very idea that the two of us are visible to the inhabitants of the Rupal Valley, two tiny black dots on this infinite landscape of ice and stone, is absurd.

I'm suddenly aware that Vince is standing stock still. "I hear drumming," he says. "Seriously." He holds up a hand, begging my silence. "I think I hear drumming."

Several times during my expeditions to Pakistan I've witnessed celebrations beat out on improvised instruments such as plastic barrels and kerosene jugs. These local songs are sung to jubilant rhythms and I've often been impressed by how happy these people seem to be, living off their bony herds of goats and a small hand-irrigated plot of potatoes. I can't imagine what the whole valley would be celebrating tonight.

I cock my head down towards the valley. "You're crazy." I stand still for one more moment. "I don't hear anything. I think you're hallucinating again." I turn back to building the anchor.

Rupal Face Ascent –20,000 Feet on Nanga Parbat, Pakistan: September 4, 2005, 8 am

"Rise and shine," I announce, as the brush of sunlight wakes me. I sit up and lean out of the tent to start the stove. When we crawled inside at 1 am last night we were so worked that all we managed was a bit of soup and one pot of water before we slept.

"Do or die," Vince says in a faint, ironic voice, flat on his back and groggy from lack of sleep. Indeed, it may now be impossible to descend the 10,000 feet below should we fail to make the summit. From here we must find our way up to the Messner route, and then down climb and rappel from V-threads.

Descending the way we came would require thousands of feet of rappelling where the only anchors would have to be found in the rock for which we lack the gear. Our rack consists of nine pitons, six nuts, five ice screws, and three cams. Without a radio or support team, we have no one to ask for help. If we don't get rehydrated and refueled we'll be compromised. We've breached 20,000 feet of altitude and we will eat and drink less and less as we get to more extreme altitudes.

As the snow melts in the pot I take out our three photographs of the wall. They offer few hints about the next section. From the valley our binoculars hadn't revealed any solutions. But my instinct, born of many smaller walls, tells me that we will find our way through.

Far away now, is that boy of 19 who, with a Slovenian expedition, laid at the base of this wall and wondered what he didn't know about himself. I have been shaped by 16 years and a million decisions made: what I learned, how well I trained, when we went, how long we waited for good weather, for good conditions, where we chose to climb. The sum of my past actions doesn't determine who I am, but it certainly determines who I may become.

I wonder about Vince. I don't know what seas he has crossed, what has shaped him. I have noticed that he perceives subtleties in life and art that I miss in my rush to juggle as many projects and activities as I can handle. On the outside Vince looks unapproachable. He often wears anti-religious, pornographic T-shirts. He has multiple body piercings, wears dangling chains and studded black boots. He plays music – Norwegian black metal – which virtually no one else appreciates. This veneer hides a stoic, quiet demeanor and a sensitive, thoughtful, highly articulate person.

At noon we've been climbing for two hours and we need food and water. I cut a stance in the ice. There is one big unknown left, one section of headwall still hidden. Vince arrives, but we don't speak.

I shoulder my pack and start up, uncertainty weighs heavily. "This has to go," I think as I traverse up and right. Slowly, a hidden corner opens to reveal a broad, chalky flow of ice rolling upward. "Pay dirt!" I holler back to Vince. "It goes! Easy!"

Pushing too hard, 150 feet later I'm exhausted. Foolishly, I've just soloed vertical ice with my pack on at 21,000 feet. My irrational exuberance could have killed us both, but I realized it after I was too far up to climb back down. Ashamed at my bad decision and the potential consequences for my partner, I lower the rope to Vince who waits patiently.

Some of the best ice on the route was on this pitch that I am leading in a gully that will take us through the over-whelmingly steep headwall to my right. We climbed as fast as we could throughout the afternoon; we hadn't seen a bivouac site all day. VINCE ANDERSON

As evening nudges me onwards I admonish myself: "No mistakes, Farmboy." Fifty feet above my last ice screw I start chopping at the cornice. "If I can get on top of this ridge maybe we can get a good bivy."

The cornice breaks suddenly and my body swings out over the dark valley 11,000 feet below. My full weight falls onto one tool as hard blocks of snow crash towards Vince. I hear the dull slaps as they hit him, and then I hear his moans. I step up, slam the shaft of my other tool into the newly exposed slope and pull across. Adrenaline pumping, I scurry down a few feet on the opposite side.

I call down. "Are you okay?"

"Fine," Vince responds, his voice cracking.

He doesn't sound fine, but there's nothing I can do. I continue along the ridge for 20 meters until I find solid rock and build an anchor by headlamp. As I belay Vince, my head pounds from the altitude. He rounds the corner.

"You okay?" I ask again.

"The biggest pieces missed me, but a smaller one hit me on the shoulder pretty good. How's this look?" he asks dubiously, eyeing the extremely narrow crest.

"Well," I grab Vince's pack and reach in to find the small shovel he carries, "let's find out."

With a resigned scowl, he takes the shovel from me. "Yeah. Let's."

Rupal Face Descent –15,000 Feet on Nanga Parbat, Pakistan: September 7, 2005, 7:45 pm

We're down to 15,000 feet. We've descended 11,000 feet since leaving the summit three days ago, but we still have nearly 3,000 feet before we get off the face and another 1,000 feet of hiking down to base camp.

At the next anchor, Vince takes off his hat and his headlamp accidentally flies down the slope. We wordlessly watch the light skip down the steep ice gully and disappear. I start the next rappel and my headlamp batteries die when I reach the ends of the ropes. At midnight I rappel by starlight.

Summitting Nanga Parbat had stripped us to our most basic essential selves. Now each step of this descent is a high-pressure debridement of that rawness. Pain immerses me. I don't crave food or water, just rest: to lie down and let my bones sink into a good flat piece of earth.

Earlier, Vince complained about foot pain, apparently a persistent problem for him. But now he is silent. His artistic aesthetic holds suffering in high regard. That, I think as I rappel away from Vince, his head hung forward, is a man living his ideal.

Near the end of the rope I notice a pointy blackness where no stars shine. It's a serac, a house-sized piece of ice. Toggling the switch of my headlamp I get a brief burst of faint light before it dies again. Sure enough, there is a flat area at the base of the serac. I climb over, stand comfortably and unclip. I'm too tired to notify Vince of my discovery. As he rappels toward me, I kneel and tease the tent out of its stuff sack. It's 1 am.

Inside the tent, Vince cooks our last bit of food: a single packet of instant bean soup. With the first bite he gags and spits.

"Ugh, sand!" he moans.

Without a light he hadn't noticed that the snow here is full of dirt, rocks and sand. He dumps out the soup, and in the darkness, excavates down to what he thinks will be clean snow. We dine on tepid water.

In the morning the fuel canister sputters under a half-melted pot of water. We take turns drinking down the icy broth before piling out of the tent. At such a low altitude and with such fatigue, our sleep has been sound and I am refreshed, but as I stand, the exhaustion and pain returns.

At noon we step off of the Rupal Face.

Rupal Face Ascent – 24,000 Feet on Nanga Parbat, Pakistan: September 5, 2005, 11 am

Day five and we slowly climb the upper gully, which has gradually become less steep. Our goal is to find a good bivy as early as possible so we can rest for the summit attempt tomorrow. At two in the afternoon, at about 24,250 feet, we discover a snow arête and quickly excavate a good tent platform. Our tension, drawn tight for so many days, releases like a relaxed bow. We know that from here we can reach the 1970 Messner route and descend if necessary. I lounge in the tent, enjoying the warm sun.

At half past midnight the alarm chimes. Summit day. Vince, again not having slept, starts the stove and we begin the wait. I stare at the flame, willing it to burn hotter, but the altitude takes its toll on the mechanical as well the human.

At lower altitude mixed climbing is enjoyable, but 100 feet out of the tent I struggle to make even the easiest moves as I fight my cold, oxygen-starved body. When we reach the end of the rock, we tie the climbing rope and most of the gear to a big boulder. We continue with one rucksack containing food, water and clothes, and a five-millimeter static rope for the descent. The one without the pack breaks trail.

The couloir we're following steepens, and the snow gets deep and loose. Vince wallows in the lead.

"Do you think it could slide?" I ask. An avalanche here would send us for a 12,000-foot fall.

Vince replies that it seems okay, but we both get quiet. Around us, the field of white seems to separate into individual crystals; innumerable factors that configure our success or failure, life or death. At this altitude, it's hard to know whether our perception, let alone our judgment, is reliable. I take my turn up front, pushing the snow down with my ice tools, crushing it with my knees, then stomping it with a foot so I can raise myself up a few inches. After five minutes, I step aside and Vince has a go. For over two hours we work like that, taking turns up front so we can progress together.

The sixth consecutive clear sunrise colors our rarified world in soft pink. We have gained only 200 feet in two and a half hours: Impossibly slow. We keep working. There's time left in the day. All our accumulated actions push us forward: all the steps, all the swings, all the luck. And before that, the hours, days and years of preparation.

In the sunlight, I discern a ripple of wind texture on the snow near a rock wall. With one crampon scratching for edges on the rock, and one in the snow, I make faster progress. Soon we've gained another 200 feet, and the snow stiffens to where it begins to support our steps. There is unspoken relief, but no certainty.

At 25,000 feet, with the sun high, I'm stripped to a shirt, gloveless, hatless and sweating. I can imagine the summit hiding just behind the crest, but my confidence is so shaken that it seems improbably far. Vince leans his head against his axe, exhausted from four mostly sleepless nights and six marathon days.

The wall drops away below. On its crest we scratch out a place to rest.

"How...ya...doin'," I spit the question between breaths. It's so hard to breathe here. Vince looks up, holds his fingers like a pistol and points it at his temple. It hurts to laugh, but I do. If he still has his sense of humor, black as it may be, then he is in good enough shape to continue. Vince shuts his eyes and looks peaceful as he gasps for air. He has pushed beyond all limits, beyond all pain into this, a solitary state of grace.

I strip my sweat-soaked socks, attach them to the rucksack, and reboot with bare feet. When we start again, our pace is slow and our altimeter reads only 25,250 feet, 1,400 feet below the summit. I hope it's wrong. We wanted to be on the summit by 2 pm, and now I realize how much the deep snow set us back. The sky is clear and windless.

At 2 pm I pause, turn, and announce the time to Vince. The steady look in his eyes tells me what I need to know. There will be no turning back now. I keep breaking trail toward the summit.

At 4 pm we crest a false summit and see the true summit 100 yards away. We rest on a big flat rock, the first place we are able to sit unroped in six days. Vince lies back and soon falls asleep. I put my now-dry socks back on, shake Vince awake, and follow him as he makes the last steps.

Rupal Face Descent – 12,000 Feet on Nanga Parbat, Pakistan: September 8, 2005, 2 pm

Back at tree line Vince and I each follow our own cow trails through the juniper. Suddenly four Pakistani men are running towards us, shouting and waving. I flinch, and try to hide behind a scraggly shrub.

"Great," I think. "What a perfect time to be captured by a Taliban warlord." A tall bearded man in Muslim dress throws his arms around me; I brace weakly against the coming blows. But he hugs me, bouncing me up and down as he dances with me held tightly in his arms. I get my elbows up and push him away, trying to focus on his face. With my hands flat against his chest I squint and try to remember another human. It's our assistant cook Ghulam.

He releases me, smiling, and gleefully shouts something unintelligible and walks a few steps downhill.

"Ghulam?" but he disappears around the other side of a large juniper tree as I follow. I see Vince sitting on his pack drinking from a bottle of water as our liaison officer Aslam stands proudly, preparing to open a box of cookies.

"Steve-sab," Aslam shouts, and I endure another bear hug, before dropping my pack and taking the water from Vince. It is sweet and viscous and filling.

Rupal Face Ascent – 26,660 Feet at the Summit of Nanga Parbat, Pakistan: September 6, 2005, 5:30 pm

The light is low and the massive shadow of Nanga Parbat reaches across several valleys to the east. My crampons crunch into the summit snow; Vince follows just a few paces behind. Just before the top, I kneel in the snow, overwhelmed by emotion. Years of physical and psychological journey – to make myself strong enough, to discover whether I am brave enough – all fold into this one moment. It seems sacrilegious to step onto the summit.

Watching Vince arrive I know that I could not have completed this climb without him. I stand as he approaches, and I take one step backwards onto the summit of Nanga Parbat. Vince joins me in an embrace. Frozen tears fall to the snow at my feet, becoming part of Nanga Parbat, as it became part of me so many years ago.

An hour before sunset, two exhausted men descend from the summit of Nanga Parbat. It should be deeply frightening to gaze out over the Rupal Face at dusk – and it is. Perhaps nowhere on earth are you so far away from life. In the dark, fear and pain seem more appropriate. Home and love are just flickers of my imagination in the hollow darkness.

In that moment, I understand that on the outer edge of infinity lies nothingness, that in the instant I achieve my objective, and discover my true self, both are lost.

Vince and I with our celebratory aprons constructed of prayer cards, tinsel, and money. We had been given many flowers, leis, and bouquets. The Pakistanis love fresh flowers and they often give them as gifts to one another. STEVE HOUSE COLLECTION

CHAPTER NINETEEN

Coming Home

Rupal Valley, Pakistan: September 10, 2005

AFTER TWO DAYS VINCE AND I – and 30 men carrying our expedition equipment – walk out of base camp. We hike in T-shirts and jeans; neither of us carries a pack. Following a narrow stream, I traverse the meadow, round the rocky terminus of a glacier, and cross a small log bridge. On the far side of the bridge I sit down, exhausted by the 20-minute walk.

Fida, our base camp cook and my companion on three expeditions, comes up and sets down his towering pack. He takes out a box of cookies and breaks the seal with his teeth. I greedily eat a stack of cookies and wash them down with Fida's water. We start walking again.

We catch Vince on the far side of the next meadow. Halfway up a short hill he sits on a boulder.

"Tired?" I ask as I slowly climb towards him.

"I can't believe how tired I am."

"Fida's got some cookies. I had to stop right back there." I keep walking as Fida leans his pack against a boulder and hands Vince the remaining cookies. Fida unscrews the cap on his bottle while Vince devours cookies, two at a time.

At the top of the hill I cross the rocky surface of a dying glacier and pause at the top of the descent on the far side.

Fida approaches. "Cookie sir?"

"Yes, please Fida. Very tired."

"I know sir." He smiles. "Very tired is good sir."

I descend into a shallow canyon that leads into a small village. A collection of mortarless stone huts without so much as a chimney, let alone electricity or indoor plumbing.

"Congratulation." A gray-bearded man appears suddenly in a doorway. I stop and look at him.

"For what?" I ask.

"For cross the Nanga Parbat." He gives me a look, as if it should be obvious.

"For cross the Nanga Parbat?" I repeat, but do not understand. "Cross the Nanga Parbat? Oh, summit." But how could he know about our climb? We have been down only two days. Word must spread quickly among these herders. "Thank you. You have a very nice mountain here. A very beautiful valley." I turn to walk away.

"*Allah ak bar*. Thank you. We watch you every night."

I halt, and look at him. "What? No. Watch us?"

Mischievously he looks up at me from underneath bushy eyebrows sprouted with gray. He steps back and disappears into the dark house. Moments later he steps through the threshold with an old pair of binoculars.

"For looking goat," he says and then points up to the Rupal Face, which is now wrapped thickly in cloud. "Every night. We see light." He touches his own forehead, then points at mine.

"Ahhh. Okay." They saw our headlamps each night.

"All valley," he says spreading his hands to encompass the five villages scattered up the Rupal Valley, "watch you go summit. Then we no see. Long time no see. Very worry. Down coming in nighttime. Very dangerous. I watch, my own eye." Excitedly he points to the binoculars again and then gestures towards the upper wall. "Then next day. You coming very fast down." A tone of admiration seeps into his voice. "We make fire so you find valley. We make big fire so you come this village. We kill goat. Much drumming. All boys dancing." He demonstrates a jig in front of his house.

"Ahh. The drumming! That was you? Thank you. Thank you. Vince… we, we could hear the drumming," I say, afraid that the next step will be an offer of tea, which it is very rude not to accept.

"Every village drumming," he says, spreading his arms and looking down the valley to the other villages that we can see by the faint clouds of smoke.

"Every village drumming? Wow. That is wonderful. Thank you. I must go. Jeep come today." I try to take my leave.

"Today?" He suddenly looks concerned. "Hmm. Yes. You go. *Aslam Alekum*. Peace be with you.

"*Alekum salam*," And peace be with you, I intone the traditional reply.

The afternoon sun burns through the clouds and the heat slows us even further. Fida runs between Vince and me. Again and again he catches me on the brink of exhaustion and fuels me with cookies and water. At the last hill I grind slowly upward, taking small steps and zigzagging back and forth in the trail to find the subtlest angle of ascent. Vince stands with Fida amid a small group of porters at the top of the hill.

I crest the hill, sit and lean against a large boulder. I look down at the village 100 yards below hoping to spy our jeeps. If the jeeps are there, we can make Chilas tonight. Chilas is the first town with a real hotel: hot showers, running water, tables and chairs, and proper beds. Not to mention baked nan bread and fresh fruits and vegetables.

I see a couple hundred people, sitting in a large group just outside the village. But there are no jeeps. The American embassy in Islamabad had warned Americans against traveling in this area. They advised "American citizens to avoid all gatherings," and had cited "recent Taliban activities in the Rupal Valley."

"What's that?" I ask.

"For you sir," answers Fida, looking unconcerned.

"For us?" I look at Vince.

"Mmmhmm," Fida replies, arms crossed and leaning on a separate boulder across the trail.

My skepticism returns. "Ah, shit."

"For you to cross the Nanga Parbat," Fida says. "Not shit." As I lift my gaze from my friend's kind eyes and look down at the crowd, it dawns on me that this is a welcoming party. The people are all standing now and look like they're organizing themselves into two lines along the trail into town. I quickly recount my recent encounter to Vince.

"Really? So you think this is a good thing." Vince's arms drop and his hands go to his pockets.

"Yeah. I think it is. But I don't have much energy for it right now," I reply.

"Yes sir. For you. You very famous men now," Fida says, spreading his arms and looking at us. "This, very poor place. They like you make big climb. Good for village. All poor village. Some have no school. No electric. Water very bad."

"Ahh. Okay. P.R. I get it. Come on, let's go. The sooner we get through this, the sooner we get to that hotel," I say as I get up.

We descend the wide trail through thick trees and round a corner by the tall white brick wall of the girls' school and walk into the open meadow. Thirty or 40 men, dressed in fine, clean clothes flank the trail. One is wearing a tan sports coat, another a nice Norwegian sweater; the others wear traditional vests and flat hats rolled up at the edges. All wear shoes. They hold banners unfurled behind them and strung across our path.

I recognize the man in the sports coat: it's Aslam, our liaison officer. And the one in the nice sweater is Ghulam, Fida's assistant. They each hold a kind of ornamental apron that ties behind the neck and waist. They are adorned with bright red cards inscribed with Arabic script – Islamic prayers for prosperity –

and printed with red, purple and yellow flowers, all trimmed with gold tinsel and 10 rupee notes.

A young boy runs forward and hands each of us a glass bottle stuffed with beautiful wildflowers. I walk toward the crowd. Vince follows closely behind. Aslam and Ghulam approach and lift the aprons; we pause as they drape them over our heads. I'm laughing now, and raise my camera to snap a picture of Vince grinning and showing off his new garb. The aprons are the ultimate in Islamic formal wear – I've seen them worn at large weddings. Vince still wears the gift I gave him at the beginning of the trip: a blue, flat-brimmed baseball cap inscribed with the slogan, Hang Loose. The contrast is striking.

I hesitate for a moment, and then Vince and I walk forward. The crowd begins to applaud as we pass under the first banner, which reads, "Congratulation to Summit Team. Mr. Steve and Vincent." Several boys in school uniforms approach and hand us bouquets of flowers. One has sewn fresh flowers together in leis and we bow as he places them over our heads.

People are clapping for us as we walk past. Many hold signs. One reads, "We pray for long lives of USA expedition team." It is signed Al Iqbal, public school of Tarshing. The school is one of five in the valley to which we donated 100 notebooks and 100 pencils on our way in to the climb. Several banners read, "Welcome to Summit Team." We continue past the men. The only women are the teachers and students of the girls' school. They hold their scarves tightly to their chins and watch us pass with big brown eyes.

We are led into the town's central courtyard and the students all file in behind us. Chairs and tables have been set out. The white plastic tables are decorated with flowers stuck into bottles and laden with store-bought cookies and a selection of Western brand sodas. The children fan out and organize themselves around the grassy perimeter, squatting or sitting cross-legged. We are directed to two seats at the center, immediately across from an improvised podium adorned with a colorful tapestry.

Aslam sits next to me as a tall, thin man in a perfectly clean black shalwar qameez with overdone pleats walks to the podium. He starts talking in a loud voice, gesturing towards Vince and me, then at the audience around him that has grown silent.

Aslam leans over. "This is mayor of Tarshing. Now he saying what you do. How you first to climb Rupal Face alpine style." He pauses, listening, "and how this is great thing for mountaineers, and great historic moment for their mountain."

I twist my head sideways, and sure enough, Nanga Parbat has cleared, rising as a beautiful backdrop to this village. Puffy clouds building towards the summit in the afternoon heat make the mountain even more dramatic.

"He is telling how, as a boy, he was playing soccer with the team from Her-

The students initiated the big welcoming ceremony given to us in the village of Tarshing by lining the approach to the village with signs, banners, and loud applause. STEVE HOUSE

rligkoffer," continues Aslam. "And Reinhold and Günther Messner were playing too. How they later went to the summit and after, Günther died going down Diamir side of the mountain."

From behind me a boy taps on my shoulder and holds out two perspiring bottles of 7-Up. I take them, nod gratefully, and hand one to Vince. We suck them down quickly. The mayor continues talking, but Aslam seems to have tired of translating. Someone passes us two more bottles of soda and a plate of cookies.

Chamonix, France: September 16, 2005

A week later, I haul my three overstuffed duffel bags onto the platform of the train station in Chamonix, France.

"Steve!" I hear a familiar cry.

"Mom." My mother comes up, her legs pumping fast, and gives me a big hug. "We're so glad to have you back."

My father saunters up, slipping his pipe into his pocket. "Congratulations," he says, putting his arms around me.

"Thanks. That one meant a lot," I say as I hug him back.

"I'm sure it did. We want to hear all about it."

"You must be so tired!" Mom exclaims.

"Yeah. I'm pretty tired. Are you guys having fun?" I hoist a duffel onto my shoulders as Dad starts to lift another.

"Jeeesh. This is heavy!" he says.

"Seventy pounds. Let me take one handle and you take the other. Mom, can you get the pack. I'll come back for the third bag. How's your trip going?"

"Great. We went to Interlaken and Grindelwald, and absolutely loved Lauterbrunnen. But we can't wait to go to Slovenia with you. That will be a real treat," replies Mom.

"I'm looking forward to it, too. Marko called me while I was on the train. He's very excited for us to come. And they're planning some kind of party in Maribor, with my old alpine club. Ljubo and Dušan are both coming. I want you to meet them."

Maribor, Slovenia: September 25, 2005

Ten days later I pilot the rental car up a familiar cobblestone country road that I last traveled on a bicycle 16 years ago. It winds past three ponds, over a short but steep little pass and down into a hidden valley. The light of the rising moon silhouettes the surrounding forest. I continue to the end of the road and pull into a cobble-paved parking area half filled with shiny Volkswagens, Citroëns, Mercedes, a BMW and a red 1970's era Alfa Romeo sport coupe.

"Wow. Things sure have changed in Slovenia since 1988," I say looking over the cars and then taking in the surrounding buildings. "There used to be nothing here. Just a barn and some hayfields."

An expansive red brick porch is lit with numerous large candles stuck on poles, in planters and on the tops of the tables. A tan stone building rises three stories; an orange glow shines out of the peaked windows, which hold pots of tired red geraniums waiting for the first frost. We step out of the car and walk towards the double wooden doors.

The doors swing into a large bar room. A middle-aged man with the first signs of gray in his beard looks up. "Štef!" Dušan cries, and rushes over.

"Dušan! *Kak si?*"

He shakes my hand, laughing, and pulls me into a hug. "*Dobro. Dobro.* And this is your mother and father. No?"

I step aside for my mother. "Hello Dušan. I'm Marti. So nice to meet you."

"And I'm Don." My dad briskly shakes Dušan's hand.

"This is really wonderful! We are so happy you make visit to Slovenia. Come on, come on, have a drink. We are taking a very good Slovenian wine now." He looks down the tile bar for the barkeeper. "*Čuj! Ti! Daj tri kozarci za vino!*"

The room slowly fills. Many of the faces are familiar, though much older now. I am older too, I think to myself, shaking the hand of another climber I knew many years ago. Dušan chats with my mother in the English he's learned in his new job networking computers. Haltingly, but efficiently, he asks her all about her trip around Slovenia.

After dinner the president of the Planinsko Društvo Kozjak, the Mountaineering Club Kozjak, a part of the Slovenian Alpine Association, takes the floor.

"Štef. *Priti sem.*" He calls me forward. "Many of you knew Štef as a young boy. Not quite a man yet, he came to this club in 1988, when Ljubo was president."

"Oh. That was really a long time ago, before the mountains were so big!" someone quips from the back.

The president presses his hands down in the air in front of him to control the laughter. "In the time he was with us he made some good ascents and earned his alpinist diploma. He then enlisted on the expedition to Nanga Parbat led by Tone Golnar. As all of you know, Štef, and his partner Vince, made very great, very historic ascent only one month ago. And it is the great pride of this club that young Štef started here, with us."

A few start in with applause and the whole room picks it up. A few raise their glasses boisterously to pour more drink down their throats. "Yeah! Štef!" someone hoots.

The president again spreads his hands to quiet the crowd and reaches into his back pocket, removing a small case. "And so it is a great honor for me tonight, to give Štef this pin."

Our reception in Tarshing was entirely unexpected by us. We had no idea that our climb would be so celebrated by the local population. STEVE HOUSE

He opens the box and holds it up for all to see. A few start to applaud, this time he overrides them with a booming voice. "This gold pin is the symbol of the lifetime member of Planinsko Društvo Kozjak, and Štef," he turns towards me, "In honor of all your achievements, it is my great pleasure to make you the seventh lifetime member of our club."

The crowd stands and applauds. Behind the bar someone bangs on a pot. I blush and stand still as the club president fastens the pin securely to my breast.

Ouray Ice Festival, Colorado: February 4, 2006

The last image, showing the very tip of Nanga Parbat's summit emerging from the clouds, flashes on the screen. The standing room only crowd at the Ouray Ice Festival is silent.

"That's our story," I say into the microphone, glancing at Vince who doesn't indicate that he has anything to add. "Thanks for allowing us to share it with you." The crowd breaks into applause and I drop the microphone with relief.

∞∞∞∞∞∞∞∞∞∞∞∞∞∞∞∞∞∞∞∞∞∞

It has been a hard few months since I came home from Slovenia. I lost 20 pounds on Nanga Parbat and starting to rock climb again has been painful in my weakened state. My girlfriend Jeanne and I had been soaring on the euphoria of our new romance prior to the expedition. Since coming back my constant irritability has led to frequent bickering.

Editors hounded me for an article and photos. With great effort I'd scratched out 4,000 mediocre words and reluctantly sent them to *Alpinist* magazine. I wrote a second, very factual, account for the European climbing magazines. I now found out just how many climbing magazines exist in Europe. It seemed every country had two and all of them wanted exclusive rights to the article and images. But none wanted to pay. Most offered less than $200 for both the writing and photography. Too tired to negotiate, I sent them what they wanted. The one bit of routine I had enjoyed was traveling to California to work with the product developers at Patagonia, where I'm always treated like family.

∞∞∞∞∞∞∞∞∞∞∞∞∞∞∞∞∞∞∞∞∞∞

The audience in Ouray runs down the usual questions.

"How cold was it?" asks a man in a bright red down jacket.

"Well I don't know, we didn't have a thermometer, but I guess it was probably around zero on the summit."

"What did you wear?" A woman holding a full pint of beer asks from the back.

"Long underwear, insulated soft shell pants, and insulated overpants. Same on the top, except add one layer."

"How much did it cost?" asks a young kid wearing a Red Sox cap.

"$10,400 divided by four of us. There were two other friends of ours sharing our permit and base camp. They were attempting to climb the Schell route in alpine style. Oh, but that doesn't include airfares."

"What's next?" asks a man whose long legs stretch into the aisle.

"Another beer for me. This glass had a hole in it."

Among the 20 or 30 raised hands, I see a small woman in the back lift her hand tentatively. I try to pick the women. They often ask thoughtful questions; the men seem to focus on the somewhat banal technical details.

"Yes?" I say, looking at her. The woman looks surprised, pointing at herself. "Yes, you in the back."

"How does it feel to have done this amazing climb?" she asks.

Now someone has my attention. "Good question." I look at Vince in case he wants to take it. He gives me a "good luck buddy" glance, and I turn back to the audience. I know the answer to this one. "Honestly, it feels empty. I've been having a really hard time since we've been back. I think that this was such a huge goal for me, and such a long journey to get to the point where I could even consider climbing the Rupal Face, that instead of feeling relieved, or…" I pause, searching for the right word, "happy, I feel kind of, well, I feel lost."

My mind skims back to the low point of the last few months, waking up in a Portland hotel room, face down on the bed with my clothes on, a pool of drying vomit on the bedcover. The girl I'd met at the 7-11 store was gone. An empty bottle of whisky lay on its side; the floor was littered with empty beer cans. My wallet had been flung into their midst. I rolled onto the floor and picked it up. All my cash, the remainder of the five hundred dollars I had made for that night's slideshow, was gone.

"Steve," comes a voice from the back row. Jeff Lowe, one of the most active and forward looking American alpinists to ever live, and the founder of this festival, stands up with difficulty. He leans on a cane, necessitated by his battle with multiple sclerosis. The room becomes quiet. "You shouldn't feel bad. I know that climbing Nanga Parbat was guiding your compass. I've been there. I understand what you're going through, or at least close to it. But you've done a great thing. And you've brought it back to share with all of us. And that's wonderful." The crowd applauds enthusiastically.

"Thank you Jeff. Thanks for your words." But at heart, I feel no better.

Vince kicks in. "Yeah, thanks Jeff. That means a lot coming from you."

⟨⟨⟩⟩⟨⟨⟩⟩⟨⟨⟩⟩⟨⟨⟩⟩⟨⟨⟩⟩⟨⟨⟩⟩⟨⟨⟩⟩⟨⟨⟩⟩

In December we had received word of our nomination for the Piolet d'Or award. "When they gave the Piolet to the Russians last year, I was so disgusted," I said to Vince on the phone. "I don't want anything to do with that thing."

"Well, they didn't nominate any big siege-style expeditions this year," he replied.

"That's because none of them were successful."

"Still. If we don't go, we don't have a voice."

"Not going is telling them something, don't you think," I replied bitterly. In the end we decide to go and are leaving for France the next morning.

Grenoble, France: February 10, 2006

Vince and I stand together on the stage with a dozen other alpinists. I hold another block of crystal in my hands: this year's People's Choice award. Among the sprawling audience are both of my parents, my girlfriend Jeanne, Vince's pregnant wife, his mother and her boyfriend.

"This is not an Olympic sport," Stephen Venables, this year's award chairman and British climbing legend concludes. "There is no scientific way of measuring the value of different ascents. And that is why alpinism is so much greater and more interesting than any Olympic event. All our nominees are winners." He pauses as the audience of 1,500 applauds lightly.

"But in the end we were looking for an ascent that seemed to point to the future...a small team, working in harmony, using the absolute minimum to climb a beautiful, elegant line. The decision was nearly unanimous." I exhale, waiting to see if we will be the first North Americans to win the Piolet d'Or.

"Steve House and Vince Anderson for the Central Pillar of the Rupal Face!" The crowd launches into loud applause and a hundred flashes explode to catch our expressions. Someone hands the prize to me, a replica of a 100-year-old wooden ice axe with a shiny plated-gold head. Emblazoned on the wooden shaft is "XV Piolet d'Or 2006." I pass it to Vince and he takes one side and we each grip the polished wood of the shaft and hold it at waist level.

Vince Anderson prepares a midnight hot water bottle during the first bivouac of our ascent of a new route on the north face of Mount Alberta. We had just enough room to lie down in the partial shelter of the ice roof.
STEVE HOUSE

North Face of Mount Alberta, Canadian Rockies: March 26, 2008

I WATCH SILENTLY AS HUGE WHITE FLAKES float by on an updraft. Vince yells, and I glance down. He shouts something about retreating, rapping off this wall, and returning to the hut.

I turn to the black rock and keep climbing. By now, you know the story. No one has climbed here before. We don't know if we can get up it or not. The climbing gets hard. It becomes dangerous. The weather threatens. Survival is questioned. This is all true.

When I adopted my mission, atop a boulder in far northern Pakistan 19 years ago – to be the best climber I could become – I couldn't have foreseen the implications that decision would have. I abandoned a nascent science career and became a mountain guide. I have lived in vans and been so broke and hungry that I checked into foreign hotels, billed meals to my room, and walked into the night at 4 am, carrying a backpack containing all my belongings, the unglued sole of my boot slapping softly in the cold night. I have fathered no children. I've burned through my emotions and left inadequate reserves for a marriage. I have trained for thousands of hours: hiked, run, sprinted, lugged 40 pounds of water uphill, bounded, pedaled, skied, and lifted. I have climbed, and climbed, and climbed. Four, five, sometimes seven days a week. I have pushed to my limits and beyond.

I've taken twisted pleasure in dedicating my life to a sport where only a few survive. In my less virtuous moments, I've reveled in the gulf between my commitment to my sport and my worldly successes. At my nadir I have criticized the accomplishments of others in order to lift myself up. These transgressions too, are part of who I am today.

I build an anchor and yell down at Vince. "Next pitch looks good!"

He leans off his belay stance and pushes the brim of his hood back to look at me. Even from this distance I can see his misery. More snowflakes float past. A gust comes up and the snow plasters onto the signature black stone of the Canadian Rockies. It's too late now anyway; we can't get back to the hut tonight. We are spending it on this mountain no matter what.

"Why?" is the obvious question. We all know Mallory's famous quip. "Because it's there." And there is Scott Backes' more elitist version. "Because I can, and others cannot." Neither answer explains this quixotic tilting against the windmill of gravity: a struggle, which at the outset one knows can never be won, though much can be experienced. Every climb ends, as does every life. And each ends where it began: on the ground, and eventually, in the ground. We always return again and again to earth, the beginning. The sum always equals zero.

I have traveled far. Through guiding I have shared this pursuit I love so much. I've gorged on commitment. I made friends with my heroes and discovered them mortal, just like me. I have wagered my life and nearly lost. I have submitted my ego to the greater good, pooled my will with other men, and entrusted them with everything. I watched another man die violently. I have lost friends and partners and witnessed the wounded families left behind. I've known romantic love and what the Greeks call philia, the love of deep friendship. I've stood atop one of the greatest climbs ever imagined.

A great climb has all the components of a good story: a worthy goal, commitment, crises, effort and resolution. Some stories end with a summit, some with the approach, some with a storm, some with death. The conclusion is unforeseeable, the lessons hard-won and costly. The unanswerable question – why climb – becomes all the more intriguing and begs us another question: What is success?

Vince does not call back. With slow, stiff movements he dismantles the anchor and starts climbing toward me in the burgeoning storm.

"You want this lead?" I ask as Vince climbs to the anchor.

"If you're fired up, you should keep going," he replies firmly.

A few minutes later I step off the belay ledge and start into the crux. I don't see the snow. I don't feel the wind. I map the tiny footholds in my mind. I still see them now, a year later, as I write this.

My search begins at the moment of danger. This moment is pregnant with both tragedy and transcendence. Though the tragic is rarely realized, the seeds are ever present. Gravity is relentless, ruin a misstep away. I have learned to accept the fear, to let it pass and not paralyze me. Once it washes through me I possess something powerful: the confidence to act.

Action is the message. Success is found in the process.

Vince hands me a water bottle to keep inside my sleeping bag and turns off the stove. It's 1 am. Eleven ounces of goose down stand between my body and the bitter night air. I sleep for a few hours but then the down wets through from the light snow and I shiver. With a gloved hand I reach out and start to make some hot tea.

Vince leads a pitch on the second day. To the left is an example of a snow mushroom, a dense block of snow built up over months of snowfall cascading down a steep rock wall and forming around a ledge or roof.
STEVE HOUSE

Vince belays me from down slope as I ascend the northeast ridge of Mount Alberta toward the summit. From the top we were unable to see any sign of humanity except for the small hut from which we'd started two days earlier. STEVE HOUSE

At 6 am Vince starts climbing out from beneath the roof that has partially sheltered us. He swings his axe sending silver slivers down the wall. He flexes his muscles and makes the move, risking a 20-foot fall onto a ledge deep in the Canadian wilderness. Up higher he tries to cross to an icefield, but the traverse doesn't go. The rock is too smooth. He has no choice but to climb a steep and foreboding right-leaning crack, so thin it barely accepts the picks of his tools.

I follow the pitch, climbing crisply featured rock through three small roofs. Even with the pack, I am compelled to try to free climb. I'm having fun. At the third roof I fall and rest, hanging from the rope for a moment before continuing to the belay.

Vince continues to lead, unlocking the secrets of our route and after three more pitches the face relents. It has the makings of a classic line of ascent. There is only one logical route and it is barely climbable. It is satisfying to imagine that someone may climb here many years after we are dirt. I tingle with the fleeting notion of immortality.

I climb for more than momentary transcendence. I enjoy the lucid, calm thoughts that come after the climb, the cobwebs sandblasted from my mind. But this alone cannot explain why the feeling after a successful experience lingers for days, months, years, a lifetime.

I also crave evidence of existence. Yukio Mishima wrote that although the core of the apple exists, you cannot see it from the outside. The only way to prove the core's existence is to cut the apple open. When the apple, or the body, bleeds, and dies the existence of the core is confirmed. I have cut open this metaphorical apple on a thousand climbs. I have seen beauty, have wept with joy; I have been astonished, and been horrified to the core.

Climbing is not an attempt to transcend gravity or death for it is these intractable forces that actually create the endeavors. Without gravity, climbing would not exist; without death, what matters life?

I take the lead as clouds rise from the valley. The rock climbing is over. We sprint for the top, simulclimbing ice until eventually we emerge from the north face onto the northeast ridge. I belay Vince in hovering cloud. We're in heaven: a land of mountains and ridges, sculpted by wind and snow, a paradise devoid of any souls but our own.

We lift ourselves on the heights, sometimes leaving bereft families in the wake. For what? They did not, cannot, live this indescribable experience.

Witnessing death is horrific. Does my panic stem from the loss of a friend or from the foreshadowing of my own demise? Or is my terror derived of Mishima's apple; his proof of existence? Facing mortality my actions carry weight, my words heft, my life meaning.

I climb a narrow corniced ridge towards the summit. Pulling onto the top, I worry the cornice will break and send me plummeting towards the wild valley on the other side. I stand up; the summit is flat and safe. I give a yell for this small victory and then kneel to belay Vince.

Five minutes. That's how long we spend. Two photographs, a bite of food, a swallow of water, and we start down. The descent is famously difficult. The thought of the frozen down sleeping bag in the bottom of my pack motivates me to hurry.

Four hours later the beam of my headlamp cuts through the darkness, but I see only fog – and Vince shoveling a narrow place for us to sleep. Beneath a smooth black rock wall, I organize our gear. By procrastinating, I hope it will clear enough so we can continue our descent. I would rather rappel and walk through the night than shiver through another bivouac.

Jeanne and I have been together for three years and we've had many ups and downs. I am willing, even driven, to take all the time and energy necessary to climb, but am unable, or unwilling, to dedicate the same to a partner or wife. It's convenient to cast aside love before a trip; I climb lighter without the tether of commitment. Would we stop loving if we knew we only had a day, a week, a year left? Jeanne says no, she would love me even more, disarming my attempted sabotage.

Vince clears a last few shovels full of snow and stands. "Well, you can sleep there, and I'll take this spot." My appointed space is narrow, but protected from snowfall by a small roof. Vince is giving me the best place.

When I point this out he looks at me. "I've done more for people who meant less."

I laugh and bend to remove my crampons. I lay a short piece of foam on my snow bed. I pull the frozen sleeping bag apart carefully.

The level of trust I have experienced has born something beyond friendship. There is nothing I wouldn't do for these men, my partners, or that they wouldn't do for me. Will I someday find this same trust, make this same commitment, with a wife?

At dawn I finally start to doze. My body heat has dried the sleeping bag and I am warmer than at midnight. The sun comes up and shines bright, but it's a cold, winter sun that brings little warmth. Vince sets an anchor for the day's first rappel. The glacier is close, about 600 feet below. We'll ski back to the road this afternoon and sleep in a warm, dry room tonight. The pink light illuminates a small band of white quartz buried among Alberta's dark rock. Winter rays cross the valley and wake the ice and stone of the nearby North Twin. Vince rappels quickly away.

I never ask Vince if there will be another climb. In 2008, Vince, Marko, and I attempted the west face of Makalu, the world's fifth highest peak and a grand prize of alpinism. Winds battered our tents, even in base camp. I returned from that two and a half-month trip not ever having tied into a rope.

With the bright, but cool, sun lighting up the east face of Mount Alberta, Vince rigs a rappel anchor on the morning of the third day. That day we would make six rappels, down climb the rest of the face, walk to the hut and ski approximately 14 miles back to the truck. The north face of North Twin is visible behind Vince. STEVE HOUSE

Beginning the most difficult pitch of what will become the Anderson-House route on the north face of Mount Alberta, I reach out around a rock corner. VINCE ANDERSON

These stories are not fairy tales. They are the thoughts and actions of a fallible person and my very human partners. Do not mistakenly assume that these portraits exalt courage, bravery, skill, or intelligence. Though these qualities bear some part, so do fear, inadequacy, and compromise. Within alpinism's narrow framework we seek transcendence and relentlessly pursue what remains hidden from us on flat ground: our true selves.

We should not be blamed for thinking our undertakings beautiful and grand, for they are. Meaning is born from struggle, and each of us has our own unique battle. My truths are not universal, which is one reason they are so difficult to express. My ice axe may be your paintbrush. One man's Slovak Direct is another's West Buttress.

I move slowly, arching my back to take in the light and the scenery. I stretch my arms to bathe in it. Absorb it. It is difficult to leave this solitude and beauty. I cannot stay here indefinitely. Mechanically I slide down the ropes after Vince, reluctant to abandon this state of grace we have achieved, here, together, beyond the mountain.

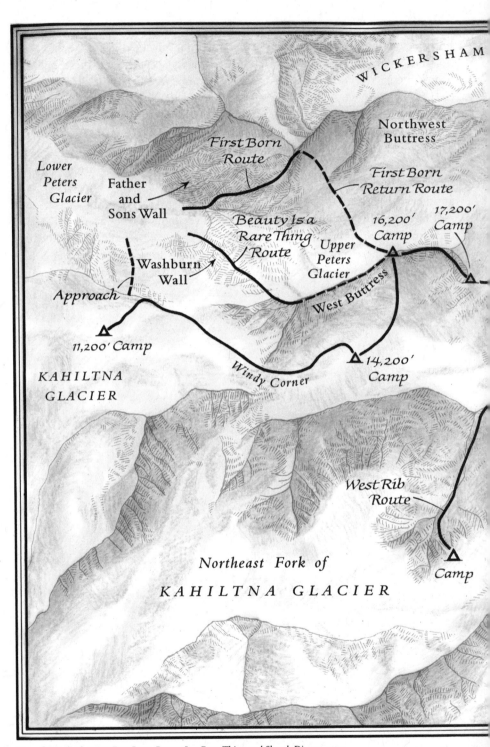

Map of Denali, showing First Born, Beauty Is a Rare Thing and Slovak Direct routes.

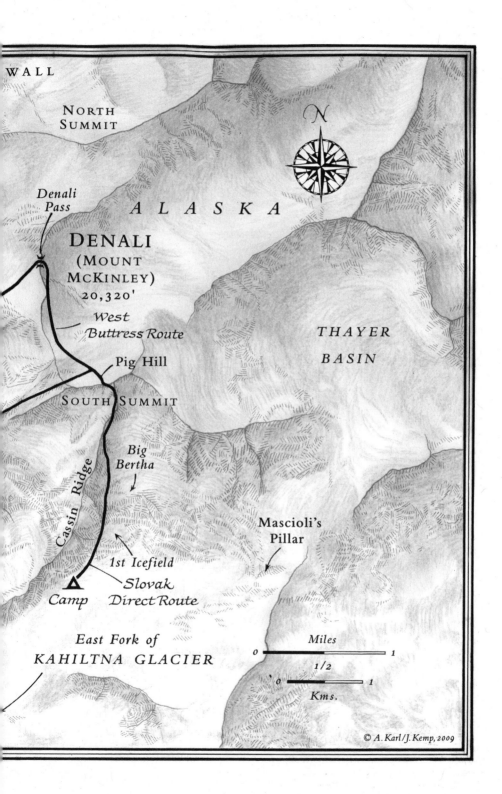

WALL

NORTH
SUMMIT

*Denali
Pass*

DENALI
(MOUNT
MCKINLEY)
20,320'

*West
Buttress Route*

Pig Hill

SOUTH SUMMIT

*Big
Bertha*

ALASKA

THAYER
BASIN

Mascioli's
Pillar

Cassin Ridge

1st Icefield
*Slovak
Direct Route*

Camp

East Fork of
KAHILTNA GLACIER

Miles

0   1

1/2

0   1

Kms.

© A. Karl / J. Kemp, 2009

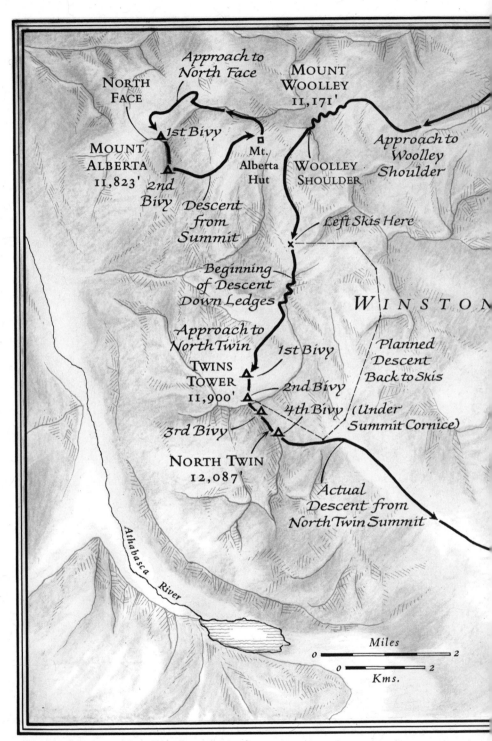

NORTH
FACE

*Approach to
North Face*

MOUNT
WOOLLEY
11,171'

△ *1st Bivy*

□
Mt.
Alberta
Hut

MOUNT
ALBERTA
11,823' 2nd
⚑ Bivy

WOOLLEY
SHOULDER

*Approach to
Woolley
Shoulder*

*Descent
from
Summit*

Left Skis Here

*Beginning
of Descent
Down Ledges*

WINSTON

*Approach to
North Twin*

1st Bivy

*Planned
Descent
Back to Skis*

TWINS
TOWER
11,900'

△

2nd Bivy

△
△

*4th Bivy (Under
Summit Cornice)*

3rd Bivy

△

NORTH TWIN
12,087'

*Actual
Descent from
North Twin Summit*

Athabasca
River

Miles

0 — — — — 2

0 — — — — 2

Kms.

Map of the Winston Churchill Range in Alberta, showing the ascent
and the descent route of North Twin and Mount Alberta.

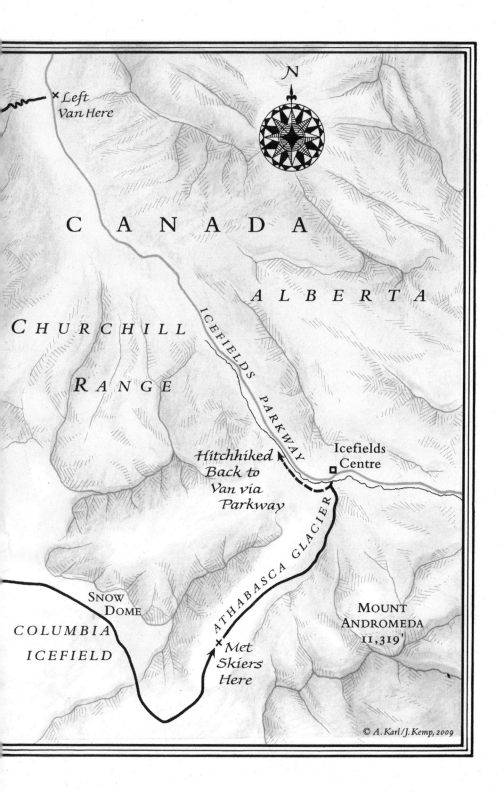

N

× Left
Van Here

C A N A D A

A L B E R T A

C H U R C H I L L

R A N G E

ICEFIELDS PARKWAY

Icefields
Centre

Hitchhiked
Back to
Van via
Parkway

ATHABASCA GLACIER

SNOW
DOME

COLUMBIA
ICEFIELD

× Met
Skiers
Here

MOUNT
ANDROMEDA
11,319'

© A. Karl / J. Kemp, 2009

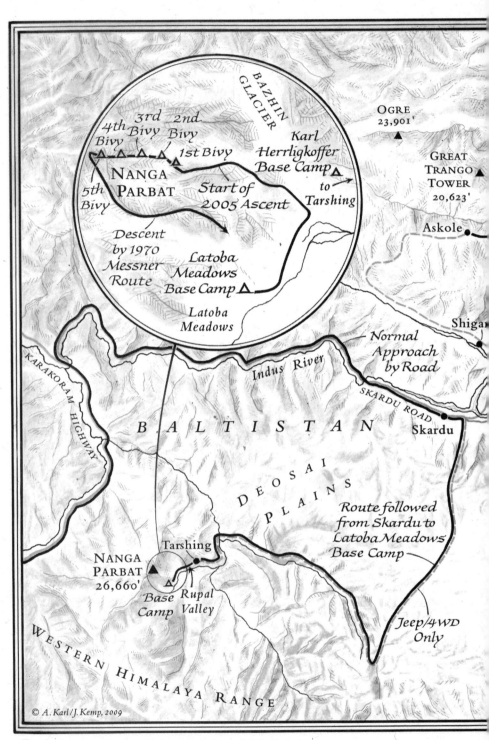

Map of Northern Pakistan, showing the Nanga Parbat and K7 regions.

The labels within the map include:

BAZHIN GLACIER

4th Bivy
3rd Bivy
2nd Bivy
1st Bivy

NANGA PARBAT

5th Bivy

Start of 2005 Ascent

Karl Herrligkoffer Base Camp

to Tarshing

OGRE 23,901'

GREAT TRANGO TOWER 20,623'

Askole

Descent by 1970 Messner Route

Latoba Meadows Base Camp

Latoba Meadows

Normal Approach by Road

Indus River

Shiga[r]

SKARDU ROAD

KARAKORAM HIGHWAY

B A L T I S T A N

Skardu

D E O S A I P L A I N S

Route followed from Skardu to Latoba Meadows Base Camp

NANGA PARBAT 26,660'

Tarshing

Base Camp

Rupal Valley

Jeep/4WD Only

W E S T E R N   H I M A L A Y A   R A N G E

© A. Karl/J. Kemp, 2009

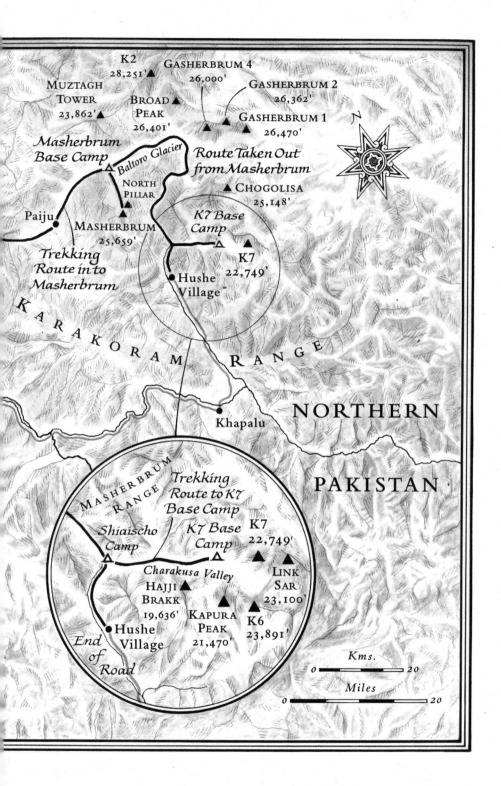

K2
28,251'▲

MUZTAGH
TOWER
23,862'▲

GASHERBRUM 4
26,000'

BROAD
PEAK ▲
26,401'

GASHERBRUM 2
26,362'

GASHERBRUM 1
26,470'

*Masherbrum
Base Camp* △ Baltoro Glacier

NORTH
PILLAR
▲

▲ CHOGOLISA
25,148'

*Route Taken Out
from Masherbrum*

Paiju ●

MASHERBRUM
25,659'

*K7 Base
Camp*
△ ▲

K7
22,749'

*Trekking
Route in to
Masherbrum*

● Hushe
Village

K A R A K O R A M   R A N G E

● Khapalu

NORTHERN

PAKISTAN

MASHERBRUM RANGE

*Trekking
Route to K7
Base Camp*

*Shiaischo
Camp*
△

*K7 Base
Camp*
△

K7
22,749'
▲

LINK
SAR ▲
23,100'

Charakusa Valley

HAJJI
BRAKK ▲
19,636'

KAPURA
PEAK ▲
21,470'

K6
23,891'

*End
of
Road*

● Hushe
Village

Kms.
0   20

Miles
0   20

A

Aid climbing
A climbing technique in which the climber places anchors into the rock to support his or her weight to make upward progress.

Alpine climbing
A synonym for mountain climbing. Alpine referring to being above the tree line or being on glaciers.

Alpine style
A style of climbing in which all equipment and supplies are carried with the team at all times.

Anchor
An anchor is a placed hex, piton or cam, or solid feature of the rock that the climber ties webbing around, and then clips the rope to in order to protect him or herself from a fall.

Ascender
A mechanical device used for ascending a rope. An ascender employs a cam, which allows the device to slide freely in one direction, but grips the rope when loaded in the opposite direction.

B

Belay
The practice of controlling the rope fed out to a climber as a means of protecting the climber in the event of a fall. The climber places anchors in the rock, clips the rope into those anchors and is thereby protected from a fall to the ground.

Bergschrund
A large crevasse found at the upper limit of the glacier. A bergschrund is formed where the moving glacier breaks away from the stationary ice on the mountain wall.

'Biner

See carabiner.

Bivy, Bivouac

A minimal overnight stay with little or no protection from the elements: sometimes planned, sometimes not.

Blade, Knifeblade (thin piton)

A very thin piton used for thin cracks. Not as strong as other, thicker pitons.

Bolt

Permanently placed protection that is screwed or driven into a hole that has been drilled into the rock.

C _____

Cam

A generic term for a type of protection used in a crack consisting of three or four cams mounted on an axis connected to a trigger mechanism. When the trigger is pulled the cams retract and when the trigger is released the cam lobes pressure the sides of a crack. The cams are oriented such that a pull in the direction of load forces them outward and tighter against the rock.

Carabiner, Locking carabiner, 'Biner

A metal loop with a sprung gate used to belay, rappel, ascend, or clip into anchors. A locking carabiner has an extra sleeve that screws down so the biner can't accidentally open. A climber typically carries 20 to 40 carabiners at one time.

Chockstone

A stone lodged in a crack.

Climbing sling

A sewn loop of nylon webbing. A climber typically carries five to 20 of these in many lengths.

Crampons
Metal devices that attach to climbing boots with teeth pointing down and forward to provide traction on snow and ice.

Crevasse
A fissure formed by the friction generated between the ice of a glacier and the terrain the glacier is flowing over. A lateral crevasse is caused by the friction of the ice moving against the sides of the glacier bed.

D

Denali
At a height of 20,320 feet (6,194m), Denali is the highest mountain in North America. The Alaska Board of Geographic Names uses Denali as the official name of this mountain. The U.S. Board on Geographic Names maintains the name Mount McKinley. A very complex mountain, it is usually climbed by the West Buttress route, though many other routes have been established on nearly every one of its many walls. Denali's most impressive wall is the south face, which is very steep for 9,000 feet. The north face, or Wickersham Wall is much less steep – it has been descended on skis – but has 13,000 feet of relief.

Drytooling
Rock climbing on rock that isn't covered in ice, but using ice-climbing equipment such as crampons and ice axes.

E

Expedition style
The original style of climbing big mountains whereby multiple camps are established and stocked in order to establish a final camp suitably close to the summit. Technically difficult sections of the route are often protected with fixed lines. These expeditions typically comprise 10 to 20 members and often employ paid high-altitude porters, often referred to as Sherpas. In extreme cases fixed

ropes protect even the very easy sections of the climbing routes. In almost all cases fixed ropes, supplies, and often entire camps are abandoned on the mountain at the end of the expedition. Popular climbs, such as the easiest (South Col) route on Everest and the West Buttress route on Denali and several other popular climbs have become badly polluted by this practice in the past 20 years.

F

Free climbing
A type of climbing in which the climber uses only hands, feet and other parts of the body to ascend. No artificial aids are employed to make upward progress. Ropes and protection are used as insurance against falls and their consequences.

Free soloing
A style of free climbing that does not use any ropes or anchors to protect the climber. Falls while free soloing are almost always fatal. This technique differs from soloing, where the climber may alternate between free soloing and employing some form of self-belay utilizing a rope and protection.

Front pointing
A technique using crampons with two front-facing points or spikes, which allow traction to be concentrated at the toe of the climber's boots. Used for climbing steep ice.

G

Grade
A number, sometimes called a rating, created to rank the difficulty of a pitch. Each discipline of climbing has a specific rating system.

Gendarme
A large rock pinnacle.

Glacier
A glacier is formed in an area where the annual accumulation of snow exceeds the melting of that snow. Given sufficient time that

snow compresses into ice and, due to its own mass, starts to slide downhill. A permanent snow or icefield that does not move is not defined as a glacier.

<hr>

H

Hexes

A type of nut placed in a crack for protection while rock climbing. It is a hollow, eccentric hexagonal prism with tapered ends, usually threaded with webbing, a swaged cable, or a cord. Not commonly used since the advent of '"cams" in the early 1980s.

<hr>

I

Ice axe, Ice hammer

A multipurpose ice and snow tool used for both ascending and descending routes involving frozen conditions.

Ice bulge

A place where the ice bulges, or becomes steeper.

Ice dagger

A very large icicle.

Ice screw

A screw used to protect a climb on steep ice. They are made from steel tubes, have teeth machined into their ends, threads on the outside and an eye for clipping a carabiner into.

<hr>

K

K7

A major peak of the Karakoram Range in Northern Pakistan, K7 is 22,770 feet (6,942 meters) high. The name is derived from the Great British Survey of India. They named the major summits Karakoram-1, Karakoram-2, etc., starting with what they thought to be the highest peak. In the case where mountains were discovered to have local names, such as Masherbrum, the K-derivative name was dropped.

Lock-off

A position where a person holds himself or herself up on fully flexed arms, such as at the top of a chin-up. It is easier to hold a lock-off than to hold oneself with arms flexed somewhere in between.

Munter hitch

A knot commonly used by climbers as part of a belay system.

Nanga Parbat

Nanga Parbat is the ninth highest mountain on earth and lies wholly within Pakistan. Nanga Parbat means Naked Mountain in the Urdu language. Hermann Buhl made its first ascent on July 3, 1954 without the use of supplementary oxygen. At that time, 31 men had already died attempting to climb it. (It is interesting to note that this was accomplished seven weeks after the first ascent of Everest, which relied heavily on the use of supplementary oxygen cached along the route by Tom Bourdillon and Charles Evans, who incidentally climbed within 300 feet of Everest's summit just days before the successful ascent.) Geologists using the Reduced Spire Measure, which is a system of measuring a peak by height and steepness, rank Nanga Parbat as number one. (See Rupal Face)

North Face of North Twin

North Twin is an 11,910-foot high peak on the northern edge of the Columbia Icefield and lies within Jasper National Park in Alberta, Canada. Properly it is the North Face of Twin Towers, a sub-peak of North Twin, but in practice this minor distinction is rarely made. The dark colored limestone wall is over 5,000 feet high and is unusually steep. The face has been climbed three times. The first was by George Lowe and Chris Jones in late-July 1974 and was graded 5.10, A4 and was, without a doubt, the most difficult alpine route in North America, and quite probably the world, at that time. The wall's second ascent was made by Barry Blanchard and David Cheesmond in August 1985 by a route up a pillar right of the Lowe-Jones route and was graded 5.10d A2. In April 2004 Steve House and Marko Prezelj became the third party to complete any route on the wall by a variation to the Lowe-Jones route. Their climb is described in Chapter 15.

Nut
A type of artificial protection that is a tapered piece of aluminum with a loop of cable that hangs below it. The tapered aluminum is wedged in a constriction in a crack to create a point of protection.

P

Piton, Pin, Peg
In climbing, a piton is a metal spike – usually tempered steel, but sometimes soft-steel or titanium – that is driven into a crack in the rock with a hammer, which acts as an anchor to protect the climber against the consequences of a fall, or to assist progress in aid climbing.

Pod
A flare, or sudden widening, of a crack in rock.

Point of aid
An anchor (piton, nut, cam, or bolt) that is pulled on or stood on to make upward progress.

Pump
Fatigue of the muscles. Usually refers to the climber's forearms and often is a precursor to muscular failure which usually results in a fall.

R

Rappel
The controlled descent down a rope. Typically using a lightweight aluminum device that also can be used for belaying.

Running belay (Simulclimbing)

When the leader reaches the end of a pitch the leader may place a good piece of protection and the second – previously the belayer – begins to climb. This allows both climbers tied to opposite ends of one rope to climb simultaneously which is much faster than belaying each climber one at a time. The risk is that if the second climber falls he can pull the first climber off, causing them to fall. Because of this the technique is usually used on moderate ground where a fall is unlikely.

Rupal Face

The southeast face of Nanga Parbat, the Rupal Face is considered to be the largest mountain wall in the world. It rises approximately 15,000 feet above base camp and 13,500 feet from the final crevasse, or bergschrund, of the Bazhin Glacier at the base of the wall to the summit. Reinhold and Günther Messner supported by a large expedition organized by Karl Herrligkoffer first ascended the Rupal Face in 1970. Their ascent was very controversial as they elected to traverse the mountain and Günther died on the subsequent descent. Two more climbers followed them to the summit the next day and descended safely. Herrligkoffer is a major figure in the history of the mountain as he organized four Nanga Parbat expeditions, including the mountain's first ascent in 1954. A joint Polish/Mexican team accomplished the second ascent of the Rupal Face in 1984. The 1970 Messner route was repeated in July 2005 by a large Korean team, giving the Rupal Face its third overall ascent. The Anderson-House route was the Rupal Face's fourth ascent and the first time it was climbed alpine style.

S

Self-belay

A method that can be used by a climber to protect him or herself while solo climbing. Cumbersome because it requires the solo climber to rappel the pitch and re-ascend it to clean the gear placed for protection on the original lead. There are many methods, the one used by the author requires the end to be tied to a solid anchor and the climber ties in a long loop that is clipped to pieces of protection. The loop ensures that any fall will be quite long, but the simplicity and the fact that this works in any conditions, such as icy ropes, has it's advantages.

Simulclimbing
See Running belay.

Slovak Direct Route
Sometimes called the Czech Direct, which was short for the Czechoslovakian Direct. The three climbers, Adam Blažej, Tono Križo, and František Korl, who made its first ascent were, in fact, of Slovak nationality. The route is considered the most difficult on Denali as it rises 9,000 vertical feet and has climbing rated to 5.9 rock and 100-degree ice (one short roof). Kevin Mahoney and Ben Gilmore did the second ascent over seven days in May 2000. The third ascent (but without the last hundred feet to the summit) is the subject of Chapter 12. In 2008, three Japanese alpinists completed the route's fourth ascent as part of an enchainment, first climbing a route known as the Isis Face.

Snice
Snice is a combination of snow and ice. It refers to a type of frozen water whose physical characteristics make it an intermediate between snow and ice.

Snow mushrooms
A frozen piece of snow or snice that often develops on steep rock walls in mountains with a lot of snow.

Solo climbing
Solo climbing or soloing is a style of climbing in which the climber climbs alone without somebody belaying him or her.

T _____

Toproping
A style of climbing in which a rope runs from a belayer at the foot of a route to an anchor system at the top of the route and back down to the climber. Toproping is usually the safest way to climb.

V

V-thread

A method of making an anchor in ice, where an ice screw is used to make two intersecting tunnels bored into the ice. Typically, cord or webbing is then threaded through the tunnel and tied to form a sling. In conditions where the ice is not moist, as is often found in the mountains, it may be possible to thread the ropes directly through the V-thread, thereby leaving no trash behind.

W

Water ice

Ice formed by running water. Water ice is typically hard and brittle. Also referred to as frozen waterfalls.

Acknowledgements

This book is dedicated to the memory of my friends who will never return from the mountains. I miss you.

Jože Rozman and Marijar Frantar who pushed too far on Kanchenjunga. Mugs Stump was lost to a crevasse on Denali. Julie Cheney-Culberson whose death on Mount Temple saddened me in a way I couldn't understand then. Caroll Robinson, whom I tried to save, but couldn't. Steve Mascioli who died suddenly on Mount Hunter. Janez Jeglič, whose mysterious death on Nuptse still haunts me. Alex Lowe and Dave Bridges are still buried under ice at the foot of Shishapangma. Hans Saari, who slipped on unseen ice while skiing the Gervasutti Couloir, I wish we'd had more time together. Thierray Braugier who died soloing a hard route on Chamonix's Aiguille du Peigne. Karl Nagy, who was lost on Mount Little. Seth Shaw whose death on Mount Johnson was so unexpected. Sue Nott and Karen McNeil, whom I wish had come back from Mount Foraker. Charlie Fowler and Christine Boskoff whose deaths on China's Mount Genyen were incredibly sad, but, dare I say it, poetic. Jean-Christophe Lafaille: I was amazed and deeply saddened when he didn't return from his attempted winter solo of Makalu. I hope he stood on the summit. Jules Cartwright died guiding the Piz Badile and the UK lost its best alpinist, again. Jim Ratz, who was a mentor to so many climbers and guides. Chad Vanderham and Doug Coombs died skiing on La Meije near La Grave, France. George Gardner was one of the best, most positive, happiest men I knew, which made his death on the Grand Teton so difficult to bear. Pavle Kozjek, a surprise death on Pakistan's Muztagh Tower. Miha Valič, whose skill and spirit were both so high, the future of alpine climbing is not the same since your death on Cho Oyu.

A great shout of appreciation goes out to Scott Backes for not apologizing. Mark Twight for being open, intelligent, and caring. Barry Blanchard and Catherine Mulvihill for always being there. Joe Josephson for sharing your rope. Rolando Garibotti, you're still the prototype. Bruce Miller for saving my life. Mr. Clean for showing everyone that it can be done and especially for the use of your beautiful photographs. Vince Anderson for being the right man at the right time for the right reason.

Thanks to Dušan Golobič, Ljubo Hansel, Branko Starič, Boris Strmšek, Marko Lukič, Mira and Zdenko Zorič and all the members of AD Kozjak and PD TAM in Maribor, Slovenia, for climbing with an eager young boy. You changed my life. Thanks to Tone Golnar for organizing the 1990 Nanga Parbat Expedition, and the Špindler family, Franci, Ani, Jure, and Nataša, for allowing me to find my own way to be at home with your family.

Thanks to all my climbing partners over the years: Todd Millay, Marty Treadway, Jeremy Coate, Brad Williams, and all the "Cliffhangers," Mark Hauter, Ken from Olympia, Michelle Burlitch, Paul Przybylowicz, Todd McDougald, Michael Powers, Doug Chabot, Stan Price, Todd Cozzens, Joe Reichert, Eli Helmuth, Kevin Mahoney, Ben Gilmore, Colin Haley, Alan Kearney, Steve Swenson, Tom Hargis, Flash Clark, Katharine Bill, Sean McCabe, Matic Jost, Scott Johnston, Kevin Doyle, Will Gadd, Grant Statham, Sean Easton, Scott Semple, Conrad Anker, Jeff Hollenbaugh, Rebecca Carmen, Brittany Griffith, Jonathan Thesenga, Ian Yurdin (thanks for tying a knot in the end of that rope), Brian McMillan, and all the Smith Rock regulars, it's like "Cheers" down there.

To all the clients I guided on ascents and descents throughout the world: you put bread on my table, taught me patience, and gave me endurance. I can never thank you enough.

Thanks to: Chris Kulp for your friendship and hard work on the epilogue. Joel Haskard for talking me into writing the crevasse-fall chapter. Michael Kennedy for your criticism; without your brave and hard words this book would have been a disaster. Yvon and Malinda Chouinard for creating Patagonia and supporting this particular project from its inception. Rick Ridgeway for believing I could do this. Rob Bondurant for always being in my corner. Michael Gilbert for forcing me to write what I meant. John Dutton, you were the firm hand of reason throughout this project and made it readable in the end. Andy Ornberg, for listening. Lisa Twight, one of my greatest friends. Chris Torgerson for coming out of your academic shell once and a while. Amber Jean for the inspiration. Mom and Dad and my sister, Chris, for never flinching, at least in my presence. Jeanne Young for teaching me how to rock climb and loving me for me.

A special thanks to the team at Patagonia Books that worked and commented on this project: Rick Ridgeway, Vincent Stanley, John Dutton, Jennifer Sullivan, Jane Sievert, Annette Scheid, Jen Rapp, Melissa Beckwith, Alyssa Firmin, and Charlotte Overby.

Thanks to the sponsors and contributors to the Mugs Stump Award for your far-sighted and generous grants program. Thanks to the American Alpine Club for your support by way of the Lyman Spitzer Grants.

Lastly, all my great sponsors, especially the big four: Patagonia, Grivel, GU Sports, and La Sportiva. We've been together a long time now and without you most of these stories would never have been lived.